BERBERS
AND
OTHERS

PUBLIC CULTURES OF THE MIDDLE EAST AND NORTH AFRICA
Paul A. Silverstein, Susan Slyomovics, and Ted Swedenburg, editors

BERBERS

AND
OTHERS

Beyond Tribe and Nation in the Maghrib

EDITED BY
KATHERINE E. HOFFMAN
AND
SUSAN GILSON MILLER

Indiana University Press

BLOOMINGTON AND INDIANAPOLIS

This book is a publication of

Indiana University Press
601 North Morton Street
Bloomington, Indiana 47404-3797 USA

www.iupress.indiana.edu

Telephone orders	800-842-6796
Fax orders	812-855-7931
Orders by e-mail	iuporder@indiana.edu

Manufactured in the United States of America

Library of Congress Cataloging-in-Publication Data

Berbers and others : beyond tribe and nation in the Maghrib / edited by Katherine E. Hoffman
and Susan Gilson Miller.
    p. cm. — (Public cultures of the Middle East and North Africa)
    Includes bibliographical references and index.
    ISBN 978-0-253-35480-8 (cloth : alk. paper) — ISBN 978-0-253-22200-8 (pbk. : alk. paper)
1. Berbers. 2. Berbers—Africa, North. 3. Berbers—Africa, North—Social life and customs.
4. Berbers—Africa, North—Politics and government. 5. Ethnicity—Africa, North. 6. Africa,
North—Social life and customs. 7. Africa, North—Politics and government. I. Hoffman,
Katherine E. II. Miller, Susan Gilson.
    DT193.5.B45B468 2010
    305.89'33061—dc22
                                                                          2009048650

1 2 3 4 5 15 14 13 12 11 10

For
G. D. M.
and
S. K. H.

For
M.C.M.
and
J.X.M.

CONTENTS

ACKNOWLEDGMENTS

The present volume is the outcome of a two-day workshop held at Harvard University on April 28–29, 2006, under the heading of *Berbers and Others: Changing Parameters of Ethnicity in the Contemporary Maghrib*. The goal of the gathering was to examine contemporary Berber activism in Morocco and Algeria and its impact on politics, language, the economy, culture, education, the arts, and the writing of history. The workshop brought together an outstanding international group of scholars from the United States, Europe, and North Africa who presented papers on the state of the art in Berber Studies. Organization and funding came from the Moroccan Studies Program and from the Center for Middle Eastern Studies (CMES), both at Harvard, with additional help from the Moroccan American Institute.

The group of participants represented a stellar cross-section of scholars working on the Maghrib. In addition to the contributors to this book, they included Lahouari Addi, Rachid Aadnani, Fatima Agnaou, Mina Elmghari, Philip Schuyler, and Jocelyne Cesari. The list of discussants was no less impressive; among them were Wilfred Rollman, William Granara, Susan Slyomovics, Suzanne Blier, Virginia Danielson, and Abdeslam Maghraoui. Their participation enriched the proceedings and helped make the workshop into an absorbing intellectual experience. The staff of CMES were instrumental in providing logistical support. Special mention must go to Hannah-Louise Clark, who coordinated events and people, and to Alison Howe, who handled the budget. The manuscript was improved by the far-ranging reflections of anonymous readers, but the editors would like to thank in particular Steve Caton, whose trenchant comments helped mold the final product. Finally, we offer our gratitude to Rebecca Tolen of Indiana University Press, who graciously but firmly induced us to see this project through to completion.

NOTE ON TRANSLITERATION

The transliteration of Arabic to English is made difficult by the predominance of French spellings in the literature and by the complex system of diacritical marks used to distinguish Arabic letters. With the general reader in mind as well as the regional specialist, we have made some adjustments by using a system based on *The Hans Wehr Dictionary of Modern Written Arabic*, without introducing diacritical marks other than the ʿayn (ʿ) and the hamza (ʾ). We have chosen not to assimilate the al- to the following consonant (*al-dawla* instead of *ad-dawla*) and we use English usage to guide spelling (*wad* rather than *oued*). For terms from Moroccan Arabic (*darija*), we have kept pronunciation conventions (e.g., *blad as-siba*). In transliterating place names, we have been faced with equally difficult choices, but generally we have used the common English spelling, such as Fez rather than Fès, Marrakesh rather than Marrakech, and so on.

There are multiple systems for transcribing spoken Tamazight/Berber in Morocco and Algeria. We have retained authors' preferences for transcription that reflect both emerging regional conventions and a principle of one grapheme per sound. Subscript dots or doubling of a letter indicate emphatics. Other symbols are as follows:

γ or ġ for what otherwise is transcribed in Arabic as gh (غ)
ε for the ʿayn (ع)
x in the place of kh (خ)
š in the place of sh (ش)

BERBERS
AND
OTHERS

Introduction

Katherine E. Hoffman and Susan Gilson Miller

More than thirty-five years have passed since the publication of Gellner and Micaud's *Arabs and Berbers*, a landmark social scientific investigation into ethnicity in the Maghrib.[1] Reflecting concerns of that time, its central theme is North Africa's transition from tribal politics to nationalism. Some of the chapters in that book have been superseded by events, but on the whole, the work retains its value and provides the critical starting point for our investigations: first, as a foil for returning to issues raised in the seventies, in order to trace their evolution, and second, as a departure point for a new set of problems not considered by an earlier generation of scholars.[2] Contributions to the present volume span a broad spectrum of topics in the fields of history, anthropology, political science, literary studies, education, and art history. Even within its broad scope, it would be impossible for one book to comprehensively cover the growing field of Berber studies. Instead, we offer various perspectives on Berber identity that challenge received wisdom and problematize an understanding of the place of Berbers in the world today. Most significantly, we have set aside an a priori dichotomization of Arab and Berber and replaced it with a perspective that situates Berbers at multiple poles of identification, allegiance, and affinity.

This volume also builds on a refreshingly new environment of openness to research on Berber ethnicity. From the mid-sixties until the late 1990s, it was difficult to conduct original ethnographic research on Berber issues because of a hostile political climate in North Africa, where recognition of ethnic or linguistic "difference" was considered a challenge to the legitimacy of the state and the unity of the nation. Publications in English treating the dialectic processes of identity construction in which Berbers participated were scarce. Today, a more relaxed political climate in both Morocco and Algeria allows for a greater appreciation of multiculturalism and diversity as positive attributes of the modern nation-state. The purpose of this volume is to seize upon this political opening as a departure point for considering how Berbers define themselves, how others conceive of them, and how these new definitions are reproduced in actions and representations. The contributors consider both framing issues, or what the colonial linguist Émile Laoust called *mots et choses berbères*, as well as more specific cases that demonstrate current thinking about Amazigh people and culture.

For the last half-century, ideas about Berber particularism have been deeply shaped by colonial policies, especially colonial strategies of divide-and-rule. This is surely one of the reasons why Berber studies were avoided by Anglophone scholars of North Africa. Fear of perpetuating colonial stereotypes or appearing complicit in imperialist projects underscoring Berber "uniqueness" drove researchers away from Berber topics and toward the "safer" ideological program of Arabo-Islamism. Beyond the academy, aversion to appearing divisive led many Berber speakers to submerge, hide, or even reject their Amazigh roots by shifting their language use away from Berber and toward dialectal Arabic, and by weakening ties with ancestral homelands. Individual language practices were shaped by both practical needs and ideological convictions as the state reached deeper into rural communities through the schools and the expansion of local government. Increased rural migration to the cities also brought large numbers of Berber speakers into a largely Arabophone environment. At the same time, the post-colonial North African states drew closer to the Arabic language and the Islamic religion that undergirded nationalist discourses. With Arabic and Islam as key pillars of nationhood, Amazigh language and heritage had little opportunity to find their place in the public sphere. For scholars everywhere, this adverse environment inhibited the academic study of Berber-related topics. For American scholars in particular, the Cold War focus on Arabic language and regional studies meant that non-Arab components of North African and Middle Eastern society and culture received limited attention and support. All these factors directed Anglophone—and to a lesser extent, Francophone—scholarship on North Africa toward Arab and Arabophone populations.

Almost a century ago in 1915, the French linguist Edmond Destaing wrote an impassioned plea to Lyautey, the first Resident-General of Morocco, calling for the creation of a Berber Studies Center in Morocco. Destaing noted that there were already numerous social-scientific initiatives for the study of Morocco, but that "this inquiry progresses too slowly for our liking . . . there are Arab sciences, Arab art, medersas, oulemas, Muslim saints and courts, or otherwise translations of Arab works," but there was little research of significance about Berbers.[3] Yet they were the ones who should concern us, Destaing noted. Like many scholars and policymakers in his day, Destaing conceived of Moroccan society as made up of a Berber foundation thinly veiled by an Arab veneer. Destaing could hardly have imagined that much of what he called the "precise information" about Berbers would, in the post-colonial period, come from North Africans themselves. In this volume, a new generation of scholars, some Maghribi, others not, engages in a close and concentrated look at various aspects of Berber experience within North Africa and beyond, revealing that Berber studies are finally approaching maturity.

Shifting Possibilities, Shifting Analyses

Many factors have changed the face of North African and Berber studies over the last three decades. Historiographical and qualitative studies are now possible that could not have been conceived when Gellner and Micaud edited their volume. The first shift is the recognition of the Amazigh element of North African identity on the part of state officials and Berber activists. This opening is by no means thoroughly institutionalized, given the ongoing tensions between activists and governments that block constitutional reform to protect minority rights. Indeed, both the Tunisian and Libyan regimes have consistently refused to recognize the Amazigh components of their populations—even as inhabitants of villages in southeast Tunisia continue to speak Tamazight.

Social science and history have changed since the 1960s and 1970s when scholarship was heavily influenced by structuralism and segmentary theory. Earlier studies focused especially on patterns of authority and leadership internal to Berber communities, in an effort to understand the relationship between elites and the largely apolitical Berber masses. Writing in the wake of two failed military coups in Morocco in 1971 and 1972, which were largely orchestrated by Berber officers, contributors to the Gellner and Micaud volume strove to understand the radically evolving place of Berbers in Moroccan public life. Power in all its political forms was their preoccupation, along with the ways in which Berbers would exercise—or fail to exercise—their potential for leadership in the newly independent Maghribi states. The questions that concern us here were not their concern: issues of process and social dynamics, the constantly changing paradigms of human agency, and the means by which individuals are able to reconfigure their lives to take advantage of new economies and new forms of communication.

The cumulative body of work on Berber studies that precedes us remains relevant, however. It molds and informs each contribution to this collection and constitutes the background to every effort in this domain of research. At the same time, we must be clear about the differences between earlier approaches and those of the present, particularly in connection with the concept of ethnicity. Frederik Barth's highly influential argument that ethnicity is relational and historically situated was not widely accepted until after the publication of *Arabs and Berbers*. In Barth's view, it is the boundaries people construct between their own and other ethnic groups that matter, not the "cultural stuff" the borders contain. Working from this argument, we understand Berber ethnicity through its relation with others. In this respect, then, the project of Amazigh studies must include a consideration of elements in the environment that impinge on constructions of identity, such as the pressures and constraints of state-imposed linguistic and educational policies. But we also have to be sensitive to the specific practices that allowed an Arab hegemony to take hold.

Here we regard ethnicity as a historically contingent construct whose characteristics fluctuate but may include such factors as shared language, expressive and material culture, beliefs, customs, social organization, norms, or shared ancestry. Whereas colonial scholars searched for absolute truths about Berber culture, today's scholars see ethnicity as a constantly changing orientation, shaped and reshaped by forces both within and outside the group. The contributors to this volume document this unfolding condition in a variety of contexts both past and present. Moreover, they are not only aware of changing situations, but also of changing ways of talking about, picturing, and concretizing Berber experiences. They reject the frozen, embrace the contingent, and situate categories and representations within their specific historical milieus. As James McDougall points out in his chapter, the very terms "Berber" and "Amazigh" have histories that have been made and remade over time. Moreover, this fluctuation is not only evident from the outside; it is also deeply felt within the group. What it means to "be" Amazigh/Berber is often different for today's urban activists than it is for rural agriculturalists; activists conceive this category as comprising a transnational ethno-linguistic group, while rural people see it in terms of a linguistic opposition to Arabs. The contextual field is always

Katherine E. Hoffman and Susan Gilson Miller

present and is not one-dimensional; rather, it resides at the nexus of axes central to the North African experience: religion, politics, class, and community.

Noticeably absent from this formula is the idea of the nation, so central to the thinking of the contributors to *Arabs and Berbers*, who wrote during the early years of independence. There was no place for ethnic particularism at a moment when scholars had to deal with the reality of an overwhelming Arabo-Islamic definition of social identity. While the idea of the nation as the sole arbiter of public life is now long past, we must still concern ourselves with the state in its various forms. Our contributors, through both direct and subtle means, draw readers' attention to the sites where nationalist ideology has become embedded. Benedict Anderson's thesis of nations as "imagined communities," first published in 1983, is most useful in this regard. His work stripped bare the collective processes and state initiatives through which a group of people comes to consider itself a nation. While this orientation rejects notions of authenticity and resistance, it does provide a comfortable position for contemplating the nation as an entity that is less exclusive and oppressive. Amazigh activists appeal to the same primordial, essential, and enduring qualities of group membership as do other nationalists, differing only in the extent to which they see Berber identity as compatible or in conflict with broader national identities.

A longstanding objection to the inclusion of Amazighness in the vocabulary of the nation-state was the argument that being Berber was merely a linguistic category, and a fractured one at that, given regional variations in the language. From this ideological perspective, it was difficult to see how it might fit into state plans for modernization and economic expansion. It is true that Tamazight has long been primarily an oral rather than literate language, as documented most recently by Nico van den Boogert.[4] The recent standardization and codification of Tamazight places it in the same category as other oral indigenous languages that are now being written down, whether through state sponsorship, missionary activity, or community activism. In order to counter the claim that Tamazight is an inadequate communicative medium, Amazigh activists are undertaking translations in order to build a corpus of literature, along the lines of what was done for Catalan in Spain. Even Modern Standard Arabic, widely considered as suited to modern needs, has undergone revision, and its use as a truly national language in North African countries is uneven at best. There are those who argue that the focus on literacy is misplaced and that orality should be revalorized. Somewhat ironically, one way of valorizing Berber oral traditions has been through the textual rendering of proverbs, song lyrics, and stories using Latin, Arabic, or *tifinagh* script. However, examples taken from other cultures suggest that while such efforts may build self-esteem, they do little to encourage the use of the language in every-day life.

Recognition by the state now allows Tamazight to be present in the public sphere. In Morocco, this process began in 1994, with the introduction of short televised news summaries in what were officially called "dialects" (*al-lahajat*), now called Amazigh language (*al-lugha al-amazighiya*). More significant, however, is the ongoing effort to teach Tamazight language in the state primary schools, a move that brings the language into the home in a more pervasive way than previously thought possible. The main objective here was to integrate Tamazight language and Amazigh history into discussions of national heritage in order to valorize Tamazight and slow its decline. We might ask whether there is any evidence from other cultures for the assertion that formal instruction ensures language maintenance. This is of particular interest since languages learned in school in Morocco—Classical Arabic, French, English, and now, Tamazight—are not spoken outside the classroom, and are generally viewed as foreign. The new curriculum confronts the same problems as the rest of the language curriculum by not taking into account students' linguistic backgrounds.

Another novelty of this age is better access to the sources needed for original scholarly research. While an earlier generation of scholars, such as historian Robin Bidwell, had the advantage of conducting oral histories, contemporary scholars are privileged to have access to archival materials in both Western and Maghribi repositories. Soon almost all colonial and protectorate archives will be available to researchers. The historical chapters by McDougall, El Mansour, and Ghambou not only bring to light new facts about Amazigh history, but also challenge the prevailing historiography as it was elaborated under the influence of Arab nationalism. Indeed, one can safely argue that Berber/Amazigh studies are relevant to a broad spectrum of disciplines and a variety of academic endeavors. Significant social scientific theory that engages with the Berber subject at some level has emanated from North Africa in recent decades; one has only to mention the names of Pierre Bourdieu, Clifford Geertz, Paul Rabinow, Kevin Dwyer, and Abdellah Hammoudi to note the salience of their research for advancing our knowledge of the way that cultures work.

Revisiting known sources and seeing them through a different lens is another aspect of the new Berber historiography. In this book, the chapter by Mohamed El Mansour recreates the life of Abu al-Qasim al-Zayani, an eighteenth-century Moroccan Berber scholar whose trajectory spanned multiple worlds. Berber by birth, an official of the *makhzan* (government apparatus) by occupation, he shifted identities depending on places and circumstances. The dearth of self-referential, autobiographical narratives in the historical corpus useful for establishing Berber identities is a major problem. Instead we must resort to a close reading of familiar texts, aided by a large dose of the historical imagination. In al-Zayani's case, personal perspectives are teased out of the narrative of his travels to Mecca and the Ottoman Empire. Still, we are not able to interrogate al-Zayani about his language use, or his multilingualism, or the conditions under which he moved away from a rural Berber identity and adopted a more encompassing Moroccan/Maghribi one (if indeed he did), or at what point his membership in the community of Islam became the decisive factor in his social identity. We can, however, conjecture about the stresses and strains implicit in these border-crossings and appreciate the intellectual flexibility that such transitions entailed.

On the question of source material, print media has joined the array of instruments available for publicizing Berber self-awareness. Older, yet still valid scholarship on the Berbers is now being reproduced for popular consumption. Monographs on Berber lifeways produced during the colonial period are appearing in new editions and are being sold in North African bookshops; classic texts by Laoust and others are now priced affordably. The classic series *Archives berbères* was recently reprinted and made available to the reading public in Morocco. Whereas these texts were once dismissed as biased, they are now widely appreciated for their attention to detail and information on Berber communities previously overlooked.

Multiple Poles of Otherness: Local, National, International

The title of this book is meant to emphasize the multiplicity of compass points by which Berbers have imagined themselves and various Others, and through which Others have in turn imagined them. These Others emerge from local, national, and transnational encounters. Earlier scholars concerned with the tribe's potential political power vis-à-vis the central state focused on points of similarity binding tribes together with rural Berber communities. Today, we can no longer suggest that there is social solidarity between speakers of the same language, descendents of those speakers, or residents of the same village or region. As these chapters demonstrate, there is significant heterogeneity even at the local level in expressive practices, group identification, economic positions, and individual and group interests. One can speak the same variety of Berber and participate in the same village life, yet still be an Other. As Paul Silverstein demonstrates, the Other can be a Tamazight speaker who occupies a competitive position in the local political economy. Silverstein's ethnographic material comes from southeastern Morocco, where Berbers sometimes occupy competing ethno-linguistic niches that are racially defined. Excluded from the category "Imazighen" are the dark-skinned, Tamazight-speaking ex-*haratin*, farmers of sub-Saharan African descent. Once considered socially inferior, their new wealth and land ownership threaten light-skinned Imazighen who have long dominated local political councils. Suspicion runs both ways as these two groups of Tamazight speakers see each other not as co-ethnics but as groups in conflict over access to economic and political resources.

Aspects of the Other may become part of what a Berber group considers its own local authenticity, especially in the rural communities that are sites of contact between Arabophones and Berberophones. In her chapter, Katherine Hoffman argues for attention to the "intermediate zones" of plains communities whose cultural expressive practices include both "Arab" and "Berber" components. This mixing comes from longstanding intergroup contact and the spread of state institutions into the countryside. Parsing through the processes leading to shifting cultural practices is an important but difficult task. Verbal expressive practices such as local genres of community song are considered authentic, valuable, and enjoyable by plains residents. Yet outsiders to these communities, laypeople as well as activists, criticize these Imazighen for adopting Arab practices labeled as inauthentic. Given the current preoccupation with safeguarding rural Berber expressive traditions as testimony to Berber uniqueness and distinction, these "in-between" communities fare less well than their mountain co-ethnics in the new politics of culture.

Amazigh activists have shown a great aptitude for strategic thinking in their agitation for equal rights, even against powerful actors such as the state. Sometimes the state itself may become the Other, either in terms of suppressing basic rights, such as speaking and writing Berber, or preventing the peaceful gathering of Amazigh militants. As Jane Goodman points out, the Berber movement in Algeria became internationalized when Algerian Berberist activists agitating for cultural rights allied themselves with heroes of the Algerian Revolution who enjoyed impeccable credentials in the collective mind. By adopting this strategy, they legitimated their own status relative to the state; eventually, they achieved their objectives by positioning Berber cultural rights as human rights.

In France, another set of strategies was employed to gain attention for the Berber cause. Museum curators sought ways to use colonial-era collections to redefine France's relationship with its former colonial subjects. In her chapter on the opening of the new Musée du quai Branly in Paris in 2006, Lisa Bernasek demonstrates that Berber advocates in France saw an opportunity not to be missed. The emphasis on "first arts"—in the case of the Berber collections, a theme that underscores their pre-Islamic character—gave activists the opportunity to hijack official rhetoric and graft it onto their own pro-Berberist cultural agenda. Cynthia Becker offers yet another perspective on the subject of representation. She demonstrates how Amazigh artists working today in North Africa and the West have appropriated and integrated into their work images and icons sanctified by colonial scholar-ship and associated mainly with a pre-Islamic past. The use of these sym-bols deliberately reproduces long-discarded notions of an Amazigh essence. The irony of this reversion does not seem to disturb these new "inventors of tradition." Finally, Mokhtar Ghambou observes the consummate creativ-ity of Berber activists in the historiographical field and their willingness to reach back into the corpus of Greco-Roman texts on North Africa to rein-vent a Berber past disassociated from what he calls the "holiness" of Islamic and Arab hermeneutics.

As the range of papers in this volume illustrates, the arenas in which Berber/Amazigh identities are created, contested, and validated are now both local and international. Rural and urban Berbers now engage in horizon-tal communication across North and West Africa in ways not thought possible a generation ago. Today, virtual ties surmount the political divide. The internet, satellite television, and video compact discs (VCDs) have in-creased access to a growing array of representations. These influences do not negate longstanding forms of contact among Berbers and between Berbers and non-Berbers; rather, they broaden the repertoire of images used to fashion a sense of self. Activists are now able to make comparisons with other indigenous groups, such as Native Americans and Australian Aborigines. Activists have also been inspired by the transformation of He-brew from a scriptural to a living language, hoping that Tamazight, if simi-larly reworked, could emerge unified from today's various regional geolects such as Tashelhit, Tarifit, and Taqbilit.

Other areas of inquiry are matters of migration and transnationalism. Berbers have long been migrating from the countryside to cities in both North Africa and Europe.[5] Migration has taken on multiple forms: at first, single men, then whole families, and more recently, young girls seeking employment as domestic servants (Fr. *petites bonnes*) in urban households. As David Crawford points out, migration raises questions of social solidar-ity. Whereas earlier generations of scholars assumed that solidarity thrived at the tribal or village level, today such presumptions must be ethnographi-cally substantiated. Primary allegiance, Crawford argues, is to the household where resources are accumulated, distributed, and organized. Moreover, migration to Europe has shifted from being temporary and circular to a pattern that is closer to permanence. A significant Amazigh diaspora has emerged in Europe and North America whose goals and aspirations re-flect an engagement with Western values, aspirations, and institutions.

Moving Forward, Looking Back

While the wealth of new cultural forms in which Amazigh personhood presents itself is a primary topic of our investigations, this phenomenon is not free from its own self-induced hazards. In their contemporary articulations, the more accessible aspects of Amazigh identity tend to receive the bulk of scholarly and popular attention. Iconic practices and symbolic systems, such as music, dress, and language, have come to stand in for whole populations. Moreover, cadres of indigenous and foreign "experts"—gatekeepers, scholars, and other culture makers—are actively engaged in the production and consumption of things Berber. Representations of culture circulate and are debated, adopted, and disregarded; lines blur and objects merge in a continuous and energetic recreation of old genres along with the invention of new ones. Managed and promoted largely by urban Berber elites, the circulation of new cultural forms manipulated for political ends dominates our understanding of contemporary Berberness and its historical antecedents. Yet it must be kept in mind that activist and elitist representations do not necessarily stand for the experiences of the Berber masses, who are largely rural, often politically disengaged, and frequently economically deprived, and whose concerns tend to diverge widely from those of the urban intellectuals. To what extent, we may ask, do such images and representations return to the homeland and influence a sense of self? How are these broader conceptions being reabsorbed, digested, and changed in the very contexts that are their source? Is the reification of local culture, whether through state-sponsored folklore festivals or locally organized and staged musical performances, becoming the accepted standard of what constitutes Berberness? What happens to sense of self and community when the standards for authenticity and expertise are established by outside authorities?

Another topic worthy of study, not covered in this volume, is the commodification of Berberness for tourism and mass consumption. It is expressed not only through the sale of material objects such as carpets, textiles, and jewelry, but also through performances—often state-sponsored—that package Berber cultural practices for a mass audience. The Imilchil Moussem or "bridal fair" in the Eastern High Atlas, site of an annual pilgrimage observed by significant numbers of both foreign and Moroccan tourists, is one well-publicized example of the increasingly blatant marketing of Amazigh cultural practice. Media coverage of this annual event, at which certain women "select" their husbands from among hundreds of suitors, is recreated and promulgated in such a manner that it perpetuates longstanding and outmoded stereotypes about Berber society: that liberated Berber women are better off than "repressed" Arab women; that Berbers as a society are racially "distinct"; and that Berber marriage is the product of a handshake, a wink, and a nod. Morocco's oft-stated ambition is to welcome ten million tourists by the year 2010, nearly doubling the number of visitors that arrived in 2006. The effects of this increased flow are certain to extend to rural areas that already attract considerable tourism. How this flood of curiosity-seekers will affect Berber lives and livelihoods is beyond anyone's capacity to predict, but surely there will be an impact.

It is not our aim here to propose an agenda for future research. Rather, we have tried to expose some of the strengths and weaknesses of the current state of research, and to point out the direction in which scholarship is moving. Maintaining momentum in this field of study requires that Tamazight language be retained by its present speakers and that aspiring fieldworkers be given the opportunity to learn it. While institutional actors like the Royal Institute of the Amazigh Culture (IRCAM) could play a major role in this endeavor, it is the rural populations, the village dwellers, the women who stay home and instruct the next generation in language arts, who are the principal agents of language maintenance. To some degree, the continuing vitality of Berber cultural studies is dependent on stabilizing rural economies and providing improved services, better conditions of life, and greater economic opportunities that will induce Berber speakers to remain in or relocate back to the countryside. In the long run, the ability to sustain rural life is a crucial part of a larger framework in which the continuity of a living Berber consciousness resides. As cities fill with more Berber speakers, research on all social categories of the urban population—not just intellectual elites—becomes pressing as well. Fieldwork in both rural and urban settings—and on the interconnections between them, as several of this book's chapters suggest—is essential to keeping Amazigh matters on the public agenda.

Whether the current exuberance for things Berber is ephemeral or will be sustained over time is still unclear. Critical to supporting a broad research agenda is the need to liberate from their desks the cadre of professional Maghribi scholars who have been co-opted into institutional settings and loaded down with administrative tasks. Hopefully, they will soon return to the field where their sources thrive. Younger scholars need training and resources to conduct field and archival research so that they are not dependent solely on memory and personal experiences. Beyond a doubt, the judicious deployment of resources and talent in the Maghrib itself is still the most important factor in the future growth and expansion of Berber studies.

Notes

1. Ernest Gellner and Charles A. Micaud, *Arabs and Berbers: From Tribe to Nation in North Africa* (Lexington, Mass.: Heath, 1972).

2. Many of the contributions in the Gellner and Micaud volume have indeed withstood the test of time and have become canonical, not only in Berber studies, but also with respect to the broader fields of Maghribi and Middle Eastern studies.

3. Centre des Archives diplomatiques de Nantes, Maroc Protectorat, DAI 59, document AB22.

4. Nico van den Boogert, *The Berber Literary Tradition of the Sous*: with an edition and translation of "The Ocean of Tears" by Muḥammad Awzal (d. 1749) (Leiden: Nederlands Instituut voor het Nabije Oosten, 1997).

5. A notable foray into this subject in the Gellner and Micaud volume was John Waterbury's chapter on political aspects of migration from the Sus to Casablanca: "Tribalism, trade and politics: The transformation of the Swasa of Morocco," 231–258.

Bibliography

Anderson, Benedict. *Imagined Communities: Reflections on the Origin and Spread of Nationalism*. New York: Verso, 1983.

Barth, Frederik. Introduction. *Ethnic Groups and Boundaries: The Social Organization of Culture Differences*. London: George Allen and Unwin, 1969.

Bourdieu, Pierre. *Outline of a Theory of Practice*. Cambridge: Cambridge University Press, 1977.

Dwyer, Kevin. *Moroccan Dialogues: Anthropology in Question*. Baltimore, Md.: Johns Hopkins University. 1982.

Geertz, Clifford. *The Interpretation of Cultures*. New York: Basic Books, 1973.

Gellner, Ernest, and Charles Micaud, eds. *Arabs and Berbers: From Tribe to Nation in North Africa*. Lexington, Mass.: D. C. Heath and Co., 1972.

Hammoudi, Abdellah. *The Victim and Its Masks: An Essay on Sacrifice*. Chicago: University of Chicago, 1993.

Hobsbawn, Eric, and Terrance Ranger, eds. *The Invention of Tradition*. Cambridge: Cambridge University Press, 1983.

Hoffman, Katherine E. "Berber Language Ideologies, Maintenance, and Contraction: Gendered Variation in the Indigenous Margins of Morocco." *Language & Communication* 26(2) (2006): 144–167.

Rabinow, Paul. *Reflections on Fieldwork in Morocco*. Berkeley: University of California, 1977.

van den Boogert, Nico. *The Berber Literary Tradition of the Sous*. Leiden: Nederlands Instituut voor het Nabije Oosten, 1997.

PART 1

SOURCES AND METHODS

1

Histories of Heresy and Salvation: Arabs, Berbers, Community, and the State

James McDougall

This history is, perhaps, nothing but a heresiology. [. . .]
Indeed, throughout North African history, people may
always have been labelled as "puritan" or "heretic," just as
they have been as "nomad" or "peasant." Or even "Arab"
or "Berber."

"Arab" and "Berber," in most accounts of Maghribi history, are both logically and chronologically prior categories. They precede history, are present at its inception, and move through it; they serve as the ground on which authority is asserted and rights are claimed; they are a constant factor of, and an explanatory mechanism for, social structure and conflict. "Arab-Berber" antagonism has often been seen as one of the several binary mechanisms—overlaying or correlating with others[1]—that have supposedly produced the vicissitudes, or the cyclical stasis, of Maghribi history. Ethnicity has thus tended to be written into Maghribi history as a foundational and causal category, whether (as scientifically ascribed) based on allegedly biological "race," lifestyle and habitation, language and cultural practice, or (as politically assumed) on community of blood, origin, home, or custom. The French scholar de Slane became an early and influential exemplar of this practice, when, in the mid-nineteenth century, he chose L'Histoire des Berbères as the title for his translation of the section of Ibn Khaldun's Kitab al-ʿibar that aimed to incorporate the North African populations encountered by the Arabs into a more general history of the peoples of the earth.[2] In the early 1970s, Gellner and Micaud did much the same when they documented what they thought of as the transition "from tribe to nation in North Africa" as a story defined by modernizing state-formation faced with the primordial ties and conflicts of "Arabs and Berbers."[3] Histories of nationalism written from the 1920s through the 1970s as the recovery of (Arab-Islamic) sovereignty and selfhood, and narratives of Amazigh revival seen in the 1980s and 1990s as an ethnic minority movement reclaiming its indigenous place in history, also operated in these same terms.

Practices of ethnic classification—the categorization of social groups on the basis of cultural and linguistic commonalities and differences—have their own history. The categories that such practices produce become "naturalized" in individual self-consciousness and community self-definition, thus acquiring a socially organizing force and a political potential of their own, but they cannot be considered as trans-historical constants. The history of North African ethnicity seen as the pre-existing relationship between Arabs and Berbers, whether as conflict, cooperation, or submersion of one by the other, poses the wrong questions. It is no more useful, as an explanatory device for historical change or continuity, than those other perennial couples, "peasants and nomads," or "puritans and heretics." We might more usefully consider ethnicity neither as "primordial" nor as contingently articulated at the relational boundary between groups, as Fredrik Barth suggested,[4] but rather as located historically in changing discourses and practices of *self-narrative* and ascriptive naming that occur within social competition, struggles for recognition and prominence, and claims to legitimate sovereignty.[5] The argument in this chapter is that we ought, in reexamining "Arab" and "Berber" as terms of analysis and as self-designations, to seek a more nuanced understanding of Maghribi history than has generally been afforded by the mechanistic deployment of these terms as a permanent ethnic dualism. This should not mean simply the "rehabilitation" of an essentialized Berber identity that has been suppressed since the independence of the Maghribi states by officially Arab-Muslim "national identities" in which "Berberism" was a kind of heretical and backward sectarianism. The officialization, codification, and patronage now afforded Amazigh culture and language in both Algeria and Morocco do not mean a final salvation of Berber identity,[6] however overdue its recognition as a legitimate part of Maghribi socio-cultural reality. It is, rather, a new, and in many respects problematic, rearrangement of the relationship between cultural self-definition, formulations of political community, and the claims of the state. As this chapter will suggest, it is this relationship that ought itself to be the focus of enquiry.

The history of how "Arab" and "Berber" have operated in social organization, as designations of selfhood or difference, should then become visible in a more subtle light. In necessarily general terms, this history can be summarized as follows: both "Arab" and "Berber" are ethnographic inventions of late antiquity. In the medieval and early modern periods, both terms were employed in practices of naming in which heredity or ethnolinguistic self-definition were crosscut by, and refracted through, other concerns. What really mattered were competitions for socio-cultural and political legitimacy whose primary horizon of reference was not "ethnicity" as such, but notions of value, authority, and belonging codified by Islam, and within which both "Arab" and "Berber" (and other labels) gained meaning. When outside observers of this period ascribed ethnic labels to the Maghrib's populations, attempting to distinguish "Arabs" from "Berbers" (and others), they were attempting to codify boundaries that they themselves did not understand, and that cannot be assumed to have had any correlative existence in the minds or practices of the people described. This situation changed when the meanings of "Arab" and "Berber" were politically reinvented and codified in the nineteenth century sciences of ethnographic classification and rational government. Both terms were then reproduced with new meanings within Maghribi societies, especially from the mid-1940s onward: first, in the service of simultaneously emancipatory and disciplinary nationalist mobilizations; subsequently, in the institutionalized official culture of the Maghrib's post-colonial states; then, in reaction to those states' practices of domination, selection, and exclusion; and, most recently, in the states' attempted co-option and neutralizing of "Berberism" as an oppositional force.

In what follows, I concentrate on one part of this argument; namely, on the role of Islam as a conception of universal history and as a normative social code in the creation of cultural community and political sovereignty in the Maghrib. It is within this nexus of universal history, moral value, community definition, and sovereignty that the signifying practices of ethnicity, and the meanings they have carried, have been primarily located. This is not—and this point must be emphasized—an argument for a distinction of "religion" from "ethnicity" or for the primacy of the former over the latter, as if, this being a "Muslim society," everything in it must be explained by Islam.[7] The point is rather, as David Crawford observes of contemporary Berber society in the High Atlas, that "the practices central to being Muslim are so embedded in daily life that they do not constitute a separable category of experience."[8] The history of Maghribi ethnicity, of "Arabs" and "Berbers," cannot adequately be understood without this third term—which in fact has generally been primary, a non-isolatable and "unthought constant" in the history of Maghribis' own signifying practices.[9] On an everyday social level, local knowledge in North Africa has defined individuals and groups primarily by judgments of their moral worth. In public discourse and political practice, such groups have defined themselves and each other through claims about legitimate sovereignty. It is at the level of community and state formation that self-designation and ascriptive labeling as Arabs/Berbers has historically occurred among Maghribi peoples; it is primarily with reference to Islam that, since the late seventh century, such designations have been made meaningful.

It is striking that in ancient Greek and Latin sources, no single ethnographic term comparable to those that name the great enemy peoples of the north (Galli and Germani) serves to designate the peoples of North Africa.[10] There are Libyans, Numidians, Gaetulians, Garamantes, Massyli and Masaesyli, Mazices, Mauri, and Barbaroi: a variety of groups and kingdoms familiar to and, at least from the late third century BCE, incorporated into the regional politics and commerce of the Hellenistic and Roman Mediterranean. The Arabs, newly equipped with the self-consciousness of a distinct people charged by God with a historical mission and an eternal message, swept aside the relics of Byzantium in North Africa; however, unlike the Romans, they came up against people who posed a sufficient obstacle to their progress to appear as a distinct and problematic unity: *al-barbar*. The Arabic term, almost certainly borrowed from Greek and Latin (*barbaroi, barbari*, speakers of an unintelligible language), is thus the first generalized ascription of an ethnonym to indigenous North Africans. From the earliest chronicle of the conquest (the *Futuh Misr* of Ibn 'Abd al-Hakam, who died in 871) to its codification in the great historical compendium of Ibn Khaldun five centuries later, it is in fact the Arabs who "invented" the Berbers as a single, definable "ethnic" group.

But labels of cultural difference and racial identity among "the peoples of the world" in medieval Arabic ethnography and history explain nothing in themselves. They are encompassed by an understanding of human identities and actions as carrying meaning, and as being susceptible to judgment, on the basis of their place in a universal salvation history. The mythologized figures of the Kahina and Kusayla, the Berber leaders of local resistance to the Islamic conquests who should probably be seen as defending a continuity of order in Byzantine Africa during the early, tentative, and discontinuous Arab incursions, find their place in an elaborate, heroic mythography of the conquest as a predestined Muslim triumph. The *barbar* of the early Arabic chronicles are duly incorporated into the universal history of Islam, whose victory the Berbers' own religious otherness is made to foresee and accept through the Kahina's prophecies.[11]

The development of social status and labeling in the first century after the conquests was clearly a complex process of negotiation—more complex than the surviving sources can ever openly admit. Careful interpretive work has to be done on the developing meanings of *islam* (submission), *muslim* (one who has made submission), and *mu'min* (believer) in an emerging post-conquest society and a religious-ideological system only beginning to formalize its conceptual categories and organize them into hierarchies. We have to tease out the connections between religious legitimacy and patronage and client relations, the shifts and transactions between unstable, racialized, and religious group identifications.[12] In the historiography and cultural politics of nationalism that reimagined the seventh century through the struggles of the twentieth, this process was flattened out and simplified. Islamization was elided with Arabization, removing "Berber" as a legitimate category altogether. As the Algerian and Kabyle Islamic reformist activist and Muslim Brother Faudel al-Wartilani put it, writing in the Syrian and Lebanese press at the height of the crisis in the 1950s, "there are no Berbers in the Arab Maghrib." The Berbers, he says (who in any case, "as some historians tell us, were of Arab origin"), "all became Arabized after the successive Arab migrations into their lands, and there does not remain today in the land of the Arab Maghrib anyone who would say: 'I am a Berber,' or who would accept that anyone describe him thus."[13] Almost half a century later, Algerian President Abdelaziz Bouteflika gave a different twist to the same line. During his first official visit as head of state to the Kabyle town of Tizi Ouzou, faced by hostile protestors chanting "Imazighen! Imazighen!" he responded: "We are all Berbers; *Imazighen Arabized by Islam!*"[14]

The strident insistence of this doctrine is, perhaps, an indication of its tenuous grip on credibility. Berberophones living in the Maghrib in the seventh and eighth centuries were not, of course, Arabized by Islam—significant linguistic Arabicization came only in the eleventh and twelfth centuries, and when it did occur (in Morocco perhaps as late as the early twentieth century), the Arabization of the majority was due to demographic and political factors rather than to Islamic observance or education that had been rooted in the Berberophone countryside for centuries. Nor, in the inverse view most notably expressed toward the end of his life by the great Algerian novelist and poet Kateb Yacine, did the Arabs, "a minute minority within us [the Berber majority]" simply "dominate us through religion," inversing the natural cultural balance of the region and making the Berbers "a minority isolated within an Arab people."[15] As Abdallah Laroui pointed out, "Islamization [in North Africa] was the work of the Berbers themselves."[16] Historically, Islam neither equated to the category "Arab," nor effaced the category "Berber," as both official Arab nationalist and dissident

Amazigh secularist views have recently claimed. This elision of "Islam" and "Muslim" with "Arabic" and "Arab" and the opposition of "Berber" to both is a very recent invention. Before the nineteenth and twentieth centuries brought about first a colonial science of the Berber and then a nationalist doctrine of Arabo-Islamism, North African peoples, both Arabophone and Berberophone, and presumably always with degrees of "brokerage" in between,[17] had engaged in almost a millennium of historical change enacted and imagined primarily through a universal history of Islam. Into this universal history, Arab and Berber "ethnicities" were subsumed as distinct languages, cultures, lifestyles, and physiognomies. Within it, each expressed its distinctive particularities, defining itself alongside or against others.

This is not to posit a harmonious Muslim idyll before the invasion of the West. Local conflicts, racial and social stratifications, antagonisms, and particularisms manifested themselves within primarily Muslim subjectivities—Shi'a and Sunni, Maliki and Ibadi, "bad" Muslims, "good" Muslims, and "better" Muslims, "recent" Muslims (blacks and Berberophones), "original" Muslims (immigrants from Arabia and those claiming Arab ancestry), and descendents of the Prophet. The particular forms in which Islamic norms were espoused in the Maghrib were merely local variants of more diffuse tendencies within Islam: saint-mediation, Shi'ism and kharijism, the use of a local language in religious texts, the persistence of local agricultural and social rites and their inclusion within a worldview now considered "Islamic." Such practices nonetheless provided self-identifying orthodox, urban, Maliki, literate, and literature-producing "Arabs," regardless of whom their own ancestors may actually have been, with a set of denunciations with which to characterize "Berbers" as pagans, schismatics, heretics, and serial apostates.

But at the same time, the adoption of Arabic as the primary language of scriptural culture, indeed, as the only script for writings in Berber languages (except among the Tuareg), along with hypotheses of Arab ancestry and identification with Islamic salvation history, served to articulate claims among Berbers to cultural and political legitimacy. Such claims did not negate, but sought to transcend or elide Arab/Berber ethno-linguistic difference within the *umma* (the community of believers). In the centuries after the conquest, Islam served in a variety of idioms to express movements that mobilized Berberophone groups within, and not against, the broader *umma*. Indeed, these movements often claimed legitimate leadership of the *umma* itself. The Shi'i Fatimid revolution began among the Kutama people of lower Kabylia at the end of the ninth century and drove out the Aghlabid dynasty from Ifriqiya (modern Tunisia) in 909 in a claim not simply to North African sovereignty against a Middle Eastern caliphate, nor in an outburst of "Berber" hostility to "Arabs," but in an aspiration to universal legitimate rule—to state-building in the name of God. In the Kharijism that took root in the Maghrib in the eighth century, the movement of the Almoravids in the eleventh century, and that of the Almohads in the twelfth century, "ethnic" Berber as against Arab identity is nowhere demonstrably relevant as a causal factor. Kharijites, Fatimids, Almoravids, and Almohads all claimed sovereignty as Muslims over Muslims, and their revolts, in their own terms, were those of "good Muslims" against "bad Muslims," whether Berber or Arab or other. The circular argument that reads every religious particularism among Berberophones as a manifestation of self-consciously Berber resistance—resisting Arabs through sectarian Islam as they had earlier resisted Romans through sectarian Christianity[18]—is a product of the contemporary naturalization of ethnic categories, not of the historical evidence. This point can be clarified if we examine the most famous of "Berber" heresies, the Barghawata movement of the ninth through eleventh centuries.

The state and the religion created by the Berberophone Barghawata people in the Tamasna region of western-central Morocco in the mid-ninth century lasted for two centuries. They survived the initial emergence of the Almoravids, whose founder, ʿAbdallah ibn Yasin, was killed in battle against them in 1059, delaying Almoravid expansion for eleven years until the kingdom's destruction by Abdallah's successor, Yusuf ibn Tashufin, in his victorious sweep north from Marrakesh. The Baghawata case has often been seen as the point at which the argument of religious innovation as the expression of ethnic particularism is at its strongest. The great Tunisian medievalist and Islamic thinker, Mohamed Talbi, called the heresy an example of "acculturation in the service of the old and still lively Berber nationalism" and "a kind of medieval decolonization [. . . a] defensive acculturation taking from the enemy arsenal the means for a complete national liberation."[19] In Talbi's ingenious account—which tells us as much about the intellectual context of the 1970s as it does about the ninth through eleventh centuries—the Berbers of western Morocco "cleansed themselves of their complexes" relative to the Arab conquerors through "the adoption of heresy as a catalyst for national aspirations [. . . in] the creation of a truly autonomous religion [. . .] to save their humiliated and threatened national soul."[20] For Talbi, the Barghawata heresy is an anti-colonial nationalist movement, emerging from a relative acculturation to (Arab) Islam but expressing an essential and insurgent "Berber personality":

> . . . the Berbers who rebelled in the name of Bargawatism were, unbeknownst to themselves, relatively deeply acculturated in contact with the civilizational values imported from the Orient. This acculturation was, in

any case, sufficiently powerful to impose upon them the cultural models that had served as the basis for elaborating an ideological and social system which, under the name of Bargawatism, was destined to *recover their personality and reaffirm it against the alienating spiritual domination of the foreigner.* Is it necessary to underline that a similar phenomenon can be seen in certain processes of decolonization in our own time?[21]

It is clearly the politics of the 1970s, not of the 840s, that produce this interpretation.[22] H. T. Norris, another great scholar of Berber societies, Arabic literature, and Islamic traditions, following Talbi, suggests that the aim of the founder of the movement, Yunus ibn Ilyas, "was to radically Berberize Islam in a local and wholly independent form."[23] Yunus apparently devised the sect's doctrines during or after his return from pilgrimage to the Hijaz, and imposed them on the state he had inherited from his grandfather, Salih ibn Tarif. It is Salih who is seen in the Arabic accounts as the originator of the heresy, disappearing into the Mashriq and promising to return as the *mahdi* ("the rightly guided": a messianic redeemer), identifying himself with the *salih al-mu'minin* ("comforter of the faithful") mentioned in the Qur'an (LXVI, 4). For Talbi and Norris, Salih ibn Tarif is a good Muslim as well as "a Berber patriot" onto whom the origin of the new movement was projected in the mythical history invented by his grandson. In accounting for the actions of Yunus, the inventor of the Barghawata doctrines, and very possibly of their Berber Qur'an with its eighty chapters,[24] Norris, paraphrasing Talbi, also goes to extremes of interpretive latitude. It was, he suggests, "either out of perverse religious zeal or from mental derangement, or because of some hatred which had entered his heart while he was in the East" that he "drew from the enemy arsenal such weapons as would enable him to achieve a cultural liberation for the Berbers who had attained political freedom through the Kharijites."[25]

This is all very problematic, first of all because it attributes to the actual content of the movement a mere instrumentality that cannot be justified except by modern conceptions of political ideology that do not belong in the story, and secondly, because it is far from clear that the movement was conceived of as a *departure* from, a revolt *against*, an Islam identified as a foreign and "alienating spiritual domination." "The name of Bargawatism" under which the people of Tamasna formed their kingdom is Talbi's own shorthand for a religion that has no name in the sources. If it seems unlikely that its adherents called it simply their "Islam" (as have most non-Sunni "heretics," from the Shi'a to the Ahmadiyya), it is, nonetheless, a decidedly Islamic sectarianism. The Barghawata professed supernumerary prayers (five during the day and five at night) and other signs of zealous one-upmanship, such as fasting one day a week, additional dietary rules, strict social morality including a ban on concubinage, stoning for illicit sexual intercourse, the execution of thieves, and banishment of liars. Along with these went a doctrine of concealment (*taqiyya*) and the promised return, in the reign of the seventh king of the dynasty, of the *mahdi*, the "comforter of the faithful" alongside Gabriel and the angels, behind whom Jesus son of Mary would pray. This is a hyper-rigorist inflection of Islam informed by Shi'ism and Kharijism, and, perhaps, by pre-existing notions of prophetic kingship and practices locally associated with Judaism. The Qur'an of Salih (or Yunus), however original its content, was apparently calqued for its form and its legitimacy as an idiom of revelation on "the Qur'an of Muhammad." The Qur'an itself may or may not have been well known to the people of Tamasna, but its existence and some of its themes and personalities must have been familiar.[26] The revelation brought to the Barghawata follows the Qur'anic model of messengers sent to different locales to bring their people to God, and it does not seem at all inappropriate to regard it as basically akin to other local prophetic or messianic movements that punctuated Islamic history from its beginning through the nineteenth century, by re-actualizing the founding dynamic of the faith in moments of crisis.

This is a story that lies within—on the fringes of, but not beyond— Islamic history.[27] Brett and Fentress are right to remark on "the *false Islam* of the Barghawata," a localized "imitation" of the conquering model that the people saw triumphant around them—but it was "false" only because it failed to survive as a viable sectarian variant.[28] Most importantly, this story—to the extent that its sources can safely be interpreted[29]—is not about decolonization or cultural liberation. The movement's proselytizing zeal to massacre fellow Berberophones while sending embassies to the Umayyad caliphs in Cordoba can hardly be read as "ethnic" assertion or proto-nationalism. It was a state-building movement, better seen as a local (as distinct from "ethnically" particularist) expression of a normative religious system engaged in local struggles for authority and community cohesion. Brett is right again to find the significance of the Barghawata in the fact that "they pointed to the possibility of a new *Muslim* revolution."[30] Their mahdist idiom of authority and their millenarian promise of justice, borrowed and radicalized from the Khariji revolt of the 740s, prefigured the emergence of the Fatimids.

Anxiety about status in the first decades of the conquest, in which Muslim, Arab, and Barbar connoted positions in a newly coalescing social order, quickly gave way, with the fragmentation of the early caliphate, to a diverse set of social and cultural self-identifications in which Islamic idioms were formed, appropriated, and put to use in local struggles for authority and legitimacy. The Barghawata are only the most inventive, a limited case of a more general trend. Shi'ism and Ibadism, the status of *shurafa'* (descendants of the Prophet) and saints, are all part of the same story, one also told in terms of collective genealogy and narratives of origin. The dynamic political landscape and mobile societies of the ninth through the thirteenth centuries laid down rich stores of origin myth, stories of migration and genealogical tradition that would nourish local histories into the modern period.[31] All were loosely but crucially linked together by a symbolic language of Islam that was shared, but also locally diverse and contested. Questions of preeminence and hierarchy, of equality or subordination, and of local social value and legitimacy within the *umma* would be played out in religious movements, from the wars of the Barghawata against their Arab and Berber neighbors in the ninth century to the revolt of the Darqawa against the Ottoman state in the nineteenth. The same purpose was served by Ibn Khaldun's tortuous genealogies, which tried to put legibility and order into the considerable chaos of his own time, and in the everyday labeling of "self" and "other" through derisive anecdotes, invented *hadiths* (statements attributed to the Prophet), the *mafakhir al-barbar* ("Glorious Exploits of the Berbers") and the *sirat Beni Hilal* ("Saga of the Beni Hilal").[32] These again are expressions of social identity in which the moral value and social legitimacy of individual figures and groups are expressed in terms of Islam.

By the sixteenth century, the Maghrib had seen the fragmentation and recomposition of a series of states, and the proliferation of forms of religious authority and practice left in their wake. Along with them came the migration and resettlement of populations—of Berberophones into the Djurdjura and Arabophones into the western Sahara, merchants and refugees from Andalusia into Fez and Tlemçen, soldiers and adventurers from the Ottoman East into Algiers and Tripoli. Early modern observers thus confronted a diverse and polyglot community. Hassan al-Wazzan, a refugee from Granada, brought up in Fez and writing in Italy in the mid-1500s as Leo Africanus, describing his country to a European audience, was necessarily expert at the blurring of neat dividing lines. His description of the inhabitants of Africa distinguishes Berbers ("Moores") from Arabs ("Arabians"), and even posits a level of linguistic unity among the former:

> The tawnie Moores are divided into five severall people or tribes: to wit, the tribes called Zanhagi, Musmudi, Zeneti, Hacari, and Gumeri [. . .] The foresaid five families or people, being divided into hundreds of progenies, and having innumerable habitations, doe notwithstanding use all one kinde of language, called by them *Aquel Amarigh* [i.e., *awal amazigh*, the Amazigh language], that is, the noble toong: the Arabians which inhabite Africa, call it a barbarous toong; and this is the true and naturall language of the Africans.[33]

But this is only a first level of description. Further on, we learn both how this distinction is linguistically attenuated and in what sense group belonging is really understood:

> the Arabians began to inhabit Africa, and to disperse themselves among the Africans, who [. . .] used to speake their language: and hence it is, that the naturall and mother-toong of the Arabians, which hath great affinitie with the African toong, grewe by little and little to be corrupted: and so they report that *these two nations at length conioined* [conjoined] *themselves in one. Howbeit the Arabians usually doe blaze their pedigree in daily and triviall songs; which custome as yet is common both to us* [i.e., Andalusis], *and to the people of Barbarie also.*[34]

Here we are back from an apparently binary ethnolinguistic map to the narratives of "pedigree," of inclusion, adoption, and competition which structure Leo's history of identity-formation more generally, rooted as it is in the genealogical and salvation-history myths of origin that he, and Ibn Khaldun before him, had inherited from earlier medieval scholarship. Thus, in a restatement of a series of medieval migration stories, "the originall of the tawnie people," that is to say, "of the Numidians and Barbarians," come into an "altogether disinhabited" North Africa from southern Arabia, from Asia via Greece, or from Palestine. *Barbar* has either the usual etymology "to murmur, because the African toong soundeth in the eares of the Arabians, no otherwise than the voice of beasts," or (in a less common spin on a common story), because the ancient Yemeni king Ifriqish "seeing himselfe so oppressed with his enimies, that he knew not what should become of him and his followers, he asked his people how or which way it was possible to escape, who answered him *Bar-Bar*, that is, to the desert, to the desert [. . .]."[35]

The terms of Leo's ethnography illustrate the unsettled lexicon in use during this period. "Moors," derived from the ancient *Mauri*, is a term, like "Turk," sometimes meaning simply "Muslim" (just as for the Spanish, who would call the Muslims of the Philippines "moros"). Here they are synonymous with (Muslim) "Africans," whether black or white, but all Berberophone and primarily rural.[36] More usually, especially in English, however, "Moors" are urban sophisticates, descendants of the Andalusian refugees to North Africa like Leo himself.

From the sixteenth century through the first decades of the nineteenth, endless energy was expended on the classification of a population that constantly eludes categorical capture. One careful account asserted that "Shelluhs" (*ishelhin*) in southern Morocco speak a language entirely separate from that of "Berebbers" (of the Middle Atlas and Rif) further north.[37] The first European Berber grammar and dictionary, assembled between

1788 and 1790 in Paris and Algiers, on the other hand, insists that from the Sous to Jerba, the "Berbers" (who live in tents on the plains, like the Arabs) and the "Chuluhs" and "Cabayles" (inhabitants of the mountains) speak "the same language" and "are everywhere nothing but one selfsame people . . . the remnants of Carthaginians, Romans, Greeks and Vandals."[38] As for "Cabayles" or "Qabyles," the term generally appears to mean simply "tribes" (from the Arabic *qaba'il*), i.e., rural people—most likely Berberophone, but not labeled as such. Those that Napoleon's spy, Boutin, found among the "Turks, Jews, Negroes, Greeks, and Armenians, Moors or 'Algerians' and Mozabites" of Algiers in 1808 were to him *"mountain Arabs called Kabyles."*[39] The term was applied to the populations of the Atlas and the Dahra south and west of Algiers as well as to those of the Djurdjura and Babors to the east, and in 1830 the French army's first proclamation was addressed *"ila sukkan madinat al-jaza'ir wa ahali al-qaba'il,"* "to the inhabitants of the city of Algiers and the people of the tribes," i.e., to the rural population at large. In the early 1840s, an English traveler still described Algeria as the land of "the Moors, Kabyles, Arabs, Turks, Jews, Negroes, Cologlies [*kuluğlari*, descendants of Turkish fathers and local mothers] and other inhabitants."[40]

If the inexact nature of this "ethnic" map seen from outside is itself instructive about the practices of categorization that our sources felt were important, it also illustrates how all such sources are external attempts to categorize a social reality that is not fully grasped. What their terms may or may not have meant to those so designated, and how they might have designated *themselves*, is far from self-evident. The appropriate question here is, how useful is it to look in these sources for the ethnic distinctions of the sociological knowledge familiar to us, and how useful is that knowledge for understanding the cultural differences of the world they describe? Of course, there are Arabs and Berbers, in some sense—as communities of language and heredity—in these narratives. But this distinction is far from clear; much less can it be assumed to convey adequately self-designations, or understandings of cultural difference, among the people concerned.[41]

The classifications of outside observers, however, do carry a naturalizing force of their own, especially when combined with the particular kinds of categorizing practice enacted by the modern state. Sociological "error" is, after all, a way of making history, and perfectly capable of producing the conditions of its own truthfulness. From the mid-nineteenth century onward, new social and political dispensations structured around observations of linguistic and legal practice materialized categorical distinctions between "Arab" and "Berber" in more "orderly," but much less subtle, ways. It was not so much that, for the first time since the fourteenth century, French ethnography amounted to a "rediscovery of the Berbers as a nation in their own right" via the discovery and publication of Ibn Khaldun.[42] Rather, the discovery of Ibn Khaldun and the reading of his categories—the great *umam* (in nineteenth-century terms, "nations") of the world—through nineteenth-century preoccupations with romanticism and antiquity as well as with imperial rule and scientific racism, *constituted* "the Berbers" as a single, definable "nation" (and/or "race") in their own right—or rather, in the eyes of their self-appointed rediscoverers. As Brett and Fentress observe, "Just as the Berbers [as such] had been invented by the Arabs for the purpose of the Arab conquest and the Arab empire, so now they were finally resurrected by the French as a subject race to be kept apart from their Arab neighbors in the interest of French hegemony," and in the interest of their own "civilizational" advancement.[43] French colonial mythology portrayed "Barbary," Berber North Africa, as an eternal "land of conquest" destined to be the domain of a Western imperial vocation.[44] Writers in this vein thought to find in "the Berbers" a hardy, enterprising and martial race of uncertain provenance but clearly distinct from "the Arabs," naturally belonging to a renewed Mediterranean sphere of Occidental influence.

In response, the Arab-Islamic cultural nationalism of the mid-twentieth century created a doctrine of Maghribi nations rooted in ethnic and spiritual homelands further east. The Berbers, as *bani Kanʿan* ("sons of Canaan"), having migrated from the Middle East in the depths of protohistory, were "Arab" in temperament and ancestry, Muslim by adoption and destiny. Nationalism riposted to the narrative of a salvific, civilizing empire rescuing the Maghrib from "anarchy" and "despotism" with a civilizing mission of its own, rooted in the distant past of an independent people now promised their ultimate redemption from local "superstition" as well as foreign oppression.[45]

Three converging factors reordered North Africa's ethno-cultural landscape between the 1880s and the mid-1940s, all products of the combined and interdependent development of colonialism and nationalism. First came a newly widespread, newly canonical definition of Islamic orthodoxy advocated by the *salafi* reformist movement.[46] Second was the exclusive identification of "Arabs" and Arabic with Islam, both by colonial observers obsessed with the dangers of "Arab" subversion and "fanaticism," and by the spokesmen of cultural nationalism fascinated by the intellectual and political reinventions both of "Islam" and of the "Arab" taking place in Egypt and Syria. Third was a correlative reimagining of "Berbers" as something other than primarily Muslims. Even as Berberophone nationalist activists adopted Amazigh (meaning "free" or "noble") identity in the service of anti-colonial struggle, Arabophone nationalist ideologues were redefining "the Berbers" as primordial ancestors destined to disappear in a sacred salvation history now imagined as that of the *Arab*-Muslim nation. For colonial writers, they would indeed "disappear" if prudent colonial policy could not "save" them.

By the 1950s crisis of decolonization, the nationalist movements had crystallized into forces of social discipline with a new set of dominant institutions, and the redefinitions of "Arab," "Berber," and Islam had produced a newly reified and dominant frame of reference. The Arab-Berber dichotomy as a basic ethnic antagonism was superimposed onto what had historically been more subtle expressions of social relationships. Colonial knowledge, refashioned by nationalism, elided Islam with Arab and Arabic, producing sharply distinguished Arab (-Muslim) and Berber/Amazigh subjectivities as operative political categories in which the former meant salvation, the latter, heresy. The effective force of this categorization was such that Berber language and culture would be forcibly excluded, for half a century, from legitimate conceptions and expressions of society and nation. Pushed out of their place in the nation, Berber language and culture became instead the expression of a minority, oppositional political identity, especially in Algeria.

This was not ineluctable. At the time of Maghribi independence, the inhabitants of the High Atlas, the Sous, the Rif, the Mzab, Kabylia and the Aurès, the Hoggar and Tassili, Djerba and Jebel Nefusa, understood themselves as Muslims, as members of immediate and extended families, as tied to specific places and toponyms, and (more recently) as Moroccans, Algerians, Tunisians, or Libyans who spoke a language and practiced a culture that were "Moroccan" or "Algerian" without being Arabic. They had not generally thought of themselves as "Berbers," and not, at least before the mid-1940s and outside particular parts of Morocco, as "Imazighen," a term whose emergence as a generally recognized and self-ascribed ethnonym among Berberophone groups is the product of a recent history of ethnicity formation, beginning around 1945.[47] And if a particularly dogmatic adoption of Mashriqi Arab nationalism had not so powerfully influenced the cultural doctrines of North Africa's independence movements, then Arabic-speaking Maghribis (many of whose grandparents or great-grandparents would have spoken a Berber variety) might also have avoided ethnic reductionism while defining their cultural community axiomatically as "Arab." Up to the 1950s, it was still possible to express Maghribi culture and identity in the elision of Arab-Berber difference, foreseeing a national community which would be Arab, Berber, and Muslim without there being any essential "otherness," coercion, or alienation in any of those terms. One eloquent exponent of such a view was the Kabyle poet Qasi Udifella N'Ait Sidi Braham, born in 1898, who wrote between 1936 and his death in 1950.[48] For Qasi, salvation both temporally and eternally lay in Islam, and in a salvation history shared by "Arabs" and "Berbers" and their distinct but equal languages and cultures.

Wa yenna-t id Weqbayli	These are the words of a Kabyle
Mazal yessuli	Who has not finished (speaking)
Kullas irennu-d kra	Each day he says more
Yethibb' ayen n lɛali	He loves what is good
Maččid d lwali	He is no saint
Yebɣ' a-ṭ-idd-yeǧǧ d ccira [. . .]	But desires to leave clear signs [. . .]
Yeffeɣ-ed waggur n tziri	The bright moon has risen
Tedwa Laljiri	Lighting Algeria
Ya lqari fhem lhedra [. . .]	You who know, understand what I say [. . .]
Yusa-d lɛilm aɛsri	The science of the age has arrived
Yeld' i-medden izri	That opens the eyes of men
Feqden medden ccaǧara	Who seek for their origins
S-ttarix lansari	About the history of the *ansar*
Seqsit lqari	You should ask those who know
ɣed zzman n lhijra	And about the time of the *hijra*[49]

For Qasi, the promise of nationalism was still emancipatory, whether in Kabylia, the Atlas, or the Aurès, and "there was no need to speak Arabic to be a good Muslim."[50] The poet could still tell his listeners in Kabyle to "seek for their origins" in "the history of the *ansar*" and "the time of the *hijra*": this did not mean abandoning "Berber identity" for an "Arab religion." But the mobilization of a disciplined, authoritarian Muslim moral community as the grounds for nationalist political belonging forbade cultural plurality along with all other "divisions" and "deviations." Attempts to assert more inclusive, historically complex visions of the "nation" were treated as heresies to be stamped out. Officially legitimate self-definitions in independent North Africa would relegate Amazigh languages and cultures to signifying backwardness and ignorance—the rural, the illiterate, the *jahili*—leaving Arabic as the only legitimate language of the national state and of national culture.

It has hardly been possible here to follow adequately the history of the construction and reconstruction of the meanings of ethnic difference in the written record of Maghribi history, from antiquity through the early Islamic period, to early modern travelogues, colonial ethnographies, nationalist politics, and contemporary social struggles. It would be even more difficult to construct a satisfactorily historical account of social signifying practices from the inside, or from "below," beyond those glimpsed in the documentary sources. I have simply attempted to illustrate, with only a few examples and across a long chronological span, how the construction of social identity in the Maghrib has occurred primarily through Islamic idioms of community, and how claims about status within Islam have transcended the meanings of "Arab" and "Berber." These processes, in turn, have fundamentally turned on the expansion or the retrenchment of the power of the state and the reconfiguration of local social status and community cohesion. State formation and the exercise of sovereignty, incorporation into or dissidence against the state, its categories of legitimacy and illegitimacy, loyalty or exclusion, or, in a sacred idiom, heresy and salvation, have been crucial to these formulations and reformulations of the lexicon of social subjectivity. The patronage and "nationalization" now offered to Amazigh cultures by the two largest Maghribi states, far from indicating a radical break with this previous history, provide simply a further episode in it. It remains to be seen whether this rearrangement of the relationship between community-formation, the state, and the region's inextricably interrelated Arab/Berber peoples can contribute to another redefinition of Arabs and Berbers, not simply as equals in their subjection to the state, nor as utopian *imazighen* ("free men"), but as self-determining citizens of states whose sovereignty might be the expression of their own.

Notes

The epigraph is from Jacques Berque, "Qu'est-ce qu'une 'tribu' nord-africaine?" in *Maghreb, histoire et sociétés* (Algiers: Société nationale d'édition et de diffusion, 1974).

1. See Kamel Chachoua, 'Cité arabe/cité berbère: archéologie d'une division', in Hélène Claudot-Hawad, ed., *Berbères ou Arabes? Le tango des spécialistes* (Aix-en-Provence: Édisud, 2006) on the function of the Arab-Berber dichotomy in nineteenth-century French sociology relative to notions of sedentarity, rurality, and urbanity. The other studies in the same volume offer a multifaceted, critical reexamination of the history of the study of Berber societies more generally.

2. *Histoire des Berbères*, 4 vols. (Paris: Geuther, 1927) [2 vols., Algiers: Imprimerie du gouvernement, 1847].

3. Ernest Gellner and Charles Micaud, eds., *Arabs and Berbers: From Tribe to Nation in North Africa* (London: Duckworth, 1973).

4. Fredrik Barth, ed., *Ethnic Groups and Boundaries: The Social Organization of Culture Difference* (Boston: Little, Brown, 1969).

5. I concur here with Anthony Cohen's account of group and individual identity construction as "self-conscious" rather than as purely relational, though I prefer Paul Ricoeur's emphasis on the narrative construction of identity to Cohen's "core self." Anthony P. Cohen, *Self Consciousness: An Alternative Anthropology of Identity* (London: Routledge, 1994); Ricoeur, "Narrative Identity," in David Wood, ed., *On Paul Ricoeur: Narrative and Interpretation* (London: Routledge, 1991). For group formation located within social struggle and political competition, see Pierre Bourdieu, "The Social Space and the Genesis of Groups," *Social Science Information* 24(2) (1985): 195–220. For recent Amazigh/Berber self-narratives mobilizing local discourses of indigenity and transnational ones of human rights, see Susan Slyomovics, "Self-determination

as Self-Definition: The Case of Morocco," in Hurst Hannum and Eileen Babbit, eds., *Negotiating Self-Determination* (Lanham, Md.: Lexington, 2006).

6. The High Amazigh Commission (HCA) was established in Algeria in 1995, followed by the Royal Institute of the Amazigh Culture (IRCAM) in Morocco in 2001, both having particular responsibility for programs to implement the teaching of Berber/Tamazight in schools.

7. For a critique of such a view, see Sami Zubaida, "Is There a Muslim Society? Ernest Gellner's Sociology of Islam," *Economy and Society* 24(2) (May 1995): 151–188.

8. David Crawford, *Moroccan Households in the World Economy: Labor and Inequality in a Berber Village* (Baton Rouge: Louisiana State University Press, 2008), 21.

9. Fanny Colonna, "The Nation's 'Unknowing Other': Three Intellectuals and the Culture(s) of Being Algerian," in James McDougall, ed., *Nation, Society and Culture in North Africa* (London: Routledge, 2003), 155–170.

10. I owe this point to Salem Chaker.

11. The Kahina, the iconic Berber prophetess-queen, foresees the Arabs' victory and provides for her sons to join them after her own defeat. On the historiography of the Kahina, see Abdelmajid Hannoum, *Colonial Histories, Postcolonial Memories: The Legend of the Kahina, a North African Heroine* (Portsmouth, N.H.: Heinemann, 2001).

12. For an overview, especially on enslavement and clientship, see Michael Brett, "The Arab Conquest and the Rise of Islam in North Africa," in J. D. Fage, ed., *The Cambridge History of Africa*, vol. 2 (Cambridge: Cambridge University Press, 1978), 501–506. On classical Arabic definitions of Berber racial provenance, see Aziz al-Azmeh, *Al-'arab wa'l-barabira* (London: Riyad al-Rayyis li'l-kutub wa'l-nashr, 1991), 55, 83.

13. Al-Wartilānī, "Laysa fi'l-maghrib al-'arabi barbar," in his *Al-Jaza'ir al-tha'ira* (Beirut: Dar al-kitab al-'arabi, 1956), 49–54. Quotes at 49, 51.

14. Emphasis added. The incident was widely reported in the Algerian press; see *Liberté, El Watan*, Sept. 20, 2005. A few days later, in Constantine, the President announced that while Tamazight had been declared a "national language" alongside Arabic, Arabic must and would remain the country's only "official" language (*Liberté*, Sept. 24, 2005).

15. In the foreword to Amar Ouerdane, *La question berbère dans le mouvement national algérien, 1926–1980* (Quebec: Septentrion, 1990), quoted in Maya Shatzmiller, *The Berbers and the Islamic State* (Princeton, N.J.: Markus Wiener, 2000), xi.

16. Abdallah Laroui, *History of the Maghreb* (Princeton, N.J.: Princeton University Press, 1977), 87.

17. Leo Africanus noted in the sixteenth century regarding "the tawny Moores" (Berbers) that "they which dwell neere unto the Arabians, and exercise much traffique with them, doe for the greater part use their language." *Geographical Historie of Africa*, English trans. and ed. of *Descrittione dell'Africa* by John Pory (Amsterdam: Theatrum Orbis Terarum, 1969, facsimile of London, 1600 edition), 8.

18. Such exemplary "Berber resistance" to the Roman empire has frequently been located in so-called "Donatism," the fourth–fifth century crisis in African Christianity viewed by Western Latin church writers as a sectarian heresy. Its foot soldiers, the "circumcellions," were painted as a violent and deranged suicide cult. In more recent historiography, they have become a revolutionary social movement—perennial Berber insurgents. But the term "circumcellions" originally probably meant no more than seasonal agricultural laborers, and the allegedly heretical "Donatists" (followers

of Donatus, Bishop of Carthage), as their enemies called them, never recognized themselves in this abusive label and considered themselves (as the records of the great debate at Carthage in 411 demonstrate) as defenders of a legitimate and orthodox tradition which a campaign of state-sponsored intimidation and violence had not broken. For discussion of this, I am very grateful to Brent Shaw. See his "Who were the circumcellions?," in A. H. Merrills, ed., *Vandals, Romans and Berbers: New Perspectives on Late Antique North Africa* (London: Ashgate, 2004), and "African Christianity: Disputes, Definitions and 'Donatists'," in Shaw, *Rulers, Nomads and Christians in Roman North Africa* (London: Ashgate, 1995).

19. "Hérésie, acculturation et nationalisme des Berbères Bargwata," in *Proceedings of the First Congress of Mediterranean Studies of Arabo-Berber Influence* (Algiers: Office des publications universitaires, 1973), 217–233. Quotes at 217, 220, and 228. Talbi suggests that the sect existed until 1148, eventually surrendering to the Almohad caliph 'Abd al-Mu'min ibn 'Ali, while the main source, al-Bakri (see note 31, below), erroneously understands them to have been exterminated in 1029.

20. Ibid., 228, 221, and 225.

21. Ibid., 225, emphasis added. Nahum Slousch, who emphasized Jewish elements of the movement, referred with similar anachronism to the Barghawata as "the most national and African of religions." "L'empire des Berghouata," *Revue du monde musulman* 10(3) (1910): 396, quoted in H. T. Norris, *The Berbers in Arabic Literature* (London: Longman, 1982), 95.

22. It should be pointed out that Talbi's source criticism, which enabled him to resituate the chronology of the origins of the movement, is exemplary and remains important to understanding the Arabic accounts. It is the presentism of his interpretation that is problematic.

23. Norris, *Berbers in Arabic Literature*, 94.

24. Only a fragment of the Barghawata revelation survives, preserved in al-Bakri. Though borrowing some Qur'anic figures and themes, it was apparently a novel composition and is not to be confused with versions of the Qur'an itself produced in Tamazight in the medieval period or more recently.

25. Norris, *Berbers in Arabic Literature*, 94.

26. Norris, *Berbers in Arabic Literature* (248, n. 14), believes that Salih Zammur ibn Musa, the Barghawata ambassador to Cordoba and al-Bakri's source, was "clearly well versed in the Koran," but this is not apparent from al-Bakri's text. Zammur reportedly relied on an interpreter to converse with the Andalusians in Arabic. He refers to the relevant verse in "the Qur'an of Muhammad" to anchor the credentials of the Barghawata prophet, but from this we can hardly infer a thorough knowledge of the whole text. Norris infers that the Berbers of Tamasna knew the Quran'ic *mushaf* (orthodox recension) sufficiently well to "make use of it to compose [. . .] a liturgical document for their heresy." This surely supposes too instrumentalist (and conscious) a "composition." It would seem more likely, on the contrary, that if the Qur'an were circulating widely and more canonical forms of authority were already well established, radically inventive revelations as those of Yunus would have been considerably harder to sell. A vague familiarity with the Qur'an, a sense of its power and of some of its images and idioms, and the notion that such revelations were "in the air" seems a more likely background to the movement.

27. The appropriate modern analogy, in terms of inventiveness and geographical location "on the fringe," is the Nation of Islam of W. D. Fard and Elijah Muhammad that emerged in the United States in the 1930s—with the crucial difference that the

Barghawata doctrine does *not* seem to have included a message of ethnic or racial election.

28. Michael Brett and Elizabeth Fentress, *The Berbers* (Oxford: Blackwell, 1996), 102, 92 (emphasis added).

29. There are two principal sources: Ibn Idhari, *Bayan al-mughrib fi akhbar al-andalus wa'l-maghrib*, G. S. Colin, and É. Lévi-Provençal, eds., 2 vols. (Leiden: Brill, 1948), I, 56–57, and al-Bakri, *Kitab al-masalik wa'l-mamalik*, excerpt with translation by de Slane as *Description de l'Afrique septentrionale*, rev. ed. (Paris: Maisonneuve, 1965), 134–141 in the Arabic text, 259–271 in the French. Al-Bakri is quoted by subsequent authors, notably Ibn Khaldun, *Kitab al-ʿibar*, 7 vols. (Bulaq, Dar al-tibaʿa al-khidiwiya, 1284 AH [1867–1868 AD/CE]), II, 207–210 (II, 125–133 in de Slane's translation). Al-Bakri's account of the Barghawata and their kings is an exotic ethnography. Yunus and his successor, Abu Ghufayr Yahmed ibn Maʿad, are blood-drenched conquerors; the former destroys 387 towns that resist him and massacres 7,770 refractory subjects; the latter takes a week (from Thursday to Thursday) to slaughter the inhabitants of one town. Abu Ghufayr also proves his prowess by marrying 44 women, each one of whom bears him a son. His successor, Abdallah Abu al-Ansar—the father of Zammur's master—is, on the other hand, a model of piety, justice, peaceable rule, and clemency. This is a gallery of fictionalized types. Whatever its basis in historical information, al-Bakri's narration of the Barghawata poses obvious problems of interpretation.

30. Brett, "Arab Conquest," 555 (emphasis added).

31. See, for example, Jacques Berque, *Structures sociales du Haut Atlas* (Paris: Presses universitaires de France, 1955), chapter 5, on the Seksawa; on the Aurès, Fanny Colonna, "Discours sur le nom: identité, altérité," *Peuples méditerranéens* 18 (Jan.–Mar. 1982): 59–65; on the Beni Hilal and Beni Sulaym, Michael Brett, *Ibn Khaldun and the Medieval Maghreb* (Aldershot, UK: Ashgate, 1999), chapter 9.

32. Text of the *Kitab mafakhir al-barbar*, an Islamic panegyric to the people of North Africa, in Muhammad Yala, *Tres textos árabes sobre berébere en el Occidente islámico* (Madrid: CSIC, 1996), 125–272. For the Hilali saga, the history of the eleventh-century Arab migrations to North Africa transmuted into an epic romance, as recounted in twentieth-century Algeria, see Youssef Nacib, *Une geste en fragments* (Paris: Publisud, 1994); for a Tunisian version, Lucienne Saada, *La geste hilalienne* (Paris: Gallimard, 1985); for an Egyptian version, Susan Slyomovics, *The Merchant of Art* (Berkeley: University of California Press, 1987).

33. Leo Africanus, *Geographical Historie*, 7.

34. Ibid., 10, emphasis added.

35. Ibid., 5–6.

36. John Pory, the Cambridge scholar who translated and edited Leo into English, understood Africa to be inhabited "by five principall nations, to wit, by the people called Cafri or Cafates [*kuffar*], that is to say outlawes, or lawlesse, by the Abassins [Ethiopians], the Egyptians, the Arabians, and the Africans or Moores, properly so called; which last are of two kinds, namely white or tawnie Moores, and Negros or blacke Moores." Ibid., preface, 6.

37. J. G. Jackson, *An Account of the Empire of Morocco, and the District of Suse and Tafilelt* (London: Bulmer, 1811).

38. Jean-Michel Venture de Paradis, *Grammaire et dictionnaire abrégés de la langue berbère* (Paris: Imprimerie royale, 1844) from Venture's manuscript of 1790. His informants were two Moroccan Berberophone entertainers working in Paris, and two Algiers *madrasa* students from the Iflissen in Kabylia.

39. V.-Y. Boutin, *Reconnaissance des villes, forts, et batteries d'Alger*, ed. G. Esquer (Paris: Champion, 1927). The distinct position of the Ibadi, Berber-speaking Mzab in these ethnic classifications deserves a study of its own.

40. J. H. Blofeld, *Algeria, Past and Present* (London, 1844). Blofeld's understanding of North African geography and ethnicity, which are interdependent, is still structured by Ptolemy, Pliny, and Strabo. See also, for example, Louis de Chénier, *Recherches historiques sur les maures*, 3 vols. (Paris, 1787; English trans., *The Present State of the Empire of Morocco*, London, 1788); Joseph Morgan, *Complete History of Algiers* (London, 1731); Thomas Shaw, *Travels or Observations Relating to Several Parts of Barbary and the Levant* (Oxford, 1738).

41. Chantal de la Veronne attempts to build a case for a clear distinction in European sources between "Berbers" and "Arabs" in the later fifteenth century, a distinction disappearing "as the Berbers lost their influence" in the sixteenth century. ("Distinction entre Arabes et Berbères dans les documents d'archives européennes des XVIème et XVIIème siècles, concernant le Maghreb," in *Proceedings of the First Congress of Mediterranean Studies of Arabo-Berber Influence* [Algiers, Office des publications universitaires, 1973], 261–265). The evidence adduced, however, in the multiple and manifestly overlapping uses of *mouros*, *moros*, *barbaros*, and *alarves* does not support so neat a division, even assuming that one "ought" to exist. Place of habitation, lifestyle, language, and religion are all designated in these sources by imprecise and ascribed ethnonyms which do *not* reflect a stable underlying "ethnic" reality. Much less can they be assumed to map onto the self-understandings of the people in question.

42. Brett and Fentress, *The Berbers*, 184.

43. Ibid., 190.

44. See René Basset and Charles Pellat in the *Encyclopaedia of Islam*, 2nd ed., 1960, vol. 1, s.v. "Berbers: Literature and Art," 1185: "As far back as one can go in the past, Barbary, 'the land of conquest' . . . has never possessed any other language of civilization than that of its foreign conquerors"; see also, G.-H. Bousquet, *Les Berbères* (Paris: Presses universitaires de France, 1957), where North Africa's history "is nothing but 'the history of the [foreign] dominations it has endured' . . ." (28–29).

45. For a nationalist reading of the Berbers' place in history, see my "Myth and Counter-Myth: 'The Berber' as National Signifier in Algerian Historiographies," *Radical History Review* 86 (Spring 2003): 66–88.

46. See s.v. "Salafiyya" in *EI²*; Jamil Abu-Nasr, "The Salafiyya Movement in Morocco: The Religious Bases of the Moroccan Nationalist Movement," *St Antony's Papers* 16 (1963), 90–105; Ali Merad, *Le réformisme musulman en Algérie, 1925–1940: Essai d'histoire sociale et religieuse* (Paris and the Hague: Mouton, 1967).

47. Previously, only *tamazight*-speakers in central Morocco used the term as a collective self-designation, though cognates—*imuhagh* and *imajeghen*—existed in the Sahara. See Jane Goodman's observation of the term's novelty in the cultural socialization of one of her Kabyle informants, *Berber Culture on a World Stage: From Village to Video* (Bloomington: Indiana University Press, 2005), 11; Salem Chaker, "Amazig (Amazigh), 'le/un Berbère'," *Encyclopédie berbère* (26 vols., in progress, Aix-en-Provence: Édisud, 1984–), IV, 562–568. The term's recent institutionalization in both Arabic and French texts establishing Amazigh state institutions in Morocco and Algeria is testimony to its very remarkable success.

48. Qasi and his poetry are the subject of Tassadit Yacine, *Poésie berbère et identité* (Paris: Maison des sciences de l'homme, 1987).

49. Ibid., poem 11 (198–199). Transliteration retained from the original; English translation adapted from Yacine's French version. The *ansar* were the Prophet's "helpers" in establishing the first Muslim social order in Medina after his *hijra* (migration) from Mecca.

50. Mohand Khellil, *La Kabylie ou l'ancêtre sacrifié* (Paris: L'Harmattan, 1984), quoted in Gabriele Kratochwil, *Die Berber in der historischen Entwicklung Algeriens von 1949 bis 1990* (Berlin: Klaus Schwartz Verlag, 1996), 146. On the same question for Morocco, see Kratochwil, *Die Berberbewegung in Marokko. Zur Geschichte der Konstruktion einer ethnischen Identität* (Berlin: Klaus Schwartz Verlag, 2002), 392.

Bibliography

Abu-Nasr, Jamil. "The Salafiyya Movement in Morocco: The Religious Bases of the Moroccan Nationalist Movement." *St Antony's Papers* 16 (1963): 90–105.

Al-Azmeh, Aziz. *Al-ʿarab waʾl-barabira*. London: Riyad al-Rayyis liʾl-kutub waʾl-nashr, 1991.

Al-Bakri, Abu Ubayd Abdallah. *Description de l'Afrique septentrionale*. Excerpt from *Kitab al-masalik waʾl-mamalik* with translation by Baron MacGuckin de Slane. Rev. ed. Paris: Maisonneuve, 1965.

Barth, Fredrik, ed. *Ethnic Groups and Boundaries: The Social Organization of Culture Difference*. Boston: Little, Brown, 1969.

Basset, René, and Charles Pellat. "Berbers: Literature and Art." In the *Encyclopaedia of Islam*, 2nd ed., vol. I. Leiden: Brill, 1960, 1185.

Berque, Jacques. "Qu'est-ce qu'une 'tribu' nord-africaine?" In Berque, *Maghreb, histoire et sociétés*. Algiers: Société nationale d'édition et de diffusion, 1974.

———. *Structures sociales du Haut Atlas*. Paris: Presses universitaires de France, 1955.

Blofeld, J. H. *Algeria, Past and Present*. London: T. C. Newby, 1844.

Bourdieu, Pierre. "The Social Space and the Genesis of Groups." *Social Science Information* 24(2) (1985): 195–220.

Bousquet, G.-H. *Les Berbères*. Paris: Presses universitaires de France, 1957.

Boutin, V.-Y. *Reconnaissance des villes, forts, et batteries d'Alger*. Edited by G. Esquer. Paris: Champion, 1927.

Brett, Michael. *Ibn Khaldun and the Medieval Maghreb*. Aldershot, UK: Ashgate, 1999.

———. "The Arab Conquest and the Rise of Islam in North Africa." In *The Cambridge History of Africa*, vol. II, ed. J. D. Fage. Cambridge: Cambridge University Press, 1978.

Brett, Michael, and Elizabeth Fentress. *The Berbers*. Oxford: Blackwell, 1996.

Chachoua, Kamel. "Cité arabe/cité berbère: archéologie d'une di-vision." In *Berbères ou Arabes? Le tango des spécialistes*, ed. Hélène Claudot-Hawad. Aix-en-Provence: Édisud, 2006.

Chaker, Salem. "Amazig (Amazigh), 'le/un Berbère'." In *Encyclopédie berbère*, vol. IV, 562–568. Aix-en-Provence: Édisud, 1984–.

Cohen, Anthony P. *Self Consciousness: An Alternative Anthropology of Identity*. London: Routledge, 1994.

Colonna, Fanny. "Discours sur le nom: identité, altérité." *Peuples méditerranéens* 18 (Jan.–Mar. 1982): 59–65.

———. "The Nation's 'Unknowing Other': Three Intellectuals and the Culture(s) of Being Algerian." In *Nation, Society and Culture in North Africa*, ed. James McDougall. London: Routledge, 2003, 155–170.

Crawford, David. *Moroccan Households in the World Economy. Labor and Inequality in a Berber Village*. Baton Rouge: Louisiana State University Press, 2008.

de Chénier, Louis. *Recherches historiques sur les maures*. 3 vols. Paris: 1787. (Translated into English as *The Present State of the Empire of Morocco*. London: 1788.)

de la Veronne, Chantal. "Distinction entre Arabes et Berbères dans les documents d'archives européennes des XVIème et XVIIème siècles, concernant le Maghreb." In *Proceedings of the First Congress of Mediterranean Studies of Arabo-Berber Influence*. Algiers: Office des publications universitaires, 1973, 261–265.

Gellner, Ernest, and Charles Micaud, eds. *Arabs and Berbers: From Tribe to Nation in North Africa*. London: Duckworth, 1973.

Goodman, Jane E. *Berber Culture on a World Stage: From Village to Video*. Bloomington: Indiana University Press, 2005.

Hannoum, Abdelmajid. *Colonial Histories, Postcolonial Memories. The Legend of the Kahina, a North African Heroine*. Portsmouth, N.H.: Heinemann, 2001.

Ibn Idhari, Muhammad. *Bayan al-mughrib fi akhbar al-andalus wa'l-maghrib*. Edited with a translation by G. S. Colin and É. Lévi-Provençal. 2 vols. Leiden: Brill, 1948.

Ibn Khaldun, Abd al-Rahman ibn Muhammad. *Histoire des Berbères*. Translated excerpt from *Kitab Al-'ibar* by Baron MacGuckin de Slane. 4 vols. Paris: Geuther, 1927 (1st ed., 2 vols., Algiers: Imprimerie du gouvernement, 1847).

———. *Kitab al-'ibar*. 7 vols. Bulaq, Dar al-tiba'a al-khidiwiya, 1284 AH [1867–1868 AD/CE]).

Jackson, J. G. *An Account of the Empire of Marocco, and the District of Suse and Tafilelt*. London: Bulmer, 1811.

Khellil, Mohand. *La Kabylie ou l'ancêtre sacrifié*. Paris: L'Harmattan, 1984.

Kratochwil, Gabriele. *Die Berberbewegung in Marokko. Zur Geschichte der Konstruktion einer ethnischen Identität*. Berlin: Klaus Schwartz Verlag, 2002.

———. *Die Berber in der historischen Entwicklung Algeriens von 1949 bis 1990*. Berlin: Klaus Schwartz Verlag, 1996.

Laroui, Abdallah. *The History of the Maghreb: An Interpretive Essay*, trans. Ralph Mannheim. Princeton, N.J.: Princeton University Press, 1977.

Leo Africanus. *Geographical Historie of Africa*. English translation and edition of *Descrittione dell'Africa* by John Pory. (Facsimile of London, 1600 edition.) Amsterdam, Theatrum Orbis Terrrarum, 1969.

McDougall, James. "Myth and Counter-Myth: 'The Berber' as National Signifier in Algerian Historiographies." *Radical History Review* 86 (Spring 2003): 66–88.

Merad, Ali. *Le réformisme musulman en Algérie, 1925–1940. Essai d'histoire sociale et religieuse*. Paris and The Hague: Mouton, 1967.

Morgan, Joseph. *Complete History of Algiers*. London: 1731.

Nacib, Youssef. *Une geste en fragments: contribution à l'étude de la légende hilalienne des Hauts-Plateaux algériens*. Paris: Publisud, 1994.

Norris, H. T. *The Berbers in Arabic Literature*. London: Longman, 1982.

Ouerdane, Amar. *La question berbère dans le mouvement national algérien, 1926–1980*. Quebec: Septentrion, 1990.

Ricoeur, Paul. "Narrative identity." In *On Paul Ricoeur: Narrative and Interpretation*, ed. David Wood. London: Routledge, 1991.

Saada, Lucienne. *La geste hilalienne: version de Bou Thadi (Tunisie)*. Paris: Gallimard, 1985.

Shatzmiller, Maya. *The Berbers and the Islamic State*. Princeton, N.J.: Markus Wiener, 2000.

Shaw, Brent D. "African Christianity: Disputes, Definitions and 'Donatists'." In Shaw, *Rulers, Nomads and Christians in Roman North Africa*. Aldershot, UK: Ashgate, 1995.

———. "Who Were the Circumcellions?" In *Vandals, Romans and Berbers: New Perspectives on Late Antique North Africa*, ed. A. H. Merrills. Aldershot, UK: Ashgate, 2004.

Shaw, Thomas. *Travels or Observations Relating to Several Parts of Barbary and the Levant*. Oxford: The Theatre, 1738.

Slyomovics, Susan. "Self-determination as Self-definition: The Case of Morocco." In *Negotiating Self-Determination*, ed. Hurst Hannum and Eileen Babbit. Lanham, Md.: Lexington, 2006.

———. *The Merchant of Art: An Egyptian Hilali Oral Epic Poet in Performance*. Berkeley: University of California Press, 1987.

Talbi, Mohamed. "Hérésie, acculturation et nationalisme des Berbères Bargwata." In *Proceedings of the First Congress of Mediterranean Studies of Arabo-Berber Influence*, 217–233. Algiers: Office des publications universitaires, 1973.

Venture de Paradis, Jean-Michel. *Grammaire et dictionnaire abrégés de la langue berbère*. Paris: Imprimerie royale, 1844.

Al-Wartilani, Fudayl. "Laysa fi'l-maghrib al-ʿarabi barbar." In Wartilani, *Al-Jazaʾir al-thaʾira*, 49–54. Beirut: Dar al-kitab al-ʿarabi, 1956.

Yacine, Tassadit. *Poésie berbère et identité: Qasi Udifella, hérault des Ait Sidi Braham*. Paris: Maison des sciences de l'homme, 1987.

Yala, Muhammad. *Tres textos árabes sobre beréberes en el Occidente islámico*. Madrid: CSIC, 1996.

Zubaida, Sami. "Is There a Muslim Society? Ernest Gellner's Sociology of Islam." *Economy and Society* 24(2) (May 1995): 151–188.

2

Internal Fractures in the Berber-Arab Distinction: From Colonial Practice to Post-National Preoccupations

Katherine E. Hoffman

In his classic 1967 book, *The Structure of Traditional Moroccan Society*, Bernard Hoffman was reluctant to argue that there are distinct Berber and Arab components of the Moroccan population. But he did make a spatial distinction: "There is in reality a Berber core-area, situated in the very high mountains; an Arabic-speaking core area, situated in the plains and desert; and a very wide intermediate zone, where the two groups interpenetrate in varying proportions."[1] Like his predecessors and his successors, this scholar avoided the particulars of the "very wide intermediate zone." Yet a growing proportion of rural and peri-urban Morocco consists of such zones, particularly since the end of the French Protectorate in 1956.[2] It is common to think of urban areas as zones of contact between Arabic and Berber speakers. Yet many originally Berberophone rural areas have also been contact zones, having undergone partial or full linguistic Arabization and cultural Arabization, whether prior to the arrival of French administration (consolidated between 1912 and 1934), during the Protectorate period, or subsequent to Independence in 1956. These contact zones are key sites in which to investigate the practices and symbolic systems central to negotiations over the very constitution of Arab and Berber/ Amazigh/Ashelhi identities. The boundaries between groups arguably are more important to ethnic group formation and maintenance than is the "cultural stuff" the boundaries enclose, as Barth classically posited.[3] This is even more striking given the multiplicity of expressive culture and material practices found within these zones. Intra-group variation may be as pronounced as inter-group differences. This appears to be the case in the Tashelhit-speaking Sous plains I discuss in this chapter.

In sorting through group-internal differences, researchers often have resorted to a kind of fractal recursivity, meaning that differences between groups on one level or in one domain are projected onto other levels or domains.[4] French Protectorate taxonomies exhibited this semiotic tendency when they assessed the relative level of Berber assimilation into Arab society by placing populations on a continuum with purist ideals at either end.[5] As Bidwell summarizes, in the early Protectorate period, Berbers could be subdivided into four categories: "almost untouched by Arab influence except for Islam," "slightly Arabized, with their notables speaking Arabic," "half-Arabized with the men bilingual," and "almost completely Arabized with women also bilingual, intermarrying with the Arabs and tending to adopt such habits as the seclusion of women."[6] Yet the recursion inherent in such categorization involved varying conceptions of Arab-ness depending on the semiotic elements used to mark boundaries, only one of which was the vernacular or spoken language in widespread use in the community. In this chapter, I argue that there are consequences to such Berber group-internal fractures that are specific to the present historical moment while simultaneously echoing aspects of the French *politique berbère*.

One glaring consequence is that little scholarship has bothered to investigate contact zones or what their residents call "mixed" cultural practices. There seems to be a presumption that scholars, administrators, and laypeople inside and outside of Morocco can easily identify the people, expressive and material practices, and histories particular to Imazighen or Berbers. The documentary goal here is familiar from as early as Franz Boas's advocacy for salvage anthropology.[7] Yet anthropological case studies from other corners of the world suggest that the documentation and standardization of formerly oral language forms have little effect on their maintenance and do little to halt language shift toward the more prestigious national languages, although those efforts may be good for morale.[8] Language maintenance requires the identification and redressing of the social conditions that disfavor a language's use among a given group of people. In Morocco, the nationalist project grounded in the 1920s, particularly through its central symbols of Arabic language and Islamic religion, has been perhaps the most significant force in encouraging language shift away from the Berber vernaculars and toward the Arabic vernacular. Since the 1970s, with both Pan-Arabism at its peak and significant rural–urban migration, the ideological association between Arabic language and urban modernity has further accelerated language shift and decreased linguistic diversity in Morocco. These different semiotic projects, at different historical moments, have led to a similar outcome: Berber language contraction. The changing parameters of Amazigh ethnicity, meaning the ways in which the categories of Berbers and Arabs are constituted, have conflated the historical processes of Arab nationalism, cultural Arabization, and linguistic Arabicization. To understand how and where language shift has occurred, it is crucial to establish historically situated political economic patterns that have shaped responses to social change.

With the early twenty-first century political opening toward Amazigh matters, resistance to Arabization and Arabicization has been lauded among activists and Berberist scholars.[9] Yet for many Tashelhit-speaking rural agriculturalists and wage laborers in the bilingual plains around Agadir, Marrakech, and Taroudant, rejecting Arab expressive and material culture simply is not a viable option. In bilingual rural communities, Berber speakers typically linguistically accommodate monolingual Arabic speakers. Material culture follows suit: the mass-market commodities that are tied to life-cycle rituals are increasingly homogenized across Morocco and more uniformly circulated in markets, much as Kapchan argues for the Middle Atlas region of Beni Mellal.[10] More specifically, the rural absorption of seemingly ethnically neutral "modern" Moroccan cultural practices has resulted in a stable diglossia between Berber and Arabic vernaculars, with language use mapping onto social or spatial domains. Bilingual language brokers mediate between monolinguals, who often develop communicative strategies that allow for greeting and celebrating with Arabic speakers, as well as sharing economic, religious, and social activities. This kind of diglossia is a model of reason and integration, a resourceful alternative to an indirect state-encouraged Arabization.

As a case in point, rural Berberophone populations have been particularly influenced by the ways that state employees speak and by their language ideologies. This is particularly true for the teachers assigned to their communities who are often young, insufficiently trained, non-Berber speaking, and originally from northern, Arabic-dominant urban areas such as Casablanca and Kenitra. As a result, schoolchildren's understanding of the inherent relationship between language use and social orders has become freighted with political significance.[11] Through their role in the socialization of Arabic language and civics, teachers have been central to the rural linguistic Arabization of Amazigh populations. Teachers may well have encouraged the disemic tendencies that extend beyond linguistic diglossia to competing semiotic systems involving as their constitutive elements musical preferences, dress styles, informal political organization, and patterns of avoidance and interaction.[12] Oftentimes for a rural Tamazight speaker, access to institutions, state administration, and public services is mediated by an Arabic speaker. The feeling of exclusion becomes acute when, for instance, the monolingual Amazigh person in the hospital calls for the nurse who cannot understand her request, or applies for an identity card and is told repeatedly to return with papers that he does not possess, or is mocked by a teacher who tells her to remove her *tamlhaft* overwrap in the classroom because such garments are signs of the community's backwardness, ignorance, and provinciality. These are the kinds of tensions that I witnessed in the Sous and Anti-Atlas regions during extended fieldwork (1996–1999 and 2008–2009) and short visits (2001, 2005, and 2006); they are only a few among the many challenges faced by contemporary Imazighen in everyday life.

Among Tamazight speakers, or even a subset of them such as the Tashelhit speakers of southwestern Morocco, verbal expressive practices are heterogeneous with regional particularities in phonology, lexicon, pragmatics, and the ideologies that govern them. Scholars of language and society typically expect variegation within the speech community, regardless of what the criteria for this community are believed to be.[13] In contrast, the discourse of Moroccan mass media, state institutions, and even Amazigh rights organizations tends to stress commonalities between Imazighen while erasing differences. Berberist scholarship, for its part, vacillates between the homogenizing and the radically micro-differentiating, with the latter particularly (and necessarily) evident in descriptive theses in linguistics. Precision was once a political necessity in order to substantiate claims that Tamazight constituted a language, not "merely" an unwritten and inconsistent dialect, and that Amazigh heritage should be considered integral to Moroccan national identity. Yet in the burgeoning popular market of locally printed Tamazight-language materials, set in Arabic, Roman, or Tifinagh script, reading audiences are typically predetermined by geolect (regional language variety). With the exception of specialists, readers of these affordable materials tend only to be interested in their native Tamazight, Tashelhit, or Tarifit.

This market tendency feeds the claim by some detractors that Imazighen, Ishelhin, and Irrifiyin are distinct ethnic groups whose language varieties are insufficiently similar to be variants of a single Tamazight language. However, this hyper-particularity has another purpose within indigenist politics.[14] Mirroring an earlier Arab nationalist tendency, there was an impulse to privilege local specificity in representations of the collective, even though this conflicted with the political expediency of Berber unity and homogeneity.[15] Given the political repression and self-censorship of public expressions of Berber language through the end of the twentieth century, it is novel and thrilling to many literate Moroccan Berbers today to see their oral heritage validated in print.

Shifting Language Hierarchies in Morocco

The symbolic and indexical values of the Arabic language shifted through the course of the twentieth century; roughly, during the Protectorate period, the use of classical, literary Arabic in particular pointed to Islamic piety. While Arabic retained these associations in the nationalist period, both classical and vernacular Arabic took on the indexical values of nationalism and Moroccan citizenship. Vernacular and classical forms of Arabic became conflated symbolically, as instantiated in the generic reference to "Arabic" (al-ʿarabiyya) for both darija (spoken, dialectal Moroccan Arabic) and fusha (literary Arabic). Of course, Moroccans knew that the varieties of Arabic were not identical. But Arabic in any of its varieties came increasingly to be something distinct from Tamazight/Berber rather than a vernacular like any other and equally hierarchically inferior.[16]

After Independence, the semiotic content of Tamazight shifted as well with the institutionalization of Arabist ideologies and policies. Whereas Tamazight had been a regional vernacular, symbolically equivalent to Arabic vernaculars, the Tamazight vernaculars were now denigrated as indices of backwardness, rurality, and defiance of a unified Arabo-Islamic identity under a central Moroccan state. In short, retaining one's ancestral Amazigh language in the post-independence, Arabo-nationalist period constituted a de facto rejection of the modern nation-state, according to a nationalist rhetoric, for the language of national unity was presumably Arabic. Thus it is no surprise that even in the last years of King Hassan II's reign, many Arabophones regarded calls for increased use of Berber in public and private domains as divisive, occasioning a self-censorship experienced as shame by many Amazigh people. For native Tamazight speakers who continued to use their language in their everyday lives, there was nothing divisive about it.[17]

Today, in the bilingual "intermediate zone" between plains and mountains, the Arab-Amazigh distinction remains central and meaningful to human taxonomies. Yet new intra-group fractures are emerging. The older boundaries between geolects (regional vernacular varieties), regions, tribes, or patrilines apply less than they used to, or rather, they have been overlaid by new criteria distinguishing different degrees of Amazigh-ness according to notions of authenticity and purity. This is reminiscent of the Protectorate authorities' preoccupation with the "contamination" of Berber society by Arab languages, institutions, and beliefs.[18]

Decisions about what constitutes Amazigh culture and lifeways reverberate in towns and villages in the form of media such as the wildly popular and inexpensive Tashelhit video compact disc (VCD) industry. Visual representations of Amazigh life in an imagined impoverished countryside and in opulent urban villas represent what Berber speakers call the Amazigh condition (*lhal n imazighn*) to an exclusively Amazigh audience. Filmmakers make decisions at every step about the "authenticity" of domestic architecture, dress, water vessels, eating utensils, food, accents, and word choice. These decisions do not pass unnoticed. The Ishelhin with whom I have watched these films comment on the details, assess their provenance and authenticity, and compare them with their own *lhal*. Under Mohamed VI, rural infrastructure and public utilities have expanded dramatically. Electricity—and almost immediately, satellite television and VCD players— have transformed growing numbers of Berber-speaking households, and shifted individuals' focus from storytelling to screen. There are no Arabs or Arabic in these films, and no bilinguals. Berber filmmakers, along with French colonial officers, scholars, Arab nationalists, and Amazigh activists, are likewise responsible for erasing the "wide intermediate zone" in representations of Amazigh society.

Arabization through Contact

Protectorate-era linguistic studies of Tamazight varieties documented the Arabic borrowings and assimilated words and phrases that were already integrated into the speech repertoires of many Berber groups.[19] Even at this earlier moment, prior to the reshuffling of linguistic hierarchies, there were factors that increased the symbolic capital of colloquial Arabic or otherwise made its influence on the vernacular permissible to Berber speakers.

For historically Tamazightophone groups that have assimilated to Arab cultural practices (which may or may not include speaking Arabic as a primary language), it is difficult to ascertain the historical moments of linguistic and cultural encounter and the eventual rejection, adoption, or adaptation of Arab practices and Arabic language. Even in the pre-colonial period, contact between at least some members of Arabic-speaking and Berber-speaking communities was common, especially in towns and market centers where such contact necessitated linguistic, cultural, and economic mediators. Educated Berbers, which then meant religiously educated, were the *talibs* (Islamic scholars) and *fqihs* (Islamic legal experts) who figured centrally in translation and interpretation. For Protectorate authorities, a Berber who read classical Arabic with the village scholar was more dangerous than an illiterate Berber who spoke Moroccan Arabic with local authorities or at the market. Literacy, which suggested a familiarity with Arabic and thus potentially with Islam and Islamic law, represented danger.[20] For these French authorities, as for many Moroccan lay people today, the modalities of speaking and writing were conflated symbolically, which fails to capture the social management of multilingualism across communicative channels. For Protectorate authorities and the scholars who advised them, both writing classical Arabic and speaking colloquial Arabic fell under the rubric of linguistic and religious "contamination." Rural Berber communities that adopted Arab linguistic and cultural practices such as wedding rites seemed to Protectorate authorities to indicate a dangerous increase in religiosity that they sought constantly to dampen. In the post-Independence period, increased integration into presumably shared Arab and Islamic symbols was crucial to national identity, at least as conceived by the Arab nationalists who assumed positions in the new government.

In the current post-nationalist period, with the political opening toward multiculturalism and the rise of Amazigh consciousness, Moroccans increasingly question the centrality of Arabic and Islam as anchors of Moroccan national unity. Yet the effects of Arab nationalist discourse and symbols from the era of Moroccan nationalism linger. One of the key tasks in nationalism's wake is to discern historically whether the accommodation of Arab linguistic and semiotic elements among plains Berbers resulted simply from cultural contact with Arabophone neighboring villagers or workmates, or whether they were instead due to individuals' perceived investment in nationalist ideologies. The outcomes of these two processes—linguistic and cultural Arabization—may be similar, but they involve different historical processes that merit consideration.

Arabization under the Protectorate: *Talibs* and "Islamic Contamination"

French Berber policy in itself may have accelerated linguistic and cultural Arabization.[21] As Anti-Atlas and Sous plains Moroccan tribes submitted to the French, their members became more mobile and participated in an expanding commodities market and greater reliance on cash income to satisfy subsistence needs. Through this movement, Berbers were increasingly exposed to Arabic language, orthodox Islamic beliefs, and Islamic institutions, foremost among them *shari'a* law. French authorities considered emigration a danger, for it exposed Berber men to the nationalism gaining momentum in the northern cities. Rural administrators then kept careful records on the quality and quantity of what they called *xenophobie*, effectively gauged as opposition to French administration. Historically, as administrators readily admitted, legal practices tended to shift in one direction only: away from customary law toward *shari'a*. This shift could be brought about by a shift in mentalities, and this in turn allegedly resulted from language shift.

When working for the French native affairs officers in rural outposts, the *talib* was supposed to draw on his knowledge of Islamic law to interpret cases. According to the sources, however, inevitable instances of ambiguity provided opportunities for him to interpret customary law in ways that made it conform more closely to Islamic law.[22] The *talib*'s literacy and religious expertise earned him respect and deference from tribesmen. With the authority of the local Protectorate officials behind him, the *talib* not only furthered Islamization of Berber customary law but also promoted Arabization; together these forces constituted a double threat, in French eyes.[23] For French Native Affairs officers, limiting the application of Islamic law among Berber *ressortissants* (lit. "citizens" but effectively subjects) meant the restriction of Arabic language in the countryside. Tribes and tribal sections that followed Islamic law—in contrast to customary law—were characterized in officers' reports as "Arabized" (*arabisées*). The purportedly more pure Berbers were characterized as "attached to custom" (*attachés à la coutume*). Judicial activities were closely related to ethnic parameters under the Protectorate.

Post-Nationalism

Keeping in mind the particulars of Arabization and Arabicization in the Moroccan case, I want to consider the role of post-nationalism in these shifts. I am conceiving of post-nationalism differently from the post-national studies positing that identities are no longer organized around national boundaries and the nation-state, but instead involve free-floating cultural attachments, so that dominant national narratives carry less weight than they did even prior to the 1980s. Post-nationalism in its popular configuration has turned our attention to migrant communities, multicultural citizens, and members of transnational diasporas whose subjectivities fall outside of nationalist projects. As theorized to date, post-nationalism has been concerned primarily with the presumed effects of an expanding neoliberal economy: namely, the displacement of employment, greater transnational migration, and a greater range of consumer commodities with foreign origins leading to a breakdown in the individual's attachment to his country of origin and nationalist values.

"Social formations" in such a post-national world "are now organized around principles of finance, recruitment, coordination, communication, and reproduction that are fundamentally postnational and not just multinational or international."[24] This approach has taken social scientific studies outside the boundaries of states and has posited similarities across transient and displaced populations in the global "transit-lounge of culture."[25] Culturally, post-nationalism refers more specifically to a condition of modernity in which national tropes no longer anchor subjectivities because of far-reaching shifts in the circulation of goods and symbols. According to this approach, the nation is rendered irrelevant because of the global exchange of goods that are often (mis)taken for culture. The ethnographic focus of contemporary post-nationalist studies (to the extent that there is one) is on migrant, transnational, and diasporic populations, for "the entire notion of cultural identity and nationalism . . . has been put into crisis in this age of global capital."[26] In their preoccupation with an allegedly shared culture and political interest, nationalisms tend to exclude minorities.[27] Yet this neglect should be a point of departure rather than a conclusion, and qualitative research can document the processes of exclusion and its effects with an eye to revising generalizations about nationalisms and cultural policy.

Despite the alleged demise of the nation-state and nationalist allegiances, remnants of nationalist discourses and practices have become solidly anchored in multiple sites from which they can be dislodged only with great difficulty. Yet the incorporation of material and symbolic culture from "outside" the immediate community, locally perceived, does not necessarily entail the rootlessness, schizophrenia, or "disjuncture" that have come to be considered endemic to a predictable post-colonial and post-national condition, or the hybridity and cosmopolitanism celebrated by others. Indeed, in important respects, the widespread focus on transnational processes and economic shifts has occluded the much more widespread processes within state boundaries by which the culture, language, and institutions of a portion of the population come to be seen as shared by all.[28]

Recent scholarship has assessed the effects of French colonialism on rural Moroccan Berbers as exemplified in Aouchar's detailed study of the transformation of Middle Atlas perceptions of time and history, the reorganization of local administrative units, and the sense of self and of group.[29] In a similar spirit, scholars of Morocco and North Africa more broadly would do well to document the Arabization and Arabicization that have resulted from nationalist policies and their underlying ideologies, and to distinguish these shifts from the more organic Arabization that has resulted from cultural and linguistic contact.

Instead of looking to migrants and diaspora to understand the post-national moment, let us turn our lens inward and examine nationalism's effects *within* Morocco, subsequent to the decline of a presumably unifying nationalism that has outlived its utility and political expediency. In this alternative formulation of post-nationalism, our attention goes instead to ways in which post-colonial peoples respond to nationalist ideologies and practices by engaging them, rather than rejecting them, and by incorporating them into their practices, whether consciously or not. At the heart of this post-nationalist project is an attention to the sites in which former nationalist hegemonies linger, anchored in material culture, embodied practices, and ideological convictions. These hegemonies may be tenacious, for practices and symbols associated with nationalism were rendered authoritative and naturalized discursively over decades or even centuries. Methodologically, the study of this kind of post-nationalism requires that we identify the locations and moments in which particular regional practices and semiotic elements that have long been associated with *Arabs* or *Arabic speakers* took on the semiotic quality of *Moroccan* collective national practices and values.

This task is particularly timely given the rise of civil society and shifting state-society expectations. Similarly, in the first half of the twentieth century, the French reorganization of rural administration led to important transformations in state-society relations and in social organization—most important for our purposes here—in terms of ethnic group formation and maintenance around questions of Arabness and Amazighness. Ultimately, the goal is to understand how, in the post-Independence period, "Moroccan" come to be grounded in "Arab." This was true not only for official purposes such as the development of political pan-Arabism, but also for the everyday purposes of ethno-linguistic differentiation that shape the ways rural and often unschooled Berber speakers classify and categorize different groups of people and their associated attributes.

We can also probe the effects of Arab nationalism in the rural Berber-speaking hinterlands, identifying the production and circulation of both dominant and alternative discourses, and establishing parameters that differ from those of urban settings. Through schools, health clinics and hospitals, civil administrations, and development projects, cultural Arabization and linguistic Arabicization have reached rural Berber populations. Rural populations may experience state ideologies as subtle, insidious pressures that shape seemingly insignificant practices over the course of time. When nationalist hegemony is entrenched, practices become mixed or abandoned and new ones adopted. These pressures may not have led to the wholesale disappearance of Amazigh practices, but they have shaped the meanings people give to them. The pressures to conform to the tastes associated with state ideologies may be experienced as fashions or trends, and therefore enthusiastically taken up by youths who are often eager to distinguish their generation from that of their parents. Yet these youths may not recognize that many of the practices they characterize as "modern" (*'asri*) are considered "traditional" in Arabophone communities. In this way, the modern and the Arab become closely identified, further increasing the desirability of rural Arab as well as urban Arab practices vis-à-vis Berber practices. These remarks about language can be applied to other signifying practices, whether material (e.g., laboring) or expressive/semiotic (e.g., dress, eating, etc.). The presence of Arabic language in a rural group does not necessarily entail a relative decline in Berber language, but it might. This depends largely on the linguistic market that holds sway in a given place at a given historical moment.[30]

Unstable Disemia: Group-Internal Fractures in a Life-Cycle Event

Let us take, for example, the semiotic elements of the crucial life-cycle event of marriage. During my fieldwork, I witnessed first steps in the process of cultural Arabization, understood by participants in terms of an opposition between "traditional" (*taqlidi*) and "modern" (*'asri*) practices. It was particularly visible in public gatherings when ritual displays of collective identity were locally understood to be important. In 1998, in the village of Arazan in the Sous Valley, for the first time, a bride insisted on taking on semiotic elements hitherto considered by villagers to be restricted to urban Arab wedding rituals. The bride hired a *nagafa*, a bridal adornment specialist, who furnished her with a number of bridal costumes that she changed into throughout the evening, including the generic "Berber" bridal dress.[31] This meant that the bride and groom were on display all evening, sitting on chairs looking down at the guests seated on mats on the ground. Without the *nagafa*, the bride would have remained cloistered with female friends and relatives prior to the consummation of the marriage. In this and other instances, I was not alone in my effort to sort through participants' signifying practices. Indeed, at weddings in Morocco as elsewhere, a good amount of talk consists of passing judgment on not only the quality and quantity of the wedding preparations, guests, and hosts, but also discussions of the "customs" of this or that place. In the case of the Arabized Berber wedding in Arazan, villagers were divided between those who, on the one hand, saw these new acts of consumption as a desirable effort at displaying the bride's modernity and familiarity with an implicitly urban fashion, and those, on the other hand, who were horrified at the couple's lack of modesty in mingling with the guests, whispering, "*ur ad hšamn* (they have no shame)."

Other Tashelhit brides I knew did not go so far as to hire a *nagafa*, but still refused to take part in the women-only pre-nuptial ceremony where, tented by a white sheet, female relatives sang and braided the bride's hair, attaching dates to the tips of the braids to be shared by the couple in the wedding chamber. Like many other practices, this women's ritual was rejected as old-fashioned and associated with Ashelhi Berber particularism. In Protectorate parlance, such a refusal would be indicative that a group consisted of "Arabized Berbers." Yet the choices I am describing here constitute the adoption of urban over rural practices, and Arab practices in the place of Berber ones. The decision to organize this kind of wedding had important implications. It shaped the type of entertainment that would be hired, the spatial arrangement of family and guests in the receiving rooms, the consumption of market and homemade commodities, and perhaps most importantly, the alignment of the couple, their families, and friends with certain social groups to the exclusion of others. No longer could the bride's relatives and friends alone dispense wisdom to the bride and calm her fears, for the bride was on display in front of hundreds of guests prior to the consummation of the marriage. Her public adornment made her even more susceptible to the evil eye of jealous wedding guests.

Here as elsewhere in the "wide intermediate zone," hegemony is rarely so complete that fissures cannot appear. Part of the deal that was struck in throwing this allegedly "modern" wedding party was that the bride and groom would wear the *nagafa*'s Berber outfits as one of their many costumes. The groom wore a long traditional robe over slacks and a shirt, with a gold and white checkered scarf tied in a turban. The bride wore an amalgam of High and Middle Atlas items with her caftan: a bright red-fringed scarf dangling over her forehead like bangs and extending down the sides of her neck, an oversized faux-amber bead necklace, and mounds of silver coin jewelry around her neck and over her chest.[32] When the couple appeared in the reception room, the all-women band of shikhat professional performers halted their Arab Houari antiphonal (call and response) song, standard entertainment in the village and to which few women were dancing. Instead the performers shifted to Tashelhit songs with their faster tempo, and soon guests were dancing. The guests' delight at the musicians' genre shift fed back to the performers, who intensified their playing. When the song concluded, the bride and groom disappeared to change their costumes once again, and the jubilant mood ended. The semiotic encoding of the dress freed up other elements of the ritual—here, code choice in song—and made possible a deviation from the script that was in step with a perceived modernity. Ironically, this involved Berbers appropriating more stereotypically "Berber" semiotic elements in dress, which triggered the shift in music. Lest one think that this signaled a preference for some sort of more originary Berber expressive culture, we might note that the shift was not only from Arabic to Tashelhit music. It also meant a shift from (Arab) community music transmitted orally to contemporary commercially recorded (Berber) music.

Participation in such "modern" practices in a single instance, as with these Arab wedding practices (but also dress, food, eating utensils and posture, architecture, and gender socializing or avoidance), is not expressly intended to shift a group's ethnic identification. But when performed on a widespread scale in life-cycle events, these practices have led to a homogenization of ritual practices and symbols across Morocco. Locally, the individuals at the Sous plains wedding interpreted this adoption of outsiders' practices as embracing a particular Moroccan "modernity" or "urbanity." More objectively, however, they substituted one local (Berber) particularity with another (Arab) particularity, all in the guise of universalism. Much as Moroccanist scholars have long done, Moroccan laypeople engage in ethno-linguistic differentiation, sorting through cultural and linguistic difference in part according to the semiotic process of fractal recursivity through which people displace differences found on one level onto other levels, and erasure, where elements that do not fit the constructed categories are simply ignored.[33] Through this process, some Berbers become more Berber or Arab than others. Arab nationalism as a process not only brought about massive linguistic Arabization of the Berber population; it also introduced language ideologies that advocated the restriction of Berber to intimate family domains. As the linguistic market consolidated around vernacular Arabic—allegedly required for upward mobility, religiosity, comprehension of media, and state schooling—the status of the Berber vernaculars decreased.[34] Competing semiotic systems encountered an ever-consolidating linguistic market.

The effects of this shift stretch into music as well as speech. We see plains Ishelhin accommodating Arab community music as well as spoken language, for many Sous villages are inhabited by Tashelhit speakers who sing in Arabic at crucial life-cycle events where neighboring Arabic-speaking villagers are also present.[35] Participation in these seemingly shared urban Moroccan practices signals an integration of dominant national symbols into dispersed communities. The associated symbols and practices are no longer considered Arab but are instead naturalized as "Moroccan," "national," "progressive," "modern," and for all these reasons, desirable. It is precisely in such ways that nationalist ideologies and practices become lodged in local ideologies, even when they are understood to be regionally particular. Indeed, the plains people of Arazan and Tazzemourt could not articulate for me why or how this practice of singing in Arabic came about, although some hypothesized that it was due to migrations during the Protectorate period, especially during years of drought.[36] While seemingly insignificant, the spread of certain cultural particularities at the expense of others makes them hegemonic, occludes their particularity, and thus marginalizes other particularities that in turn index resistance in the eyes of some, or backwardness in the eyes of others.

Herzfeld's concept of disemia builds on diglossia—a speech community's domain-specific patterning of multiple languages or language varieties, often with a language for everyday interaction and another for liturgy or institutional uses—but extends it into para- and extra-linguistic semiotic signifying practices.[37] The concept of disemia is a useful heuristic device for the patterned engagement with signifying practices among intermediate zone, "mixed," or bilingual speech communities. The particulars of the competing or co-existing semiotic systems vary by region and historical moment. Possible components that may be involved in disemia for the plains communities I discuss here may include code choice (language used in different domains of social interaction and text production); wedding rituals; musical consumption and production, and accompanying dance or dance avoidance; popular religious and orthodox religious practices, such as choices to revere a regional pious one (m. *shikh*, f. *tashikht*) and his or her associated festivals and collective meals; gendered spatial and interactive norms that govern both same-sex and mixed-sex gatherings; gendered and generation-specific laboring practices; norms around beauty and adornment that require use of plant products for face decoration (wild pistachio ink for temporary tattoos and walnut bark for yellow gums); henna for hands and feet, whether carefully traced by a professional henna artist or liberally applied to the whole hand, fingernails, and foot by oneself; and a breakfast of morning barley porridge or store-bought white bread. Each of these sets of practices has different semiotic associations.

Despite disemic signifying practices and diglossic expressive repertoires, Amazigh communities cooperating with new language policies incorporate Tamazight language into elementary schools. This is true regardless of how Arabized they have been in terms of social organization, ritual practices, cultural expressive practices, architecture, or dress. After decades during which marginalized populations negotiated this border, merging in some respects with Arabic-speaking neighboring communities, and keeping links with Amazigh populations in other respects, these communities engage in practices that are meaningful to them, but that are now (as in the Protectorate period) framed as "inauthentic." This becomes a significant issue in terms of the practices perceived as collectively meaningful, such as weddings, circumcisions, funerals, births, and the other life-cycle events where a group represents itself to itself, enacting itself through what Urban has called metaculture.[38] In many Tamazight-speaking communities, elements of this metaculture are the result of decades of accommodation with Arab neighbors, so that practices remain saturated with meaning.

Insecurities and Conclusions

This chapter has examined cultural and linguistic assimilation in Morocco due to contact between Arabophones and Berberophones and to the symbolic violence of post-nationalist ideologies. I have also attempted to consider reasons why assimilation only goes one way today—from Amazigh to Arab—whereas it went in both directions in the past. Tamazight's shaping of Moroccan Arabic, historically, is only one manifestation of this trend but an important one; the influence extends beyond lexicon to grammar and phonetics, and these are elements of spoken language that tend to resist change. Today, assimilation can go from Berber to Arab, but it rarely goes from Arab to Berber, and not even from partly Arabized Berber to more "purely" Berber. The plains Berbers simply do not shift in identification toward the mountain Berbers; mountain dwellers do not welcome them into their fold, and there is too much suspicion surrounding them because of their lack of *aşl* (roots) and lack of tribal affiliation.

This is most evident in choice of spouse and employment. Oral histories attest to the rarity with which Arabic speakers become Tashelhit-dominant later in life. Among rural Swasa in the late 1990s, some elderly Arab women had married into Tashelhit-speaking villages and became Tashelhit dominant. Occasionally, displaced individuals with no remaining roots in an Arabic-speaking place shifted toward Tashelhit. But otherwise, at least in recent times, widespread shift from Berber to Arabic or to bilingualism took place on a widespread scale. We might ask whether this process is irreversible, given the recent political opening toward Amazigh affairs. Perhaps Tamazight will be semiotically adjusted to become not just a language of folklore celebrations in isolated mountain communities, but also a fully accepted language of the country's streets, institutions, and homes. While Tamazight now has de facto recognition from the monarchy and certain governmental institutions such as the primary schools where its instruction has been introduced, this de jure recognition does not yet ensure de facto tolerance among Moroccan Arabic speakers.

A scale of authenticity seems to be reverting to values established in the Protectorate period, when some Tamazight-speaking communities were deemed more Amazigh than others. Rural Berber-speaking groups characterized by accommodation and bilingualism are once again marginalized because of their diglossic and disemic practices.[39] The emerging group-internal divide is no longer primarily demarcated by geolect (Tashelhit, Tamazight, or Tarifit). It does not even map onto the urban/rural divide.[40]

Rather, it is a divide among rural Amazigh groups according to the extent and nature of their interactions with Arabs, or at least Arabic speakers. This divide brings front and center the ways that groups have mediated ethnic, cultural, linguistic, legal, and political differences historically. In the past, ethnolinguistic units of Arab and Amazigh were not absolute, as individuals moved between them according to *larzaq* (Ar. *al razaq*, "fate") that comes with exogamous marriage, or forced displacement in times of famine—as my Arazan-native neighbor in Taroudant, Fatima Mhammd, explained, the repercussions of migration in times of drought, stress under the Protectorate, and exogamous marriage: "Whatever the people spoke in the land where they landed, they spoke it too."[41]

Today, as in the past, a group's mapping onto this scale of Arabness and Berberness has important repercussions, not only regarding access to resources, but also for the maintenance of Tamazight language on a broader scale. The linguistic insecurity I have sensed in conversations with older native Tashelhit speakers does not bode well for language survival. If members of a group see themselves as in-between and not represented in the idealizing discourses and portrayals of community types, they may ally even more with the dominant society into which they hope to assimilate, for they cannot assimilate in the other direction toward a greater Amazigh authenticity. In centers of rural–urban emigration such as Taroudant native Tashelhit speakers integrate into the Arabic-dominant population and raise their children as Arabic-dominant, hastening ethnic assimilation. When linguistic standardization leads to a modified language removed from personal experience, there tends to be a linguistic shift away from the contracting ("endangered") language (here, Tamazight) and toward the dominant vernacular (here, Moroccan Arabic). There could be increased Amazigh pride yet decreased linguistic competence to the point where Berber may drop out of the verbal expressive repertoire altogether and become instead a badge of identity, but no longer a communicative code.[42]

Anthropologists are keen to encourage cultural and linguistic preservation. Still, it is crucial not to disregard processes through which cultural and linguistic assimilation take place in particular historical contexts, and it is important to understand why some people find it in their best interest to abandon their native language, land, or customs. Assimilation into the urban, Arab fold is compelling, but far from inevitable. Some Ishelhin raised in the city return to the countryside to grow old, and some (although fewer) Arabic speakers still marry into Tashelhit-speaking families or villages. Such moves may be involuntary, as with an arranged marriage, or they may be strategic, as when a young woman from the plains secures a marriage with a man in the mountains in order to gain freedom from the relatively strict female seclusion practiced in the plains. Other times, people just want to "change the air" (*ibadl lhawa*) and live somewhere new, or take on an identity other than the one of their birthplace. Following Balzer, who writes about changing meanings of Siberian ethnicity, I too want to "empathize with a people through their changing self-definitions."[43] Yet we must also understand that changes in collective self-definitions bring about a changing sense of self. In this post-nationalist moment, we should remain attentive to the Amazigh and Morocco-specific ways in which this population is experiencing common pressures and choices shared by indigenous and minority populations worldwide, and expect that they will resolve the linguistic challenges with the *bricoleur* spirit that has long characterized them.

Notes

1. Bernard Hoffman, *The Structure of Traditional Moroccan Rural Society* (The Hague: Mouton & Co., 1967), 40.

2. The topic of language practices in urban Morocco is outside the scope of this chapter.

3. Frederick Barth, "Introduction," *Ethnic Groups and Boundaries: The Social Organization of Culture Differences* (Prospect Heights, Ill.: Waveland Press, 1969).

4. See Judith Irvine and Sue Gal, "Language Ideology and Linguistic Differentiation," in *Regimes of Language*, ed. Paul Kroskrity, Bambi Schieffelin, and Kathryn Woolard (Santa Fe, N.M.: School of American Research Press, 2000), 35–83.

5. See Katherine E. Hoffman, "Purity and Contamination: Language Ideologies in French Colonial Native Policy in Morocco," *Comparative Studies in Society and History* 50(3) (2008): 724–752.

6. Robin Bidwell, *Morocco under Colonial Rule: French Administration of Tribal Areas 1912–1956* (London: Frank Cass), 49.

7. Franz Boas, "Introduction to the Handbook of American Indian Languages," *Language, Culture, and Society*, ed. Ben Blount (Prospect Heights, Ill.: Waveland Press, 1995), 9–28.

8. On the relationship between language standardization and language maintenance, see Daniel Nettle and Suzanne Romaine, *Vanishing Voices: The Extinction of the World's Languages* (Oxford: Oxford University Press, 2000); Peter Muhlhauser, *Language Ecology* (London: Routledge, 1996); and A. Tabouret-Keller et al., *Vernacular Literacy: A Re-evaluation* (Oxford: Clarendon Press, 1997). See also a discussion of this literature in Katherine E. Hoffman, "Berber language ideologies, maintenance, and contraction: Gendered variation in the indigenous margins of Morocco," *Language & Communication* 26(2) (2006): 154. On the affective repercussions of language standardization, see Nancy Dorian, "Language Shift in Community and Individual: The Phenomenon of the Laggard Semi-Speaker," *International Journal for the Sociology of Language* 25 (1980): 85–94 and Angela Terrill, "Why Make Books for People Who Don't Read? A Perspective on Documentation of an Endangered Language from Solomon Islands," *International Journal for the Sociology of Language* 155/156 (2002): 205–219.

9. It is less celebrated by those documentarians of Amazigh culture and Amazigh activists with educational backgrounds in the *madaris al-atiqa*, the educational system with a core of religious instruction in Arabic. These scholars, particularly from the

Sous, primarily publish in Arabic, allowing for a more widespread appeal to the literate popular classes, and they use this facility with classical Arabic to their advantage in documenting and representing Amazigh culture. A few examples of such scholars are Ahmed Bouzid, who has published on *ahwash* collective song and dance; Omar Amarir, whose popular television program on rural Amazigh history and culture is widely appreciated; Ahmed Aasiid, poet-performer and author of oral narrative collections; and Id Belkasem, lawyer and activist who has appeared before the United Nations to discuss indigenous peoples. Thus among the intelligentsia, there is yet another fracture, between Arabist Berberists and the Francophone Berberists who studied and publish in French. The Francophone Berberists tend to have greater access to European and North American colleagues and resources, whereas the publications of Arabophone Berberists reach a wider Moroccan audience.

10. Deborah Kapchan, *Gender on the Market: Moroccan Women and the Revoicing of Tradition* (Philadelphia: University of Pennsylvania, 1996).

11. On this dynamic, see Richard Bauman and Charles Briggs, *Voices of Modernity. Language Ideologies and the Politics of Inequality* (Cambridge: Cambridge University Press, 2003); Irvine and Gal, "Language Ideology and Linguistic Differentiation," and the contributions to Bambi B. Schieffelin and Kathryn A. Woolard, eds., *Language Ideologies: Practice and Theory* (New York: Oxford University Press, 1998), especially Woolard's "Introduction: Language Ideology as a Field of Inquiry."

12. Michael Herzfeld develops the concept of cultural disemia, building on the more sociolinguistic concept of diglossia, in *Cultural Intimacy* (New York: Routledge, 1997), 14–15.

13. On speech community, see Nancy Dorian, "Language Shift in Community and Individual"; Allessandro Duranti, *Linguistic Anthropology* (Cambridge: Cambridge University Press, 1997); John Gumperz, "Types of Linguistic Communities," in *Readings in the Sociology of Language*, ed. Joshua A. Fishman (The Hague: Mouton, 1968): 460–472; Janet Holmes and Miriam Meyerhoff, "The Community of Practice: Theories and Methodologies in Language and Gender Research," *Language in Society* 28(2) (1999): 173–183; Dell Hymes, *Foundations in Sociolinguistics: An Ethnographic Approach* (Philadelphia: University of Pennsylvania Press, 1974); and Etienne Wenger, *Communities of Practice* (New York: Cambridge University Press, 1998).

14. On indigenism and the tension between articulations of local, national, and international identities, see Ronald Niezen, *The Origins of Indigenism: Human Rights and the Politics of Identity* (Berkeley: University of California Press, 2003).

15. See Katherine E. Hoffman, "Berber Language Ideologies, Maintenance, and Contraction: Gendered Variation in the Indigenous Margins of Morocco," *Language & Communication* 26 (2006): 60.

16. This hierarchy is detailed in my book *We Share Walls: Language, Land, and Gender in Berber Morocco* (Malden, Mass.: Wiley-Blackwell), 22–24.

17. For a discussion of the broad contours of language practices and attitudes in Morocco, see Ahmed Boukous, *Société, langues et cultures au Maroc* (Casablanca: Annajah Al-Jadida, 1995). For discussions of well-documented Tashelhit poetry, see Abderrahman Lakhsassi, "La conception de la poésie Tashelhit," *Lamalif* 183 (1986): 56–58; Claude Lefebure, *Nouveaux enjeux culturels au Maghreb* (Paris: Centre national de la recherche scientifique, 1986) and "L'Émigration au miroir de la poésie berbère du Maroc," *Hommes & Migrations* 1191 (1995); E. El Moujahid, "La dimension interculturelle dans la poésie berbère tachelhit moderne," in *L'Interculturel au*

Maroc: arts, langues, littératures et traditions populaires (Casablanca: Afrique Orient, 1994), 109–126; and Abdallah El Mountassir, *Amarg: Chants et poésie amazighs (Sud-Ouest du Maroc)* (Paris: L'Harmattan, 2005). Not analyzed to date are the contours of multiple language management, language attitudes, and language change in different corners of North Africa where Berber and Arabic speakers have long been in contact.

Descriptions of multiple language management in Morocco have generally taken a national perspective. As the majority of these studies are written by first- or second-generation urban Moroccan scholars, many of whom speak one of the Berber varieties as their first language, the languages taken into consideration include Standard Arabic and French as the codified languages of writing and administration and the vernaculars, Moroccan Arabic and the Berber varieties, as spoken restricted codes. To my knowledge, there are no published studies of multiple language management in a more restricted geographical area, or studies that focus on the micro-interaction between spoken MA and spoken Berber (other than my *We Share Walls*). While a national perspective is instructive for the broader picture, or for considerations of language planning policies, the specifics of regional and local language management vary considerably from place to place throughout the country and constitute the bulk of meaningful communicative and expressive language use for people. Once outside the cities, standard languages play a very limited role in social life. Studies of language in Morocco are freighted, too, with overly simplified symbolic associations commonly presented in the literature as inherent to the language varieties at hand—Arabic invokes religion, French indexes secularity, Berber reflects popular tradition. For an example of this approach, see Abdelali Bentahila, "Motivations for code-switching among Arabic-French bilinguals in Morocco," *Language & Communication* 3(3) (1983): 233–243.

18. Key among these authorities was Maurice Le Glay as in his *Les populations berbères au Maroc*, Conférences francomarocaines, Tome I (unpublished, n.d.), as discussed in Hoffman, "Purity and Contamination: Language Ideologies in French Colonial Native Policy in Morocco," 731–737.

19. The influence of colloquial Arabic on the Tamazight lexicon and grammar is seen clearly in some of the early Protectorate-era linguistic studies such as A. Renisio, *Étude sur les dialectes berbères des Beni Iznassen, du Rif et des Senhaja de Sraïr: grammaire, texte et lexique* (Paris: E. Leroux, 1932); Émile Laoust, *Mots et choses berbères* (Paris: A. Challamel, 1920); and Edmond Destaing's *Étude sur la tachelhit du Souss: vocabulaire français-berbère* (Paris: Leroux, 1938) and by the same author, *Textes berbères en parler des chleuhs du Sous (Maroc)* (Paris: P. Geuthner, 1940).

20. K. Hoffman, "Purity and Contamination," 736–738.

21. This argument was made, among others, by J. Mourot, *Contribution à la recherche d'une solution au problème marocain* (1948), in the CADN archives (Centre des Archives diplomatiques de Nantes), Maroc Protectorat, Direction des Affaires Indigènes (DAI) 455.

22. See de Laforcade, *Étude sur les actes en pays de coutume* (unpublished report, 1941), in CADN Maroc Protectorat DAI 455, doc. 53.

23. For the argument that Islamization did not lead to Arabization in the early Islamic invasions, see Michael Brett and Elizabeth Fentress, *The Berbers* (Oxford: Blackwell, 1996) and Maya Shatzmiller, *The Berbers and the Islamic State: The Marinid Experience in Pre-Protectorate Morocco* (Princeton, N.J.: Markus Weiner Publishers, 2000).

24. Arjun Appadurai, *Modernity at Large: Global Dimensions of Globalization* (Minneapolis: University of Minnesota Press, 1996), 167.

25. James Clifford, "The Transit-Lounge of Culture," *Times Literary Supplement* 4596 (May 3, 1991): 7–8.

26. Kanishka Chowdhury, "It's All Within Your Reach: Globalization and the Ideologies of Postnationalism and Hybridity," *Cultural Logic: An Electronic Journal of Marxist Theory and Practice* (2002), http://eserver.org/clogic/2002/chowdhury.html (accessed Dec. 12, 2008).

27. For this critique of nationalism, see Homi Bhabha, "Narrating the Nation," in *Nation and Narration*, ed. Homi Bhabha (New York: Routledge, 1990), 1–7; Paul Gilroy, *The Black Atlantic: Modernity and Double Consciousness* (Cambridge, Mass.: Harvard University Press, 1993); Stuart Hall, "Minimal Selves," in *Black British Cultural Studies*, ed. H. A. Baker, Jr., et al. (Chicago: University of Chicago Press, 1996), 114–119.

28. There is something of a self-congratulatory acknowledgement that the global transit lounge is not inhabited solely by white Westerners.

29. Amina Aouchar, *Colonisation et campagne berbère au Maroc* (Casablanca: Afrique Orient, 2002).

30. The linguistic market is elaborated in Pierre Bourdieu, *Language and Symbolic Power [Ce que parler veut dire]*, ed. and intro. John B. Thompson, trans. Gino Raymond and Matthew Adamson (Cambridge: Harvard University Press, 1991).

31. Kapchan, *Gender on the Market*, chapter 6.

32. Her dress resembled that photographed by Kapchan at an urban wedding in Beni Mellal in *Gender on the Market*, 170.

33. Fractal recursivity is further elaborated in Irvine and Gal, "Language Ideology and Linguistic Differentiation."

34. See Boukous, *Société, langues et cultures au Maroc*.

35. For a fuller discussion of this "Houara" style music (after the large Houara Arab tribe in the Sous plains between Taroudant and Agadir), see Hoffman, *We Share Walls*, chapter 7. According to Philip Schuyler (personal communication), the language, instruments, and musical forms are very similar to *hemwada*, the musical genre performed in another "intermediate zone": the northern foothills of the High Atlas and the Chicaoua/Chiadma plains. He notes that the instrumentation is so well-developed and unique to this genre that he suspects the practice pre-dates the Protectorate, but we both await future work on this topic, which should be instructive of histories of Arab-Berber linguistic contact and bilingualism as well.

36. Hoffman, *We Share Walls*, chapter 7.

37. The concept of cultural disemia is elaborated in Herzfeld, *Cultural Intimacy*, 14, and further discussed for Morocco in Hoffman, "Berber Language Ideologies, Maintenance, and Contraction," 150. Diglossia, or domain-specific use of different language varieties or different languages, is discussed in Penny Eckert, "Diglossia: Separate but Unequal," *Linguistics* 18 (1980): 1053–1064; Charles Ferguson, "Diglossia," *Word* 15 (1959): 325–340; John Gumperz, *Language and Social Identity* (New York: Cambridge University Press, 1982); and A. Hannaoui, "Diglossia, Medial Arabic and Language Policy in Morocco" (Ph.D. diss., State University of New York, 1987).

38. Greg Urban, *Metaculture: How Culture Moves Through the World* (Minneapolis: University of Minnesota Press, 2001).

39. I have argued elsewhere that this tends to correlate with their political economies, as plains dwellers are mainly rural proletariat. See my "Berber language ideologies, maintenance, and contraction," and *We Share Walls*, chapter 6.

40. A discussion of Berber urban elites, especially intellectuals and administrators, is outside the scope of the present discussion. Since the founding of IRCAM, it is increasingly the case that this elite is moving from Arabic to Berber and using more French as well. Another segment of the urban Amazigh population that is outside the scope of this discussion includes sometimes wealthy, emigrant, polyglot, and polysemic merchants from the Anti-Atlas whose political and economic lives are centered in the northern cities but who consider themselves fully Ishelhin. My discussion here is limited to rural, diglossic, disemic populations of native Tashelhit speakers. I am grateful to Philip Schuyler for reminding me of this social complexity.

41. Quoted in Hoffman, *We Share Walls*, 147.

42. See Hoffman's "Berber Language Ideologies, Maintenance, and Contraction," and Maryon McDonald, *"We are not French!": Language, Culture, and Identity in Brittany* (London: Routledge, 1989).

43. Marjorie Balzer, *The Tenacity of Ethnicity: A Siberian Saga in Global Perspective* (Princeton, N.J.: Princeton University Press, 1999), 3.

Bibliography

Aouchar, Amina. *Colonisation et campagne berbère au Maroc*. Casablanca: Afrique Orient, 2002.

Appadurai, Arjun. *Modernity at Large: Global Dimensions of Globalization*. Minneapolis: University of Minnesota Press, 1996.

Balzer, Marjorie M. *The Tenacity of Ethnicity: A Siberian Saga in Global Perspective*. Princeton, N.J.: Princeton University Press, 1999.

Barth, Frederik, ed. *Ethnic Groups and Boundaries: The Social Organization of Culture Differences*. Prospect Heights, Ill.: Waveland Press, 1969.

Bauman, Richard, and Charles Briggs. *Voices of Modernity: Language Ideologies and the Politics of Inequality*. Cambridge: Cambridge University Press, 2003.

Bentahila, Abdelali. "Motivations for Code-Switching among Arabic-French Bilinguals in Morocco." *Language & Communication* 3(3) (1983): 33–243.

Bhabha, Homi. "Narrating the Nation." In *Nation and Narration*, ed. Homi Bhabha. New York: Routledge, 1990, 1–7.

Bidwell, R. *Morocco under Colonial Rule: French Administration of Tribal Areas 1912–1956*. London: Frank Cass, 1973.

Boas, Franz. "Introduction to the Handbook of American Indian Languages." In *Language, Culture, and Society*, ed. Ben Blount. Prospect Heights, Ill.: Waveland Press, 1995, 9–28.

Boukous, Ahmed. *Société, langues et cultures au Maroc*. Casablanca: Annajah Al-Jadida, 1995.

Bourdieu, Pierre. *Language and Symbolic Power [Ce que parler veut dire]*, ed. and intro. John B. Thompson, trans. Gino Raymond and Matthew Adamson. Cambridge, Mass.: Harvard University Press, 1991.

Brett, Michael, and Elizabeth Fentress. *The Berbers*. Oxford: Blackwell, 1996.

Chowdhury, Kanishka. "It's All Within Your Reach: Globalization and the Ideologies of Postnationalism and Hybridity." *Cultural Logic: An Electronic Journal of Marxist Theory and Practice* (2002). http://eserver.org/clogic/2002/chowdhury.html (accessed Nov. 8, 2007).

Clifford, James. "The Transit-Lounge of Culture." *Times Literary Supplement* 4596 (May 3, 1991): 7–8.

Destaing, Edmond. *Étude sur la tachelhit du Souss: Vocabulaire français-berbère.* Paris: E. Leroux, 1938.

——. *Textes berbères en parlers des chleuhs du Souss.* Paris: P. Geuthner, 1940.

Dorian, N. "Language Shift in Community and Individual: The Phenomenon of the Laggard Semi-Speaker." *International Journal for the Sociology of Language* 25 (1980): 85–94.

Duranti, Alessandro. *Linguistic Anthropology.* Cambridge: Cambridge University Press, 1997.

Eckert, Penny. "Diglossia: separate but unequal." *Linguistics* 18 (1980): 1053–1064.

El Moujahid, El Houssain. "La dimension interculturelle dans la poésie berbère tachelhit moderne." In *L'interculturel au Maroc: arts, langues, littératures et traditions populaires,* ed. Groupe d'études maghrébines. Casablanca: Afrique Orient, 1994, 109–126.

El Mountassir, Abdallah. *Amarg: chants et poésie amazighs (Sud-Ouest du Maroc).* Paris: L'Harmattan, 2005.

Ferguson, Charles. "Diglossia." *Word* 15 (1959): 325–340.

Gilroy, Paul. *The Black Atlantic: Modernity and Double Consciousness.* Cambridge, Mass.: Harvard University Press, 1993.

Gumperz, John. *Language and Social Identity.* New York: Cambridge University Press, 1982.

——. "Types of Linguistic Communities." In *Readings in the Sociology of Language,* ed. Joshua A. Fishman. The Hague: Mouton, 1968, 460–472.

Hall, Stuart. "Minimal Selves." In *Black British Cultural Studies,* ed. H. A. Baker, Jr., et al. Chicago: University of Chicago Press, 1996, 114–119.

Hannaoui, A. "Diglossia, Medial Arabic and Language Policy in Morocco." Ph.D. diss., State University of New York, 1987.

Herzfeld, Michael. *Cultural Intimacy.* New York: Routledge, 1997.

Hoffman, Bernard. *The Structure of Traditional Moroccan Rural Society.* The Hague: Mouton & Co., 1967.

Hoffman, Katherine E. "Berber Language Ideologies, Maintenance, and Contraction: Gendered Variation in the Indigenous Margins of Morocco." *Language & Communication* 26(2) (2006): 144–167.

——. "Purity and Contamination: Language Ideologies in French Colonial Native Policy in Morocco." *Comparative Studies in Society and History* 50(3) (2008): 724–752.

——. *We Share Walls: Language, Land, and Gender in Berber Morocco.* Blackwell Studies in Discourse and Language. Malden, Mass.: Wiley-Blackwell, 2008.

Holmes, Janet, and Miriam Meyerhoff. "The Community of Practice: Theories and Methodologies in Language and Gender Research." *Language in Society* 28(2) (1999): 173–183.

Hymes, Dell. *Foundations in Sociolinguistics: An Ethnographic Approach.* Philadelphia: University of Pennsylvania Press, 1974.

Irvine, Judith, and Susan Gal. "Language Ideology and Linguistic Differentiation." In *Regimes of Language,* ed. Paul Kroskrity, Bambi B. Schieffelin, and Kathryn Woolard. Santa Fe, N.M.: School of American Research Press, 2000, 35–83.

Kapchan, Deborah. *Gender on the Market: Moroccan Women and the Revoicing of Tradition.* Philadelphia: University of Pennsylvania, 1996.

de Laforcade. *Étude sur les actes en pays de coutume,* unpublished report, 1941. Centre des Archives diplomatiques de Nantes, Maroc Protectorat, Direction des Affaires Indigènes 455, doc. 53.

Lakhsassi, Abderrahman. "La conception de la poésie Tashelhit." *Lamalif* 183 (1986): 56–58.

Laoust, Émile. *Mots et choses berbères*. Paris: A. Challamel, 1920.

Lefebure, Claude. *Nouveaux enjeux culturels au Maghreb*. Paris: Centre national de la recherche scientifique, 1986.

Le Glay, Maurice. *Les Populations berbères au Maroc*. Conférences francomarocaines, Tome 1, n.d.

McDonald, Maryon. *"We are not French!": Language, Culture, and Identity in Brittany*. London: Routledge, 1989.

Mourot, J. "Contribution à la recherche d'une solution au problème marocain." Centre des Archives diplomatiques de Nantes, Protectorat du Maroc, Direction des Affaires Indigènes 455, 1948.

Muhlhauser, Peter. *Language Ecology*. London: Routledge, 1996.

Nettle, Daniel, and Suzanne Romaine. *Vanishing Voices: The Extinction of the World's Languages*. Oxford: Oxford University Press, 2000.

Niezen, Ronald. *The Origins of Indigenism: Human Rights and the Politics of Identity*. Berkeley: University of California Press, 2003.

Renisio, A. *Étude sur les dialectes berbères des Beni Iznassen, du Rif et des Senhaja de Sraïr: grammaire, texte et lexique*. Paris: E. Leroux, 1932.

Schieffelin, Bambi B., Kathryn A. Woolar, et al., eds. *Language Ideologies: Practice and Theory*. Oxford Studies in Anthropological Linguistics. New York: Oxford University Press, 1998.

Shatzmiller, Maya. *The Berbers and the Islamic State: The Marinid Experience in Pre-Protectorate Morocco*. Princeton, N.J.: Markus Weiner Publishers, 2000.

Tabouret-Keller, Andrée, et al., eds. *Vernacular Literacy: A Re-evaluation*. Oxford: Clarendon Press, 1997.

Terrill, Angela. "Why Make Books for People Who Don't Read? A Perspective on Documentation of an Endangered Language from Solomon Islands." *International Journal for the Sociology of Language* 155/156 (2002): 205–219.

Urban, Greg. *Metaculture: How Culture Moves Through the World*. Minneapolis: University of Minnesota Press, 2001.

Wenger, Etienne. *Communities of Practice*. New York: Cambridge University Press, 1998.

Woolard, Kathryn. "Introduction: Language Ideology as a Field of Inquiry." In *Language Ideologies: Practice and Theory*, ed. Bambi B. Schieffelin, Kathryn A. Woolard, and Paul V. Kroskrity. New York: Oxford University Press, 1998.

3

The *Makhzan*'s Berber: Paths to Integration in Pre-Colonial Morocco

Mohamed El Mansour

To what extent does ethnicity as a category of analysis provide a methodological framework valid for all societies? It is clear that the concept of ethnicity developed within particular historical and cultural conditions that characterized Western societies in modern times.[1] What about non-Western, nomadic societies in which the conceptual reference is not so much "ethnos" or "race" as "tribe" or "lineage"?

Anthropologists often define ethnicity by using race, religion, or national character as their main parameters. In *The International Encyclopaedia of the Social Sciences*, Milton Gordon writes that an ethnic group "is defined or set off by race, religion, or national origin, or some combination of these categories."[2] However, this definition does not fit North African Berbers, since they do not conceive of themselves as a distinct race, nor do they differ from any other major group of Arabophones in terms of religion. And the criterion of a separate "national origin" as a basis for claiming a distinct ethnicity is obviously irrelevant for Berbers in the pre-modern era.

A less essentialist definition put forward by others identifies the core component of ethnicity as "the myth of common ancestry," a myth also found in tribal societies. However, Berbers see no room for ethnic differentiation from Arabs, since their genealogists claim a common ancestry with their Arab "cousins." The eighteenth century Moroccan historian Abu al-Qasim al-Zayani, the subject of this chapter, shared with his genealogist grandfather the belief that the Middle Atlas Sanhaja Berbers were related to Noah through Canaan, the son of Ham.³ This mythical lineage leading back to Noah was found in many Bedouin genealogies of Arabia, according to historian Hugh Kennedy;⁴ with the Islamization of North Africa, it was adopted by Berbers and became part of their constructed pedigrees, and by the medieval period, it was already well entrenched among Berber genealogists. In fact, Ibn ʿAbd al-Halim al-Illani, author of the fourteenth century *Mafakhir al-barbar* ("The Glorious Exploits of the Berbers") was one of the first Berber historians to advance the myth that Berbers, just like their Arab relatives, were connected to the Biblical genealogy of Ham and the Canaanites of Palestine,⁵ thus laying the basis for Ibn Khaldun's claim of the Mashriqi (eastern) origin of the Berbers—an assertion that became a well-established "fact" for later generations of North African historians and genealogists.

For Arab and Berber genealogists alike, the issue was not so much to prove a common ancestry (already taken for granted), but rather to establish credible genealogies infused with nobility and prestige. Within this "genealogical culture" spread by the Arab conquerors along with the Islamization process, genealogies differed greatly in terms of nobility, depending on one's closeness to the Prophet. In the Maghrib, the outstanding genealogy was that of the *sharif*s, or those who could prove their descent from the Prophet. Next in order were lineages related to the Quraysh, the Prophet's tribe, or to one of his companions. Finally, if neither of these options was available, the simple fact of belonging to an Arab lineage was a mark of social distinction. The claim of Arabian or Mashriqi origin by Berber genealogists was intended to underline the closeness of the Berbers to lineages valued by the Arabo-Islamic genealogical culture. By connecting themselves to Biblical figures, the Berbers were looking for a way to come closer to the Prophet of Islam.⁶

Thus it can be said that within the Arabo-Islamic tradition, genealogy was the defining social norm. While the Western concept of ethnicity has undertones of "race" and "nationality," Arab genealogy alludes more to "lineage" and "tribe." Ibn Khaldun, theoretician of tribal organization in the Maghribi context par excellence, avoids (or is unaware of) the concept of "race," and refers instead to human groupings such as Arabs or Berbers using the word *jayl*, meaning "generation": that is, a particular people at a specific time. Thus he talks about *jayl al-barbar*, or *jayl al-ʿarab*, meaning "a tribe or a group of tribes living at a specific historical moment."[7] Discussing the misreading of Ibn Khaldun in the West, 'Abd al-Majid Hannoum points out the inaccurate conflation of Ibn Khaldun's *jayl* with "race" by leading Orientalists such as Baron de Slane and Franz Rosenthal.[8] Moreover, by alluding to temporality, Ibn Khaldun suggests that group identity is not static, but changes under the influence of history and environmental conditions.

Within the same logic, Ibn Khaldun developed the notion of *'asabiya*, or group belonging, that was an attribute based not on a shared and mythical biological origin, but rather on a long-standing need for group solidarity in the face of common threats. *'Asabiya* itself is not a fixed or unchanging attribute, since tribal groups come together or disband depending on a multitude of factors. Even genealogical affiliation is subject to alteration, Ibn Khaldun acknowledged: "It is clear that a person of a certain descent may become attached to people of another descent" through interest, alliance, or a master-client relationship.[9]

The Khaldunian interpretation has shaped the vision of Maghribi historians and genealogists for centuries, and al-Zayani was no exception. The fact that he adopted without question the conventional Berber genealogies as they were reproduced in the classical texts did not mean that he believed in the sacred or immutable character of these pedigrees. Undoubtedly, he was aware of the frequent manipulations to which these genealogies were subjected for the purpose of maximizing prestige and material benefits.[10] During his lifetime, he also witnessed the dismantling or emergence of new tribal entities among the Middle Atlas Berbers, either as a result of *makhzan* (government) intervention or inter-tribal conflict.[11] Genealogy changes with the situation, as does ethnicity; instead of being trapped within a single inherited identity, the individual increases his strategic choices by acquiring multiple identities that he then displays at different times, depending on the perceived utility of each.[12] For al-Zayani, Berber identity would be an inner circle surrounded by many concentric circles representing other manifestations of his complex and layered character.

Biography and Cultural Identity

The importance of biography as a mirror of cultural identity is self-evident.[13] In the Moroccan case, cultural biography has been used effectively by social scientists as a tool to unfold multiple identities. French sociologist Jacques Berque used it to investigate the personality of the seventeenth-century Berber scholar al-Hasan al-Yusi (d. 1691), while Dale Eickelman employed the genre to analyze the less well-known but a no less interesting case of 'Abd al-Rahman Mansuri, a scholar and judge under the French Protectorate.[14] Al-Zayani's identity also gained in complexity as he moved across cultural boundaries. His travels to the Islamic East show how an ethnic "Berber" who ventures into the wider world could acquire a complex identity in which "Berberism" is only one among many facets.

Through al-Zayani's biography, we also see that paths to integration in pre-colonial Morocco were diverse. Foremost was religion that declared—in principle, at least—all Muslims, irrespective of ethnic or tribal origin, to be equal before God. Religious scholarship allowed individuals from all backgrounds to move to center stage and assume prominent roles as judges, *muftis*, and *imams*. The pursuit of knowledge not only opened the way for social mobility; it also allowed students and scholars from the countryside to settle in the cities where they could merge into the urban social tissue. Mysticism and sainthood offered another means to integration. Sufi orders that flourished during the pre-colonial period tended to cut across tribal and social boundaries, developing networks whose ramifications went far beyond tribal affiliations and sometimes even beyond the limits of a single country. Through the cultural biography of al-Yusi, Berque showed how an ethnic "Berber" was able to integrate into the wider Islamic order using Islamic scholarship and Sufism as the bridge between his local Berber culture and the outside world. For Abu al-Qasim al-Zayani, the path to integration was through service to the state. Here we shall glean notions of al-Zayani's self-fashioning by looking closely at his writings, and in particular his description of the world, the *al-Turjumana al-Kubra*, a work that provides insights into his political career under three 'Alawi sultans.[15]

Al-Zayani's Early Life in Fez

Al-Zayani was born in Fez in the year 1734. His father had left his home village in the Middle Atlas some forty years before. Behind the movement of the family from the Middle Atlas to the city was the decision by Sultan Isma'il (who ruled 1672–1727) to bring to Meknes al-Zayani's grandfather, 'Ali Ibn Ibrahim, to serve as his private *imam* (leader of prayer). Ahmad Ibn 'Ali, al-Zayani's father, left his village as a child and spent most of his life in Meknes, but as soon as Sultan Isma'il died in 1727, he decided to move to Fez.[16] This decision was probably motivated by his desire to flee the turmoil in Meknes caused by rebellious soldiers following the death of the Sultan and to provide a better education for his children. However, Abu al-Qasim's father did not seem to find the peace of mind he was seeking, for Fez, too, was caught up in the political upheavals that followed Mawlay Isma'il's death.

The scholarly biography (*tarjama*) of al-Zayani was a classical one. After learning the Qur'an, he moved to the next stage of study, acquiring the basic sciences (*al-ummahat*) such as grammar and the principles of Islamic law (*fiqh*). At the Qarawiyin mosque in Fez, he attended lectures of the leading scholars of the time, among them the *shaykh al jama'a*, the most notable authority, Muhammad al-Tawdi Ibn Suda (d. 1795). However, at some stage of his studies at the Qarawiyin, al-Zayani became bored listening to the dry lessons of *fiqh* and started to develop extra-curricular interests that led to the end of his formal education.[17] Among the books in his family library he discovered a register (*kunnash*) on Berber genealogy written in the hand of his grandfather, who was, in his words, "an unsurpassed authority in the field."[18] This finding triggered his curiosity and directed him down the path of the study of genealogy and history.

For centuries, the education offered by the university-mosque of the Qarawiyin and other *madrasas* had played a critical role in integrating students of rural origin (*afaqis*) into a more expansive corps of scholars from a variety of backgrounds. Abu al-Qasim did not achieve that integration for a number of reasons, among them his preoccupation with history and genealogy. An even more unconventional pursuit of al-Zayani concerned alchemy and fetishism. Al-Zayani relates that his teacher 'Umar al-Fasi questioned him about his secret interests and as a result embarrassed him. After this incident, he abandoned attending his master's lectures altogether.[19] His teachers' doubt about his competence in the religious sciences was later confirmed in his own writings. His knowledge of the *shari'a* (religious law) was never well grounded, and the education he acquired ranked him only as a *talib* (an accomplished laureate) rather than the more exalted *'alim* (religious scholar). His detractors would regard him as a failed scholar whose limited knowledge of the religious sciences had prepared him at best for an administrative post in the *makhzan*. As a result, al-Zayani never found his niche among the learned men of Fez. His Berber origins alone could not have been the obstacle, since hundreds of families who were successfully integrated into Fasi elite society carried names that referred to rural and tribal backgrounds.[20] In al-Zayani's case, it was surely a combination of his recent migration, an eccentric educational experience, and above all, an affiliation to the *makhzan* that kept him from fully becoming part of this select group.

After he joined state service in 1758, the rift between al-Zayani and his native city seems to have widened. Relations between the 'Alawi monarchy and the people of Fez were never harmonious, and the situation in the period of Sidi Muhammad Ibn 'Abd Allah was no exception. At the onset of his rule, the new Sultan rejected an invitation from the people of Fez to make their city the country's capital. His heavy-handed fiscal policies targeting urban-based activities were especially unpopular. Moreover, the religious scholars of Fez, along with most of the Moroccan *'ulama*, did not appreciate Sidi Muhammad's Hanbali sympathies, since they conflicted with the well-entrenched Maliki tradition of the country.[21] Toward the end of al-Zayani's life, relations between the people of Fez and Sidi Muhammad Ibn 'Abd Allah's successor, Mawlay Sulayman (r. 1792–1822), deteriorated even further, as the city came under the influence of conservative religious groups. In 1820, much of the Fasi elite allied themselves with dissenting *zawiyas* such as the Wazzaniya and Darqawiya to overthrow the unpopular sultan.[22] During this unsuccessful rebellion, al-Zayani remained loyal to the *makhzan*. As a result, he was imprisoned and his property confiscated by the rebels. Some of the Fasi ulama went so far as to accuse al-Zayani of disbelief (*kufr*) and sorcery.[23] Al-Zayani considered his suffering at the hands of the Fasi rebels the price to be paid for his loyalty to the *makhzan*. Two works he produced during the rebellion were refutations of the arguments raised by the rebels aimed at dethroning Sulayman.[24]

In these polemical works, al-Zayani is especially virulent toward the notables (*shurafa'*) who played a crucial role in the rebellion. The Sharif of Wazzan, head of the influential Wazzani *zawiya* (religious order), used his religious prestige and wide popularity to garner support for the 1820 uprising in Fez. Transgressing conventional norms regarding the respect due to holy lineages like the Wazzanis, al-Zayani brashly condemned Mawlay al-'Arbi, head of the Wazzani order, as "another wicked Satan."[25] Furthermore, he broadened his attack against the *shaykh* of the Wazzaniya to include all of Mawlay al-'Arbi's forebears. Thus he refers to the revered Sufi "pole" Mawlay 'Abd al-Salam Ibn Mashish (d. 1228) simply as "*shaykh* 'Abd al-Salam," dropping the usual honorific of "Mawlay" used to address people of the Prophet's lineage.[26] Likewise, he refers to the Wazzani *shurafa'* in general simply as "the sons of 'Abd Allah al-Sharif," not only dropping the "Mawlay," but also stripping the Wazzanis of their religious mantle and discrediting their Sufi claims.[27] Moreover, al-Zayani attacked other popular Sufi orders in Fez, such as the Darqawiya and the Tijaniya.[28]

These insults were not easily tolerated in a city where the religious nobility enjoyed great prestige and influence. Conservative religious groups gained in popularity at the end of the eighteenth century in widespread reaction to the *makhzan*'s accommodationist policies toward the West.[29] Al-Zayani was identified with these unpopular *makhzan* policies.[30] As a result, al-Zayani's image was negatively etched in Fasi memory, taking on the form of ridicule. Muhammad Ibn Ja'far Al-Kattani (d. 1927), a prominent *sharif* and author of a multi-volume history of Fez, *Salwat al-Anfas*, ridiculed al-Zayani by characterizing him as having a skull made of a pumpkin after an operation to replace part of his damaged cranium.[31] The *Salwa*, a highly authoritative biographical dictionary devoted to eminent people buried in Fez, notes that al-Zayani's burial in Fez "was carried out

on the sultan's order," implying the unwelcome character of this inter-
ment. Al-Kattani goes on to vilify al-Zayani in just a few words: "He had a
malicious tongue that spared no one; so much so that he ended up attacking the great among God's friends (kibar al-awliya). May God preserve us
from such [horrible] things!"[32]

Temptations of Power

Al-Zayani's first trip to the Mashriq took place in 1756. At the age of
twenty-three he accompanied his father on the pilgrimage (hajj) to Mecca.
His father had become disillusioned with life in Morocco as a result of the
long civil war following the death of Mawlay Isma'il. He decided to head
East with his family and settle there permanently. However, these plans
were drowned in the Red Sea after their ship sank and they lost all their
property.[33] When al-Zayani returned to Fez in 1758, he found a new sultan
on the throne, Muhammad Ibn 'Abd Allah (r. 1757–1790), who took on
the task of reorganizing the country after thirty years of civil war. Later, al-
Zayani would describe the reign of this new sultan as a period of regenera-
tion of the 'Alawi dynasty after its near-collapse during the post-Isma'ili
fatra, or power vacuum.[34] This reorganization included the strengthening
of the bureaucracy and the recruitment of many talibs (laureates) to fill
administrative positions in the new government.

Al-Zayani wished to resume his studies, but he soon discovered that
most of his schoolmates had been offered positions in the remodeled makhzan administration. His peers included Ahmad al-Ghazzal, later ambassador to Spain, Ahmad al-Wannan, poet and writer, and Muhammad
Ibn 'Uthman, later ambassador to many different Muslim and Christian
courts.[35] The need for educated people to fill the expanding makhzan bureaucracy opened opportunities even for laureates coming from rural areas. Among them was al-Zayani's close school friend, Sa'id al-Jazuli, a
Berber from the Sus region, known among his classmates as al-Shliyah, or
the "little Berber."[36] Like al-Zayani, al-Jazuli had developed a passion for
history, and the friendship between the two had grown as they read and
exchanged historical works. It was al-Jazuli who encouraged his friend's
desire to join the makhzan service. "When I saw what he had become, my
ardor to join [my schoolmates] became irresistible, and my heart was set
on [joining] the sultan's service," al-Zayani later wrote.[37]

Al-Zayani's father did not share his son's passion for state service, warning
him with the following words: "Son! Fear God and mind your affairs! . . .
You are my only son . . . and I expect you to look after me until I am put to
eternal rest." "But my friends are all gone," replied al-Zayani as he rejected
his father's advice: "They have realized their wishes and attained the

highest honor and prestige . . ."[38] Because of the unending crisis that had destabilized the country in his youth, al-Zayani had a rather cynical view of affairs. He believed that in a troubled world, one had to count on a powerful protector. After three generations away from Zayan, the land of his ancestors, al-Zayani felt stripped of his tribal-based kinship ties ('asabiya) and in need of the protection offered by a powerful patron.

Service to the *Makhzan*

States and rulers try to diversify their power base as a means of increasing their ability to maneuver. The 'Alawi dynasty lacked a tribal base and sought alliances beyond the limits of their weak '*asabiya*. They created '*asabiya* by means of a professional slave army and tribal alliances that transcended ethnic and regional boundaries. Thus Mawlay Rashid (d. 1672) and his successor Mawlay Isma'il (d. 1727) relied on the Berber tribes of the Rif to consolidate their power from Tangier to the Muluya River. These tribes assumed a permanent auxiliary military status, becoming what was known as the *jaysh al-Rifi* (the Rifian militia) stationed in Tangier and its hinterland. The 'Alawi military system also included the Udaya, a cavalry corps drawn from the Ma'qil Arab tribes of the south of the country. Their policy also rested on a system of alliances drawing into the orbit of the *makhzan* the lowland Berbers (*barabirat al-wata*) of the Middle Atlas such as the Ait Idrassen, Zemmour, and Guerwan. These tribes were then used as a buffer against the unruly mountain tribes (*barabirat al-jabal*). Although the *makhzan* never succeeded in upgrading this relationship to the level of an institutionalized military structure, the arrangement with the lowland Berbers endured long enough for al-Zayani to consider them, in his words, as "*barabirat al-dawla*" (the state Berbers).[39]

Another *makhzan* strategy consisted of winning over tribal notables and setting them up as local governors, or recruiting members of local elites into the royal entourage, thereby strengthening their ties with rural concentrations of power. Through these means, sultans would widen their administrative base at the local level and diversify their retinue at the center, thus making themselves less dependent on any single group. In the case of al-Zayani's grandfather, 'Ali Ibn Ibrahim, brought to Meknes by Mawlay Isma'il, we assume that his recruitment was part of *makhzan* policy to mend relations with the Sanhaja Berbers following the demise of the Dila'i principality in 1669. His grandfather was one of al-Yusi's teachers and maintained a small yet active *zawiya* near Adekhsan where he used to receive students. Mawlay Isma'il wanted to remove him from a milieu where every gathering, even for religious or educational purposes, looked like a plot against the regime.[40] The transfer of al-Zayani's grandfather to Meknes also gave the sultan a channel for maintaining communication with the Zayan tribal milieu that was useful in the management of this troublesome, mountainous region.

A Career with the *Makhzan*

When Abu al-Qasim al-Zayani joined the sultan's service as *katib* (clerk) in 1758, his duties were not clear. Sultan Muhammad Ibn 'Abd Allah was passionate about history and genealogy and liked to surround himself with people like al-Zayani and his friend Sa'id Al Jazuli who could entertain him with their knowledge.[41] Then, after ten years of loyal service, al-Zayani was summarily dismissed. He calls this event the second great misfortune (*nakba*) of his life, after the Red Sea shipwreck. But soon he was recalled and appointed head of the Sultan's *diwan* (secretariat). He notes this promotion with pride: "After the 'divorce'," he wrote, "he [the sultan] entrusted me with the *diwan* of his secretaries . . . and to compensate my previous losses made me the master of slaves and dependents."[42] Apparently this promotion came at the expense of his friend al-Jazuli, whom the sultan had discarded. Al-Zayani had reached the heart of the logic of the *makhzan*, consisting of a combination of ruthlessness, intrigue, and an unrepentant lust for power. Of the seven great misfortunes he encountered in his life, he noted that five were the result of the merciless game of *mahkzan* politics. Throughout his career, al-Zayani recalled his father's warning to stay away from princes; no doubt his father would have considered his misfortunes as divine punishment for having ignored his advice.

During his years in the royal service, al-Zayani took on a range of administrative tasks under the rubric of *katib*. He lived under five 'Alawi sultans, serving three of them, but it was under sultan Muhammad Ibn 'Abd Allah that he made his mark. He served as head of the *diwan*, as an advisor, as tutor to the sultan's sons, as regional governor, and as royal ambassador. One of Muhammad Ibn 'Abd Allah's reforms was aimed at putting order into the administration by assigning specific tasks to his secretaries. Thus we find al-Zayani in charge of the *makhzan*'s relations with the European diplomatic corps during the years 1778–1779.[43] This gave him the opportunity to gain direct knowledge of European affairs and to observe closely the sultan's strategic choices in shaping new approaches to the West. Muhammad Ibn 'Abd Allah is known for having placed Morocco's domestic and foreign policy on a new footing. Internally, this change consisted of removing the fiscal burden imposed on the tribes by seeking alternative income through overseas trade. It was a pragmatic choice, aimed at avoiding tribal unrest, while reducing the need for the military force normally required to collect taxes. At the same time, it required a more active tribal diplomacy and what the French would later call "*une politique des notables.*" According to this policy, tribal chiefs and other influential religious figures served as intermediaries between the central administration and the local population, in return for receiving privileges and other rewards.

Externally, the sultan encouraged more active trade relations with the West as the basis for peace at home.[44] However, this presupposed renouncing *jihad* (holy war) against the West, a policy deplored by conservative religious groups. To appease them, the sultan made an effort to support other confrontational Islamic states, such as the Ottomans. The embassies he dispatched to Istanbul were opportunities to deliver symbolic and indirect assistance to the *jihad* in the form of precious metals, saltpetre, and ships. Sidi Muhammad also exploited his friendly relations with European countries such as Spain to negotiate the ransoming and release of Ottoman captives.

Al-Zayani found a place in the *makhzan* of Sidi Muhammad because of his competence and loyalty, not because of his ethnic and tribal origins. Most of the secretaries who joined the sultan's service after 1757 were recent graduates, born in the cities and distant from their family's rural roots. However, the *makhzan* never lost sight of the need to diversify, making al-Zayani an ideal choice, since he belonged to a Berber family whose fidelity to the state had already been proven. Moreover, he had no other competing organic links; not to the Zayan tribes of his forbears after three generation of city life, nor to the Fasi milieu that had rejected him.

After the death of Sidi Muhammad, the country went through a period of extended political upheaval, during which al-Zayani and others associated with the previous reign left the royal service. With the proclamation of Sultan Sulayman in 1792, he returned and the new sultan immediately assigned him the task of pacifying the eastern provinces around Oujda where *makhzan* authority had receded in the face of intervention from Ottoman-ruled Algeria. The troops under al-Zayani's command were thrown into complete confusion and the operation was a total failure.[45] This debacle was another turning point in al-Zayani's life, and he decided to leave the *makhzan* definitively.

Like his father, he too sought refuge in the Mashriq, where he performed the pilgrimage and took a binding pledge before the Prophet's tomb to never again return to political life. "When God blessed me with removal from service to the *makhzan,*" wrote al-Zayani, "I wanted to purify my body and relieve myself from all the wrongs and misdeeds that burdened me by paying visit to the House of God and the shrine of his Prophet."[46] But by the time he returned to Morocco in 1797, he had recanted on his oath and accepted (with hesitation) the post of governor of the northern ports.[47]

In this last phase of his life, al-Zayani continued to serve the *makhzan* in various posts, including the governorate of the Tadla region near the Za-yan mountains. But he had difficulties conforming to a changing world. Trained in the accommodating practices of Sultan Sidi Muhammad, he could not easily adjust to Sultan Sulayman's confrontational policy toward the Middle Atlas Berbers.[48] By this time he was in his seventies, his acuity had been eroded by age, and good sense must have dictated that it was time for retirement.

Ambassador to the Sublime Porte

During the second half of the eighteenth century, relations between Morocco and the Sublime Porte improved greatly. While Morocco fol-lowed a policy of peaceful coexistence with the Western Christian powers, the Ottoman Empire was on a confrontational course, militarily resisting European efforts to dismantle it. During the second half of the eighteenth century, no fewer than fourteen Moroccan ambassadors were dispatched to Istanbul, mainly to show solidarity with the Ottomans in their anti-Christian *jihad*.[49] Al-Zayani's embassy to Istanbul in 1786 had the addi-tional purpose of easing tensions between Morocco and Algeria, still un-der nominal Ottoman rule.

Al-Zayani's visit to Istanbul allowed him to witness firsthand the great-est Muslim empire; on a personal level, it gave him the chance to contem-plate his own identity. He expressed high admiration for Ottoman culture, especially when compared to Morocco, and in particular the order and good management. The rational government structure and the careful distribu-tion of authority between the sultan and his grand vizier (*al-sadr al-a'zam*) also impressed him. The real ruler in the Ottoman lands, according to al-Zayani, was the grand vizier, while the sultan was no more than a figure-head. Moreover, the complex distribution of powers among religious and military authorities (muftis, judges, chiefs of the Janissaries, etc.) circum-scribed the role of the grand vizier. There was even room for the voice of the people (*ra'iyya*), and the powerful viziers could be removed and pun-ished if they were unjust.[50] Ottoman institutions such as the treasury, arse-nal, dockyards, ordnance factory, and official paper mill impressed some-one coming from a country where such institutions were either non-existent or lacked durability and efficacy. The military academy and the new engi-neering school had no parallels in Morocco.[51] Al-Zayani reported these Ottoman successes with great pride, as if they represented the achieve-ments of Muslims everywhere.

Al-Zayani's travel to Istanbul was especially revealing in terms of self-identification. Within Morocco, he identified himself as a Berber, but in a different land, the parameters of his identity changed. Regarding religious practice, the Turks were Sunni Muslims like him. Regarding their ethnicity, they were ʿajam—that is, non-Arabs—just as he was, as an ethnic Berber. Yet from his remarks, it seems that al-Zayani did not recognize this parallelism and instead opted for a placing of his own identity as distinct from that of the ʿajam. Writing about the Ottomans, al-Zayani notes that if the Turks have a vice, it is their "Arabophobia."[52] This attitude is deeply rooted in them, he observed, for

> an Arab, whatever degree of learning, nobility (sharaf), or religion he reaches, will never be respected. We have witnessed this throughout their lands and even in the seat of their government. When they want to praise someone for his virtue, religion or scholarship they will say: "How noble, virtuous and learned is this man, if only he were not an Arab!"[53]

Al-Zayani speaks here as someone who was personally involved in this controversy. At home, he no doubt considered himself as a "Berber" within an Arabo-Islamic culture; but in the Ottoman lands, he became an "Arab" of sorts, or at the very least, not a member of the ʿajam.[54]

His identification with Islam took precedence above all else. He condemned the Arabophobia of the Turks, believing that Islamic doctrine deplored discrimination among believers on the basis of ethnic origin. Al-Zayani also took a stand on this issue in Morocco, when some Fasi scholars of sharifian origin stigmatized other Fasi scholars on the basis of their Jewish ancestry.[55] Such ethnic discrimination, he believed, whether in the form of Turkish Arabophobia or Fasi snobbery toward converts, was contrary to the letter and spirit of Islam.[56]

Conclusion

Al-Zayani's life story provides the context for assessing the modalities for expressing Berber identity within a Moroccan and Maghribi context. In his case, we see a complex pattern in which neither Western notions of ethnicity, nor Maghribi understandings of genealogy, were sufficient to capture the full range of al-Zayani's personality. In fact, the "ethnic" or the "tribal" aspect of al-Zayani's selfhood was just one of several layers. He was a Berber in the sense that he was born into a Middle Atlas family of the Zayan recently moved to the city. Although he had an urban Arabo-Islamic education, he continued to speak Tamazight and never lost contact with his countrymen in the mountains. In his daily life, he remained attached to the customs, habits, and simple lifestyle of the rustic countryman who never fully accepted the manners of the city. He tells us that he preferred a diet of couscous to one of more refined foods.[57] Yet, as we have seen, al-Zayani's makeup was far more complex than that encompassed by the notion of "Berber."

In pre-colonial Morocco, the means of social integration were diverse and included religion, migration, business partnerships, marriage, military service, and state employment, to name only a few. Among these pathways, acquiring an Islamic education and enrolling in state service both played major historical roles in the formation of a cohesive Moroccan society. In fact, Islamic education allowed many from the Berber countryside to link to a more global Islamic culture. For Abu al-Hasan al-Yusi, the bridge between local Berberism and an Islamic universalism was built by means of scholarship and mysticism. For al-Zayani, state service was a means of distancing himself from tribal attachments and reaching into the wider society.

Al-Zayani's case indicates that in pre-modern Morocco, identity was far from being predetermined and fixed. Rather, it was situational in the sense that the same person could be categorized, or affiliated, depending on the circumstances in which he found himself. Social theorists refer to "salience," whereby one particular aspect of one's identity is "activated" at a particular moment so as to become the most prominent.[58] Accordingly, al-Zayani played the Berber card when he was among his Zayan countrymen; elsewhere he emphasized his standing in the *makhzan*, and in yet another situation, his Fasi affiliation. Other roles he occupied included member in the Nasiri sufi brotherhood, *talib/ʿalim*, member of the *khassa* (elite), subject of the Moroccan sultanate, "Arab" in the land of the *ʿajami* Turks, and Sunni Muslim in the land of the orthodox Ottomans. In other words, our ethnic "Berber" had a full portfolio of identities whose boundaries could be shifted and fitted to the needs of the situation. Yet despite this malleability, and in conjunction with the constraints of the moment, a hierarchical order emerges in which one dimension prevailed. For Abu al-Qasim al-Zayani, the *makhzanian* dimension was the "salient" one that dominated over the rest.

Notes

1. According to Audrey Smedley, the notion of human difference "based on a notion of heredity and permanence" was unknown in the West before modern times. "Race" as a form of social identification and stratification came into being in the eighteenth century in Europe and the New World to express a new relationship between "the civilized Europeans" and the barbaric Other. While "ethnicity" is not necessarily the same as "race," many social scientists have pointed out that the two differ "only in degree." See Audrey Smedley, "Race and the Construction of Human Identity," *American Anthropologist* 100 (Sept. 1998): 690–694.

2. Quoted by W. Isajiw in "Definitions of Ethnicity," *Ethnicity* 1 (1974): 113.

3. al-Zayani, *al-Turjumana al-Kubra* (Rabat: Ministry of Information, 1967), 548.

4. Hugh Kennedy, "From Oral Tradition to Written Record in Arabic Genealogy," *Arabica* 44(4) (Oct. 1994): 536.

5. Abu Salih al-Illani, *Mafakhir al-barbar* (Rabat: Dar Abi Raqraq, 2008), 208.

6. The Berbers also discovered maraboutism as another way of accessing holy lineage. By producing a profusion of marabouts, the Berbers were (according to J. Berque) taking revenge on the conquering Arabs who had the monopoly of ancestral nobility. See J. Berque, "Problèmes initiaux de la sociologie juridique en Afrique du nord," *Studia Islamica* (1953): 159.

7. A. Hannoum, "Translation and the Colonial Imaginary: Ibn Khaldun Orientalist," *History and Theory* 42(1) (Feb. 2003): 75.

8. Ibid. Building on this misinterpretation, later historians such as Maya Shatzmiller attributed to Ibn Khaldun the writing of North African history in terms of "race," a concept not found in the original Arabic version of Ibn Khaldun's history. See M. Shatzmiller, "Le mythe d'origine berbère," *Revue des mondes musulmans et de la Méditerranée* 35 (1983): 151.

9. Ibn Khaldun, *The Muqaddimah*, trans. F. Rosenthal (Princeton, N.J.: Princeton University Press, 1967), 100.

10. Al-Zayani, *Tuhfat al-Hadi al-Mutrib* (Rabat: Ministry of Islamic Affairs, 2008), 90–95.

11. The best illustration in this respect is the Ait Idrassen, the largest Middle Atlas confederation, to which some tribal groups were added while others broke away. See Mohamed El Mansour, *Morocco in the Reign of Mawlay Sulayman* (Wisbech, UK: Menas Press, 1990), 9.

12. Joanne Nagel, "Constructing Ethnicity: Creating and Recreating Ethnic Identity and Culture," *Social Problems* 41(1) (1994): 154.

13. Concerning the Middle East, see Martin Kramer, ed., *Middle Eastern Lives: The Practice of Biography and Self-Narrative* (Syracuse, N.Y.: Syracuse University Press, 1991) and Edmund Burke III, ed., *Struggle and Survival in the Middle East* (Berkeley: University of California Press, 1993).

14. J. Berque, *Al Yousi: problèmes de la culture marocaine au XVIIe siècle* (Paris and The Hague: Mouton, 1958); Dale F. Eickelman, *Knowledge and Power in Morocco: The Education of a Twentieth Century Notable* (Princeton, N.J.: Princeton University Press, 1985).

15. See note 3. Al-Zayani's published writings include *al-Bustan al-Zarif* (Rabat: Ministry of Culture, 1992) and *Tuhfat al-Hadi al-Mutrib* (Rabat: Ministry of Islamic Affairs, 2008). Most of his writings remain in manuscript form, the most important of them being a history of the 'Alawi dynasty: *al-Rawda al-Sulaymaniya*, MS 1275, National Library, Rabat. Polemical writings include *Tuhfat al-Nubaha*, MS K241, National Library, Rabat.

16. Al-Zayani, *al-Turjumana*, 58.

17. Ibid.

18. Ibid.

19. Ibid., 57.

20. A quick survey of family names as they appear in Muhammad Ibn Ja'far Al Kattani's biographical dictionary of Fez, *Salwat al-Anfas*, 4 vols. (Casablanca: Dar al-Thaqafa, 2004) shows that a considerable number of Fasi families carry names that refer to their rural and Berber origins: Marnissi, Zarwali, Waryaghli, Jazuli, etc.

21. The Hanbali doctrine is one of the four Sunni *madhhabs*, or methods of legal interpretation. It favors reliance on the Prophet's tradition and opposes the use of

reason and speculation in matters of belief, calling for a strict adherence to the literal meaning of the religious texts. S.v. "Ahmad Ibn Hanbal," *The Shorter Encyclopaedia of Islam* (Leiden: E. J. Brill, 1974).

22. El Mansour, *Morocco,* 184ff.

23. al-Zayani, *Sharh al-Hal,* MS 11323, Royal Library, Rabat, 28. This long poem is commented upon by Muhammad Ibn Idris al-Amrawi in his *Nafhat al-Araj,* MS 11323, Royal Library, Rabat.

24. al-Zayani, *Tuhfat al-Nubaha,* MS K241, National Library, Rabat.

25. al-Zayani, *Sharh al-Hal,* 25–26.

26. al-Zayani, *Tuhfat al-Hadi,* 61.

27. This attitude of al-Zayani mirrored that of the makhzan and of Sultan Sulayman in particular; the Sultan accused some *shaykhs* of using their religious prestige to serve their material interests. See the letter of Mawlay Sulayman to al-Tuhami al-Wazzani, undated, in 'Abd Allah al-Wazzani, *al-Rawdh al-Munif,* MS K2304, National Library, Rabat, folio 48.

28. See *al-Turjumana,* 460. Al-Zayani was a disciple of the Nasiri sufi order. In the eighteenth and nineteenth centuries, the Nasiriya became the *makhzan's* favorite order and sultans Sidi Muhamad and Sulayman were among its affiliates.

29. J. Brignon et al., *Histoire du Maroc* (Paris: Hatier, 1967), 265.

30. Al Zayani, *Sharh al-Hal,* 28.

31. Al-Kattani, *Salwat al-Anfas,* 1, 296.

32. Ibid. The veneration of saints is one of the pillars of Moroccan Islam, prevalent among common people as well as the learned elite. The *shaykhs* of the religious brotherhoods, often regarded as saints, enjoyed much respect even from those who did not belong to their orders. Sultans were known to discredit living *shaykhs* when they intervened in political matters, branding them as nothing more than self-interested opportunists having no religious legitimacy. Al-Zayani's daring attack on emblematic religious figures largely reflects the makhzan's attitude. When the makhzan's authority crumbled in 1820, al-Zayani's detractors retaliated against him, accusing him of witchcraft and heresy (*kufr*). See al-Zayani, *Sharh al-Hal,* 28.

33. Al-Zayani, *al-Turjumana,* 59.

34. al-Zayani, *al-Rawda al-Sulaymaniya,* fol. 103.

35. Ahmad al-Ghazzal (d. 1777) was a prominent figure in Sidi Muhammad's makhzan. In 1766 he was dispatched to Madrid to negotiate the liberation of Muslim captives held in Spain. Ahmad al-Wannan (d. 1773) was a distinguished poet and a member of the sultan's entourage. Muhammad Ibn 'Uthman (d. 1799) led several embassies to Spain (1779–1780), Malta, and Naples (1781–1782). He was also sent to Istanbul as ambassador in 1785.

36. Al-Zayani, *al-Turjumana,* 61.

37. Ibid.

38. Ibid., 62.

39. Al-Zayani, *al-Turjumana,* 76.

40. Ibid., 58

41. Ibid., 62–63.

42. Ibid., 62.

43. Pierre Grillon, *La correspondance du consul Louis Chénier, 1767–1782,* 2 vols. (Paris: S.E.V.P.E.N., 1970), 2: 783, 806. In 1779, the French consul general mentions in one of his reports that al-Zayani "seems to be in charge of our affairs at this court" (806).

44. A. Laroui, *The History of the Maghrib* (Princeton, N.J.: Princeton University Press, 1977), 277–278.

45. Al-Zayani, *al-Turjumana*, 140.

46. Ibid., 168.

47. Ibid., 381.

48. On Sultan Sulayman's tribal policy, see El Mansour, *Morocco*, 23.

49. A. Benhadda, *Le Maroc et la sublime porte, XVIe–XVIIIe siècles* (Zaghouan, Tunisia: Fondation A. Temimi, 1998), 168–169.

50. Al-Zayani, *al-Rawda*, fol. 149.

51. Al-Zayani, *al-Turjumana*, 99.

52. Al-Zayani, *al-Rawda*, fol. 149.

53. Ibid., fol. 149.

54. It is interesting to note that in the classical Maghribi view, the Berbers tended to occupy a position outside the Arab/*ʿajam* dichotomy, or an intermediate position between the two groups. As an indication, we might refer to Ibn Khaldun's history; according to its title, it was intended to be a history of "the Arabs, the *ʿajam*, and the Berbers." This interpretation coincides with al-Zayani's self-positioning regarding the Ottoman Turks.

55. On Fasi Muslims of Jewish origin (*bildiyyin*), see M. Garcia-Arenal, "Les Bildiyyin de Fes, un groupe de néo-musulmans d'origine juive," *Studia Islamica* 66 (1987): 113–143.

56. Al-Zayani, *al-Rawda*, fol. 150.

57. Al-Zayani, *al-Turjumana*, 283, 525.

58. On the concept of "salience" and identity "activation," see Jan E. Stets and Peter J. Burke, "Identity Theory and Social Identity Theory," *Social Psychology Quarterly* 63 (Sept. 2000): 230.

Bibliography

Al ʿAmrawi, Muhammad Ibn Idris. *Nafhat al-Araj*. MS 11323, Royal Library, Rabat.

Benhadda, A. *Le Maroc et la sublime porte, XVIe–XVIIIe siècles*. Zaghouan, Tunisia: Fondation A. Temimi, 1998.

Berque, Jacques. *Al Yousi: Problèmes de la culture marocaine au XVIIe siècle*. The Hague and Paris: Mouton, 1958.

———. "Problèmes initiaux de sociologie juridique en Afrique du Nord." *Studia Islamica* 1(1953): 137–162.

Burke, Edmund, III, ed. *Struggle and Survival in the Middle East*. Berkeley: University of California Press, 1993.

Eickelman, Dale F. *Knowledge and Power in Morocco: The Education of a Twentieth Century Notable*. Princeton, N.J.: Princeton University Press, 1985.

El Mansour, Mohamed. *Morocco in the Reign of Mawlay Sulayman*. Wisbech, UK: Menas Press, 1990.

Grillon, Pierre. *Un chargé d'affaires au Maroc: la correspondance du Consul Louis Chénier, 1767–1782*, 2 vols. Paris: S.E.V.P.E.N., 1970.

Hannoum, Abdelmajid. "Translation and the Colonial Imaginary: Ibn Khaldun Orientalist." *History and Theory* 42 (Feb. 2003): 61–81.

Ibn Khaldun. *The Muqaddimah*, trans. F. Rosenthal. Princeton, N.J.: Princeton University Press, 1967.

Al-Illani, Abu Salih. *Mafakhir al-barbar*. Rabat: Dar Abi Raqraq, 2008.

Al-Kattani, Muhammad Ibn Ja'far. *Salwat al-Anfas.* 4 vols. Casablanca: Dar al-Thaqafa, 2004.

Kennedy, Hugh. "From Oral Tradition to Written Record in Arabic Genealogy." *Arabica* 44 (Oct. 1994): 551–544.

Kramer, Martin, ed. *Middle Eastern Lives: The Practice of Biography and Self-Narrative.* Syracuse, N.Y.: Syracuse University Press, 1991.

Laroui, Abdallah. *The History of the Maghrib.* Princeton, N.J.: Princeton University Press, 1977.

Nagel, Joanne. "Constructing Ethnicity: Creating and Recreating Ethnic Identity and Culture." *Social Problems* 41 (Feb. 1994): 152–176.

Shatzmiller, Maya. "Le mythe d'origine berbère." *Revue des mondes musulmans et de la Méditerranée* 35 (1983): 145–156.

al-Wazzani, 'Abd Allah. *Al-Rawdh al-Munif.* MS K2304, National Library, Rabat.

al-Zayani, Abu al-Qasim. *al-Rawda al-Sulaymaniya.* MS D1275, National Library, Rabat.

———. *al-Turjumana al-Kubra.* Rabat: Ministry of Information, 1967.

———. *Sharh al-Hal.* MS 11323, National Library, Rabat.

———. *Tuhfat al-Hadi al-Mutrib.* Rabat: Ministry of Islamic Affairs, 2008.

———. *Tuhfat al-Nubaha fi al-Tafriq bayna al-Fuqaha wa'al-Sufaha.* MS K241, National Library, Rabat.

PART 2

PRACTICES: LOCAL,

NATIONAL, AND

INTERNATIONAL

4

The Local Dimensions of Transnational Berberism: Racial Politics, Land Rights, and Cultural Activism in Southeastern Morocco

Paul A. Silverstein

Since the mid-1960s, Amazigh activists and cultural producers have appropriated colonial and missionary studies of Berber societies and redeployed them to present a coherent representation of an endangered cultural unity. If the vision they have produced often relies on structural nostalgia for a mythical "time before [state national] time,"[1] their efforts, and the internal contestations they elicit, complicate any attempt to anthropologically represent Berber culture as a unified field of discourse or practice. In the wake of such Amazigh auto-ethnography, the line between the study of Berber culture and Berber culturalism has become very fine, if not indelibly blurred.

Several scholars have begun to explore this dialectical relation between colonial, anthropological, and activist representations of Berber culture.[2] This chapter focuses on the shifting dimensions of activist representation of Berber culture on the Moroccan periphery, where "culture" is increasingly reified as a "right" that requires national and international protection. If studies of Berber activism to this point have principally focused on the national and international dimensions of the Berber cultural movement,[3] here I will explore how these larger arenas of struggle both reflect and reciprocally influence local contests over the nature and meaning of locality. Here I examine how Amazigh activists on the periphery of Morocco strive to achieve a monopoly of cultural representation in a given territory of habitation, in multi-racial situations of a relative surplus of culture and scarcity of territory. Paying particular attention to struggles over local development between social groups racialized as reciprocal "others" in southeastern Morocco, I examine how the former *haratin* (now referred to as Iqbliyin) come to mediate Arab-Berber relations, as well as the ideological production of ethnic identity that emerges from these contests.[4]

Reflecting on these localized struggles calls for a counterpoint to the empathetic narrative which uniformly presents Amazigh activists as embattled protagonists in an uphill struggle against states historically prone to marginalize their ethnic others or assimilate them into a national (Arab) identity. In other words, as I will argue, the same global discourse on "rights" can underwrite a politics of resistance on a national scale, while bolstering a politics of domination on the scale of locality. This represents as much a scaling-up of local struggles to the national and international stage as a novel scaling-down of national and international commitments to democracy of political access, in which previously fixed, hierarchical relations of land tenure are now subject to privatization and contestation in the name of cultural rights.

Moroccan Nationalism and Amazigh Activism

Contemporary Amazigh activism in Morocco relies on a historical consciousness of continual struggle against a variety of colonizing and centralizing powers. Activists in southern Berberophone regions still refer to their areas as the *bled as-siba* ("land of dissidence"), a cartographic and ideological category of rule redeployed in the colonial period to reference the mainly Berber tribes who occupied the hinterland and who escaped the full control of the pre-colonial state (*makhzan*). The nationalist movement explicitly sought to divorce itself from these geographic-cum-ethnic divisions and forge a univocal identity for Moroccans.[5] While Mahjoubi Aherdan's Mouvement Populaire (*al-haraka al-sha'biya*) sought to introduce a "multicultural" definition of Moroccan identity (as both Arab *and* Berber), the dominant Istiqlal party, under the direction of Fasi elites, adopted an Arab nationalist position that emphasized Arabic as the official language of the newly independent, but largely Berberophone and Francophone state.[6]

This institutional elaboration of Morocco as an Arab state centered in the northern cities did not go uncontested. The early years after independence witnessed a similar use of state violence to ensure national unity, particularly in the peripheral Berberophone regions. In 1957, the army of Crown Prince Mawlay Hassan was forced to intervene in the southeastern Tafilalet province when the local governor, Addi ou Bihi, who refused to accept the Rabat-based Ministry of the Interior's nomination of provincial qa'ids, jailed local members of the Istiqlal party and took direct control over the towns of Midelt and Rich. In December of the following year, a number of Berber tribes in the northern Rif mountains fought a similar, three-month rebellion against central state rule. The revolt followed the government's arrest of leaders of the rural-based Mouvement Populaire, and the insurgents demanded neutral (non-Istiqlal) local administrators as well as more state investment in terms of employment, hospitals, schools, roads, and other infrastructure in the region. The eventual repression by Mawlay Hassan's forces was brutal. Heavy artillery and aerial bombardments were used against the dissident regions, resulting in severe casualties and the near decimation of the Beni Ouriaghel tribe.[7]

In 1972–1973, in conjunction with the aborted assassination attempt against King Hassan II led by army forces loyal to General Mohammed Oufkir (who was of Berber origin), small groups of dissidents in the Berber-speaking Middle Atlas, High Atlas, and pre-Saharan southeast amassed arms and attempted a revolutionary secession. Likewise severely repressed, hundreds of the participants were jailed, and over twenty were sentenced to death and shot.[8]

In spite of the failure of these particular movements, the history of these threats to the territorial integrity of the state continues to haunt the Moroccan regime. In response, increasingly powerful ministers of the interior have pursued the centralization of political authority, the surveillance of dissent, and the ongoing economic marginalization of Berberophone regions in favor of more loyal areas. They have also engaged in explicit processes of cultural assimilation through the Arabization of the media and the school system. Until the late 1980s, advocates of Berber culture were consistently accused of being colonial apologists and of sectarianism by the national media, and were on occasion arrested for sedition and even forced into exile. Indeed, the very notion of Berber ethnic particularity was decried by nationalist ideologists as a colonial invention.

Such heavy-handed efforts by the Moroccan state have not resulted in Berber quiescence. Already in the 1960s, Berberophone students and intellectuals in Rabat and Paris, under the aegis of the Association marocaine de la recherche et des échanges culturels (AMREC), began collecting and disseminating Berber folklore and oral traditions. In the 1970s, these activities became more politicized with the growth of several Sous-based cultural associations, such as the Université d'Été d'Agadir and Tamaynunt, which actively promoted Berber identity.[9] However, it was the Algerian-Kabyle student uprisings of April 1980 (known internationally as the "Berber Spring") and the subsequent solidification of a transnational Berber Cultural Movement (MCB) which galvanized Moroccan Amazigh ethnolinguistic militancy into a public movement, with conferences and a journal, *Amazigh*, published in the early 1980s in Agadir.

While this movement was largely repressed during the 1980s, it has seen an immense resurgence since the mid-1990s. In 1994, seven teachers, most of whom were members of the Amazigh association Tilelli (Freedom) from the southeastern oasis town of Goulmima, were arrested after their participation in a May Day parade in nearby Errachidia for carrying banners written in the *tifinagh* script. Police held the seven for several weeks, after which the courts sentenced three of them to prison terms and large fines. The three were later released on appeal and the charges subsequently dropped after the case received widespread international publicity and offers of aid. Responding to the public outcry, the Moroccan government promised reforms, with Prime Minister Abdellatif Filali opening channels for Berber-language programming in the national broadcast media. Meanwhile, the late King Hassan II declared in his August 29, 1994, Throne Day speech in Agadir that Amazigh "dialects" were "one of the components of the authenticity of our history" and thus should, in theory, be taught in state schools. Since this speech, Amazigh associations and newspapers (now numbering in double digits) have flourished throughout Morocco. In a variety of charters and international declarations, Amazigh militants have promulgated a redefinition of Morocco on the basis of its pre-colonial and pre-Islamic Berber heritage and have sought political changes that would preserve Berber culture and language as "human rights."

In an explicit attempt to address these demands, King Mohamed VI created the Royal Institute of the Amazigh Culture (IRCAM) through a royal edict (*dahir*) issued on October 17, 2001, in Ajdir. The *dahir* proclaimed Berberness to be "a principal element of national culture, as a cultural heritage present across all stages of Moroccan history and civilization," and presented this cultural inclusion as a necessary step in his project for a "democratic and modernist society." The establishment of IRCAM fit into a larger politics of national development that responded to international pressure to create a transparent regime of social justice and human rights, efforts for which Morocco has been increasingly heralded as a success story by the United States and other allies abroad. To a great extent, this discourse on rights served as an ideological prop for a larger U.S.-sponsored "war on terror" with which Morocco's compliance was demanded and—given the opening of Moroccan prisons for the rendition of U.S. terror suspects—to a great extent received.[10] Moreover, the creation of IRCAM co-opted Amazigh activists into the Moroccan state's larger efforts to present a modernist front in opposition to an expanding Islamist movement. The Institute's thirty-three-member administrative council was explicitly recruited through the Amazigh associational structure, and Amazigh militants with technical training and advanced degrees were likewise incorporated into the Institute's seven research centers.

Oppositional Politics

The establishment of IRCAM has had a profound effect on the Amazigh movement more generally. On the one hand, the Institute succeeded in bringing together Amazigh militants from different associations and ideological factions. On the eve of the Ajdir *dahir*, three distinct and opposed groups could be identified as they operated both nationally and within the transnational Congrès Mondial Amazigh (CMA): the "royalist" Mouvement National Populaire and its allied associations, which drew their major support from the Middle Atlas; the "historical," "moderate," Rabat-based Association marocaine de recherche et d'échange culturel (AMREC), whose membership was drawn from the urban intelligentsia; and the "left-wing" Tamaynunt/Université d'Été d'Agadir, which drew its base primarily from the Sous. These divisions proved unworkable and broke down in the day-to-day compromises and conversations among militants employed in the research centers, as well as during the periodic conferences and seminars which constitute IRCAM's most visible public activity.

On the other hand, the establishment of IRCAM effectively split the Amazigh movement into two macro-factions: those who support the Institute's agenda, and those who oppose it, either on principle or out of resentment for not having been recruited into it. Activists who joined the Institute acknowledge that they lose credibility in the eyes of their peers by joining, but in the end they believed that they had a better chance of facilitating change by working within the system. Today they are often denounced by some of their former comrades as having been *makhzanisés*—of literally having been transformed into de facto representatives of the state. The opponents are outspoken in their belief that the Institute works in the interest of global forces of Arab nationalism, declaiming—generally in private conversations, but periodically in the form of graffiti and signs bandied during public demonstrations—that "IRCAM = IRKAN" ("dirt" in Tashelhit).

Dissenters point to several recent Institute decisions as evidence of IRCAM's covert "divide and rule" strategy with respect to the transnational Amazigh movement. In the first place, they object to the official adoption of the *tifinagh* script as the standard means to write Berber language in

Morocco. The 2003 decision was highly contested within IRCAM, and was decided on by only a handful of votes, according to one of the members of the administrative council. Many Amazigh activists and IRCAM members supported the use of Arabic script both for pragmatic reasons—insofar as it would be more familiar to Moroccans on the rural periphery without formal education in European languages—and on the grounds of continuity with a prior Moroccan history of publication of Berber texts in the Arabic script, particularly by AMREC. Other, mostly younger activists and IRCAM members advocated the use of the Latin script to align IRCAM's policies with those of parallel state institutions and academic departments in Algeria and France, whose efforts at orthographic standardization antedated those of IRCAM. However, according to one member, the deciding committee feared Islamist reprisals if the Latin script were adopted. Thus, although officially couched in a language of cultural authenticity, the adoption of *tifinagh* was in the end a political compromise. Nevertheless, many Amazigh militants continue to view the decision as a thinly veiled ploy to separate Moroccan Berbers from those in Kabylia or in the diaspora who use the Latin script. In like fashion, they understand the production of separate textbooks in the three major Moroccan Berber dialects instead of the standard Tamazight developed by Paris-based linguists as part of a similar effort not only to divide the international Berber community, but to fragment the national one as well.

Fears that IRCAM represents an effort at cooptation designed to re-suture national hegemony in the face of Berber regional and transnational aspirations are widespread among activists unincorporated into IRCAM. While a number of these militants may harbor some resentment because they were not invited to join the Institute, others are forthright in presenting a different vision of Berber unity than that proposed by IRCAM's policies. One such group is the amorphous Amazigh Movement, a shifting set of primarily young male activists based in Rabat but made up of Berberophones from the southern and southeastern regions, most of whom had been members of Tamaynut before it affiliated itself with IRCAM. Since coming into existence with the signing of the Manifeste Berbère in June 2000, the group explicitly dropped the term "Culture" from its self-appellation in order to distinguish its members from an older group of student and intellectual activists whose associational efforts at cultural and artistic promotion had failed to influence the "street," the larger society. As one militant averred to me, "We are now done with the cultural." These men keep in close contact with Berber militants from Kabylia through internet-mediated communication, host them when they visit Morocco, and script their own visions of Berber autonomy through the discourse of the Movement for Autonomy in Kabylia (MAK) and other related groups.

Regional Identity and Development

More than simply an agenda item in urban cultural activism, Berber regional autonomy in Morocco has been an object of recent conflicts that have pitted local activists against state officials and their legal resources across a geographic spread that recapitulates the regionalist struggles of the late 1950s and early 1970s, but at a lower scale of intensity. Since the establishment of IRCAM, a large number of urban and rural Berber cultural associations have recentered their activities around socio-economic development, environmental protection, and community education, treating these areas as equally subject to a universal discourse of human rights. For instance, associations collect money and supplies for disaster relief. In the aftermath of the February 2004 earthquake in and around the Berber-speaking city of Al-Hoceima, Amazigh activists were at the forefront of organizing the relief effort, traveling to the Rif region to bring needed tents and food rations and generally publicizing the social impact of the disaster to the larger national community through the Amazigh press. Amazigh associations have likewise coordinated efforts to bring financial aid to overseas groups in critical states of emergency, such as the Berberophone Tuareg in Mali and Niger who face drought conditions and military oppression.

Moreover, an increasing number of emigrant-based organizations in Rabat, Casablanca, and overseas in Europe have reformulated themselves as cultural associations in order to receive official recognition and funding from the state and to better their efforts at small-scale infrastructural developments in their villages of origin. The Casablanca-based Association Mohammed Kheir-Eddine of Tafraout, for instance, integrates efforts at building schools and paving roads in Tafraout with the sponsorship of cultural activities in the members' home villages, including courses in written Tamazight. Other urban associations, like Tamaynut-Rabat, have forged ties with UNESCO and other European NGOs in order to facilitate their double goal of cultural advocacy and economic development in their home regions. Given the success of such organizations operating at a distance, Berber activists who have remained in their home villages have begun to form their own cultural associations that increasingly double as vectors for infrastructural improvement. They make demands on the government and solicit international agencies for the electrification of their villages, for the paving of roads, or for the provision of running water. Ironically, the success of these groups in gaining overseas support has come to work against them, as the Moroccan state increasingly demands a level of NGO commitment before it will engage in any projects for village-level infrastructural improvement. For instance, the village of Taltefraout in the southeastern Gheris oasis valley had been repeatedly refused the provision of potable running water by the state until the local rural council signed a partnership agreement with a Luxemburg-based NGO, which agreed to front 50 percent of the funding for the project.

However, development projects are not universally desired: in certain cases, they can spur local conflict. In recent years, rural Amazigh activists have been involved in a series of protests against what they perceive to be state efforts to expropriate tribal lands for municipal, national, or even private use. In February–March 2004, the Averroès Foundation for Education and Development based in the pre-Saharan town of Goulmima launched a sustained protest against the provincial governor's attempt to transfer five hectares (12.36 acres) of collective land to a non-local private investor in compensation for the latter's loss of business following the construction of a new bridge across the river bed. Five members of the association were interrogated by the municipal police and threatened with arrest and criminal prosecution before the association was able to call on connections in Rabat to pressure the governor to drop the case. A smaller conflict erupted during the same period in neighboring Tinjdad over the state electrical agency's attempts to appropriate local land for the building of an electrical relay, with similar threats of prosecution narrowly averted. Members of the Association for Integration and Sustainable Development (ASIDD) of the High Atlas region of the Tasemmit massif (near Beni-Mellal) were not so lucky when they attempted to block the state's establishment of a nature preserve for wild sheep that would cut off village inhabitants from their grazing lands and prevent easy access to local market and educational centers. Three women from the area were sentenced to two months in prison for cutting a hole in the reserve's boundary fence to reach a water source, and the president of the association was also put on trial for his role in "inciting racial hatred, tribalism, inciting destruction of public property, [and] threatening the public order."[11]

The Racialization of Land Rights

If state accusations of "racial hatred" and "tribalism" were clearly exaggerated, in the three development struggles just discussed the conflict was between state efforts at national development and local groups' attempts to control resources that they identified in Berber tribal terms. In other words, the struggle is not merely taking place within the framework of ethnicity—between an Arabized state apparatus and a Berberophone "indigenous people" seeking regional autonomy—but also on a racialized terrain of contestation over the definition and control of the "local." Berber activists' claims to autochthony within local settings are premised on a historical imaginary that dates from the time of the Protectorate. While Berberophones clearly preceded the arrival of Arabophones in southeastern Morocco, they were not unified as a group. Instead they belonged to transhumant tribal confederations—most famously the Ait Atta and the Ait Yafelman[12]—who battled each other for pastoral grazing rights and the ability to control local agriculture. This mode of livelihood was made possible in the pre-Saharan regions by the existence of an agrarian class of territorially fixed black sharecroppers, the Berber-speaking *haratin*, who tilled the oasis fields as dependent clients of the Berber tribes in a relationship known as *khumas* or working for one-fifth of the harvest. The *haratin* had no legal rights and could not own or inherit land. The arrival of the French and the "pacification" of the *bled as-siba* (unsubmitted lands) in the 1930s softened the exploitation of the *haratin*, but fixed the tribes and land-holding relations in place, with the French recognizing the Berbers' tribal claims on given lands. In the pre-Saharan region around the present towns of Goulmima and Tinjdad, the Ait Mghrad tribe made official their land rights which had been established only fifty years prior by force of conquest over lands previously held by the Ait Atta.

The independent Moroccan state endorsed the colonial legal structure that recognized tribal land claims, but at the same time it granted the *haratin* citizenship and enabled them to gain ownership over private land. No longer able to benefit from forced *haratin* labor regime, and practicing partible inheritance whereby land is equally divided among the sons of the deceased, members of the Berber tribes of the pre-Saharan periphery, like the Ait Mghrad, had to seek additional means of livelihood, either through the establishment of small businesses or through the upward social mobility enabled by the national educational system. In the 1960s and 1970s, young Ait Mghrad men were very successful on national exams and garnered high positions within the state apparatus and the army as engineers and high-level functionaries. However, this success resulted in the further fragmentation of local notable families, with male emigrants setting up households in Casablanca or Rabat and distancing themselves from local affairs. If Ait Mghrad emigrants have lent their voices to support the movement for Berber cultural and linguistic rights, they have by and large turned their backs on the economic well-being of their native regions, in spite of repeated (and often eloquent) pleas for financial support from local Berber activists.

The migration of Iqbliyin (the term used for *haratin* in the Gheris Valley), on the other hand, remained directly tied to local concerns. Lacking similar access to state employment due to institutional racism and a relative lack of educational opportunities, the Iqbliyin pursued construction and factory work in the northern Moroccan cities and in Europe (France,

Belgium, and the Netherlands). Not only did they remit a large percentage of their income, they also tended to return to their oasis communities, transforming their economic capital into local social capital in the form of land acquisition and the purchase of political influence. In this respect, both private land and political power began to pass from diminishing Berber households to demographically expanding Iqbliyin families, with Iqbliyin demanding and gaining representation on informal tribal councils (Ar. *ajmuˤ*, B. *tiqbilin*) and displacing Berbers as elected heads of municipal boards and assemblies.[13] In Goulmima, the increasing transfer of Ait Mghrad land into Iqbliyin ownership not only brought them representation in the various *tiqbilin* in the sub-communities (*ighramn*) where Ait Mghrad and Iqbliyin co-exist, but also eventually led to a doubling of official communal offices, with "black" Iqbliyin appointed alongside "white" Ait Mghrad as joint heads of the assemblies (*imgharn*) and irrigation overseers (*imgharn n-waman*). Moreover, in 2002, a returned migrant from an Iqbliyin family—who had made a small fortune as a factory worker in the Netherlands and continued to receive generous compensation for an injury received there—was elected vice-president of the municipal council, unseating the patriarch of the largest landowning Ait Mghrad clan who had held the position for years.

This shift in the racialized political economy in what Hsain Ilahiane calls the "retribalization of the village space" of southern and southeastern Morocco has only deepened the divide between Berber and Iqbliyin Moroccan citizens.[14] Iqbliyin are Berber-speakers themselves and full participants in much of the ritual life including, notably, maraboutic popular religious practices and local musical performances that mark festivities such as the celebration of the birth of the Prophet (*ˤid mawlad*) highlighted by the Amazigh cultural movement as markers of Berber culture. Yet they are suspicious of Berber associations and land-claim struggles, seeing these as fronts for a tribalist politics aimed at local resource dominance. Iqbliyin living in semi-urban areas where Amazigh activism is particularly present feel excluded from the social and economic promotion opened by Berber public politics, being under-represented within the membership of IRCAM, the leadership of Amazigh cultural associations, and the ranks of journalists and other engaged Berber intellectuals now living and working in Rabat and abroad. They regard Amazigh activists as primarily interested in personal or familial gain, referring to them as "snakes" (*lahnash*) or "foxes" (*ushshn*).

In the meantime, the Iqbliyin's lack of active engagement in Berber cultural politics has created resentment among many Amazigh activists from the region, who regard them as "self-hating" Berber-speakers, if not a Fifth Column of Arab nationalism and state (*makhzan*) politics. This resentment feeds into a larger racism that draws on an older form of ideological justification for *haratin* disenfranchisement: that blacks are without honor or *aṣl* (tribal ancestry). Some Ait Mghrad further deploy a racist discourse in everyday speech, referring to Iqbliyin as "flies" (*izzn*); they project a dystopian future where the continued out-migration of the Ait Mghrad conjoins with the expanding birth rate of the Iqbliyin to transform the oasis into a black community that would result in the death of Berber culture. Such racism persists among many Berber members of cultural and human rights associations, in spite of their avowal of universalist principles and their claim of "Africanity" as an element of Berber and Moroccan identity, and in spite of their explicit efforts to incorporate Iqbliyin representatives into their various cultural and human rights projects.

Berber resentment of Iqbliyin social and economic mobility is matched by a lack of solidarity between the Amazigh movement and the fight for Sahrawi self-determination in the disputed Western Sahara. To a great extent, the wide participation of southern Berbers in the 1975 Green March in which King Hassan II mobilized 350,000 Moroccan citizens in an *auto-da-fé* occupation of lands left behind by the departing Spanish colonial regime re-legitimized them as loyal citizens in the eyes of the monarchy. The Amazigh Movement's tacit support for Morocco's claims to sovereignty over the Western Sahara remains the condition of possibility for their negotiations with the government for Berber cultural and linguistic rights. Such lack of solidarity with Sahrawi self-determination, combined with persistent racism, marks a Black-Berber racial divide that parallels and occasionally reinforces ongoing Arab-Berber ethnic fragmentation.

These racialized social struggles between Iqbliyin and Berber tribes over local land and political capital can on occasion break out into open conflict. In one extreme case, in November 2003 at the University of Errachadia, a handful of MCA student militants were brutally knifed by members of the Marxist *qaʿidiyin* (Fr. *basiste*) student group for refusing to participate in an exam strike on behalf of the Palestinian *intifada*. The MCA's refusal largely derived from the general philo-Semitism of Amazigh activists and their recognition of parallels between Zionist and Berber struggles for linguistic standardization and self-determination.[15] Amazigh activists were increasingly reluctant to support a Palestinian struggle which they understood as part of an ideological Arab nationalist hegemony. However, the conflict in Errachidia also took on a racialized aspect, as the MCA leadership was largely made up of Ait Mghrad from the Goulmima area (Igoulmimin and Izilf *ighramn*), and many of the qaʿidiyin militants were Iqbliyin from the adjoining area (especially from the Ait Yihya *ighram*). In the eyes of a number of local residents, the Errachidia violence was part of a spillover from the Goulmima struggles.

Other less-brutal, local conflicts feed back into the land-rights claims described earlier. This was certainly the case during the Goulmima-based social movement to block the transfer of five hectares of uncultivated tribal land offered by the Errachidia governor to a non-Ait Mghrad in compensation for having his service station bypassed by the construction of a new bridge across the riverbed (Ar. *wad*, B. *asif*). The station owner planned to expand his operation on the land granted, incorporating a café, restaurant, and hotel into the complex. The project would have created a number of local jobs, and had the potential to attract tourists to a region that was generally avoided by tour operators due to the lack of infrastructure and state investment. Ironically, the project was exactly the kind of economic development which activists had been demanding for years, and indeed, a local Ait Mghrad man had proposed a similar project several years earlier, only to have it rejected by the provincial administration. Moreover, in point of fact, the land in question was part of a larger parcel ceded in 1986 by the Igoulmimn *taqbilt* to the provincial government for use in projects deemed to be in the collective interest.

To a certain extent, one could read the Ait Mghrad activists' rejection of this principle of collective interest as part of a larger generational shift, with the younger generation increasingly understanding territorial integrity as central to a cultural identity in desperate need of protection. Young Ait Mghrad men (as well as those of other allied Berber and Shurafa tribes) regularly walk the land (*tamazirt*) surrounding the Goulmima oasis, visiting the parcels of their families, trekking up the abutting hills or to the local springs to make tea and eat a meal, or visiting neighboring *ighramn* both to maintain relations with extended family members and to engage in playful flirtation (*taqrafayt*) with unmarried female age-mates. Fifty kilometer (thirty mile) round-trip excursions (on foot or by bicycle) are not unusual in this regard, and if women and older men engage in such excursions, their purpose appears to be more closely tied with the maintenance of kin groups through visiting with them, rather than simply visiting the land itself.[16]

Young Ait Mghrad men, in contrast to their female counterparts, explicitly avow their interest in the territory in question, even the non-agricultural portions, whether because of the land's potential for economic projects or for building a future home, or because of its symbolic value as a marker of identity. In March 2004, in the midst of the protest over the five-hectare transfer mentioned earlier, local Amazigh activists made use of the local celebratory masquerade marking Jewish Ashura (*udayn-t ashur*) to voice their demands.[17] Masked activists carried a banner invoking the pasha (mayor) not to cede the "lands of our widows and orphans." They also carried a wooden coffin bearing the name of the *taqbilt* and its various fractions, implying that the tribe would die should it lose its land, and posted a sign on the wall of the *ighram* declaring, "Our identity is our language and our land."

However, the opposition to the land transfer did not solely derive from a renewed cultural ideology which equated land and identity, but also from the racialized political economy of the oasis. While many of the protesters were certainly forthright in their claim of a landed identity, and were willing to risk arrest and incarceration for their principles, other more prominent activists were engaged in a very different game of local interest. As it turns out, the development project was being underwritten by several rising Iqbliyin families, including the new vice-president of the municipal council who had paid some of the costs out of his own pocket. Not only did some activists thus read the development project as opposed to Ait Mghrad material and political interests, but several of the leaders of the protest were allied affinally with the landowning family whose dominance the new president threatened, and thus had a particular stake in seeing the project collapse. In the end, the land sale did occur in spite of the widespread protest (although the development of the parcel remains to date stalled), but only after the governor initiated a police investigation against the protesters for an illegal demonstration, thus shifting the direction of subsequent activist mobilization to countering the investigation (what they decried as "state terrorism") instead of pursuing their opposition to the initial transfer.

The land-rights case points to the ways in which racialized local rivalries are increasingly playing out in the realm of social movements that have a national and even international reach. Goulmima may be a relatively extreme case of Amazigh activism even for Morocco, but it is noteworthy in its doubling of associational structures, recalling a dual classification system long observed for Berber societies and politics: two Amazigh cultural associations, two human rights organizations, and two local development agencies.[18] These doubled associations managed to garner a large membership, despite the small population (12,000) of the town and surrounding region. Moreover, the significance of these associations and their activist members within the national and international Berber cultural rights movement is palpable to Moroccan and outside observers, thus gaining Goulmima a wide reputation of being a place of "serious" and even "hard" politics. In addition to the 1994 arrest of Tilelli militants—which remains a symbolically charged moment of recognition for the contemporary national movement—Goulmima-area activists dominated the Moroccan contingent sent to the CMA and continue to be disproportionately prominent in the Rabat-based Amazigh Movement.

While this prominence might appear from the outside to attest to the strength of the Ait Mghrad's organizational skills, from the inside the picture looks very different, with internal fragmentation being the norm rather than the exception. Communiqués issued by the various Goulmima associations regularly accuse the state of "sowing internal disaffection" (Fr. *semer la zizanie*). Yet it is clear that the state is primarily only encouraging preexisting lines of fracture between racialized groups, tribes, tribal fractions, and competing landowning families. Goulmima activists admit as much, expressing amazement at outsiders' representations of regional unity, and recalling past moments when brothers (if not militants from rival households) have taken opposed positions in voting situations, or have even worked to exclude each other from leadership positions.

Indeed, the successive growth of rival cultural, human rights, and development associations is evidence of the scaling up of local rivalries to national and transnational levels and of the adoption of a global language of "rights" and "development" as a secondary means to compete for local dominance. Such local material and political interests are recognized and familiar to residents, and for this reason association leaders are regarded with ambivalence by the larger community. Activists, when they speak or act explicitly on behalf of larger community interests, are always regarded with suspicion and accused of not being "serious" and of "playing politics" for personal gain. And yet, as the land-rights case shows, the activists can become important mediators, able to mobilize support through associational networks and publicize their demands through communiqués sent to the local and national press. Activists are suspected of working solely for individual gain, but they are also objects of ambivalent desire. As one of the younger protesters related to me, "Our only interest in including [a prominent local human rights leader] was for his connections, for his organization's [literal] stamp of approval (*tampon*)."[19]

Conclusion

A focus on the interface between Amazigh activism and regional contests over land and politics adds a local dimension to analyses that up to now have principally explored the national and transnational dimensions of Berber cultural politics. When viewed from these different scales, the politicization of Berber culture as a patrimonial "right" to be protected and developed takes on a set of ethical dimensions which can exist in mutual tension. If a discourse of human rights serves as a marker of regime transparency and an ideological prop for a global "war on terror" at an international scale, it can simultaneously translate into a tactical art of resistance at a national level, as well as a local practice of territorial domination. The same activists speak on behalf of Fourth World peoples to a global audience, militate for regional autonomy to a *makhzan* historically committed to Arab nationalism, and play a racialized game of personal and familial politics in their home areas.

This points to the continued need for social scientists to play close attention to the local dimensions of the so-called "new social movements." All too often, cultural observers reproduce the neophilic, mass media celebration of the technologies of globalization in their burgeoning focus on the transnational dimensions of local struggles, and on the ways in which local cultural activists scale up their demands and become actors in the larger Fourth World movement. While such processes certainly reflect an important new reality, they only represent a partial truth. As often, the potentially disruptive effects of global discourses and technologies on local social life requires their domestication, their scaling-down. In the case of southeastern Morocco, the differential trajectories of Ait Mghrad and Iqbliyin transnational migration have transformed social, political, and landholding relations in oasis communities, disrupting Ait Mghrad hegemony. Using an idiom of cultural and territorial "rights," Ait Mghrad respond to this challenge transnationally by invoking the support of international NGOs and the overseas Berber diaspora for their Amazigh identity putatively threatened by Arabs and "Blacks." While some might view this Amazigh-Iqbliyin opposition as a recrudescence of "traditional" forms of social segmentation, in many ways the conflict is fundamentally new. From a former, vertical structure of social stratification in which *haratin* were dependent clients of Berber tribes, we are now witnessing a horizontal set of relations in which Ait Mghrad and Iqbliyin approach each other through a global idiom of race: as "Whites" and "Blacks." This process of racialization is simultaneously local and transnational, and thus defies any attempt to treat these two dimensions of social engagement as distinct.

Notes

The research and writing of this chapter were made possible through generous financial support from the United States Institute of Peace, the Fulbright-Hays Faculty Research Abroad Program, the Michael E. and Carol S. Levine Foundation, and the Carnegie Corporation of New York. Earlier versions of this essay were presented at the Harvard University Center for Middle Eastern Studies and the Hagop Kevorkian Center for Near Eastern Studies at New York University. I thank Katherine E. Hoffman, Deborah Kapchan, Susan Gilson Miller, Sofian Merabet, Kristin Pfeifer, Susan Slyomovics, and George Trumbull IV for their generous comments and suggestions. This essay draws on my article, "States of Fragmentation in North Africa," originally published in *Middle East Report* 237: 26–33 (2005).

1. Michael Herzfeld, *Cultural Intimacy* (London: Routledge, 1997), 109. See Jane E. Goodman, *Berber Culture on the World Stage* (Bloomington: Indiana University

Press, 2005), 69–93; Katherine E. Hoffman, "Moving and Dwelling: Building the Moroccan Ashlehi Homeland," *American Ethnologist* 29(4) (2002): 940–941; and Paul Silverstein, "On Rooting and Uprooting: Kabyle Habitus, Domesticity, and Structural Nostalgia," *Ethnography* 5(4) (2004): 553–555.

2. David Crawford, "Morocco's Invisible Imazighen," *Journal of North African Studies* 7(1) (2002): 53–70; Jane Goodman, "Writing Empire, Underwriting Nation: Discursive Histories of Kabyle Berber Oral Texts," *American Ethnologist* 29(1) (2002): 86–122; and Goodman, "The Proverbial Bourdieu: Habitus and the Politics of Representation in the Ethnography of Kabylia," *American Anthropologist* 105(4) (2003): 782–793.

3. Hassan Aourid, "Le substrat culturel des mouvements de contestation au Maroc: Analyse des discours islamiste et amazighe" (Thèse de Doctorat d'État, Université Mohamed V, Agdal-Rabat, 1999); Salem Chaker, *Imazighen ass-a* (Algiers: Éditions Bouchène, 1990); Bruce Maddy-Weitzman, "Ethno-politics and Globalisation in North Africa: The Berber Culture Movement," *Journal of North African Studies* 11(1) (2006): 71–83; Paul Silverstein, "Martyrs and Patriots: Ethnic, National, and Transnational Dimensions of Kabyle Politics," *Journal of North African Studies* 8(1) (2003): 87–111; and Tassadit Yacine, "La revendication berbère," *Intersignes* 10 (1995): 95–106.

4. The *haratin* (sing. *hartani*) are likely the descendents of the migration of Bafour from Mauritania. See Bouazza Benachir, *Esclavage, diaspora africaine et communautés noires du Maroc* (Paris: Harmattan, 2005); Mohammed Ennaji, *Soldats, domestiques et concubines: L'esclavage au Maroc au XIXe siècle* (Casablanca: Eddif, 1994); Remco Ensel, *Saints and Servants in Southern Morocco* (Leiden: E. J. Brill, 1999); and Hsain Ilahiane, *Ethnicities, Community Making, and Agrarian Change: The Political Ecology of a Moroccan Oasis* (Lanham, Md.: University Press of America, 2004). "Racialization" refers to the processes through which any diacritic of social personhood—including class, ethnicity, generation, kinship/affinity, positions within fields of power, etc.—comes to be essentialized, naturalized, and/or biologized. Racialization thus indicates the historical transformation of fluid categories of difference into fixed species of otherness, often (though not always) indexed by skin color. See Robert Miles, *Racism* (London: Routledge, 1989); and Michael Omi and Howard Winant, *Racial Formation in the United States: From the 1960s to the 1990s* (New York: Routledge, 1994).

5. French military scholars throughout colonial North Africa underlined the Arab-Berber divide as constitutive of the region's identity. Nationalist ideologues opposed this reified divide through a postulation of Arab-Berber unity through Islam. For the Algerian case, see Goodman, "Writing Empire"; Patricia Lorcin, *Imperial Identities: Stereotyping, Prejudice and Race in Colonial Algeria* (London: I.B. Tauris, 1995); James McDougall, "Myth and Counter-Myth: 'The Berber' as National Signifier in Algerian Historiographies," *Radical History Review* 86 (2003): 66–88; and Paul Silverstein, "The Kabyle Myth: The Production of Ethnicity in Colonial Algeria," in *From the Margins: Historical Anthropology and Its Futures*, ed. Brian Keith Axel (Durham, N.C.: Duke University Press, 2002), 122–155.

6. Gilbert Grandguillaume, *Arabisation et politique linguistique au Maghreb* (Paris: Maisonneuve et Larose, 1983), 69–94.

7. Susan Slyomovics, "Self-Determination as Self-Definition: The Case of Morocco," in *Negotiating Self-Determination*, ed. Hurst Hannum and Eileen Babbitt (Lanham, Md.: Lexington Books, 2005), 145; John Waterbury, *The Commander of the Faithful* (New York: Columbia University Press, 1970), 239–243.

8. See the compelling account of the revolt by the son of one of its leaders, Mohamed (Mahmoud) Bennouna, *Héros sans gloire: Échec d'une révolution, 1963–1973* (Casablanca: Tarik Editions, 2002).

9. For histories of Amazigh activism in Morocco, see Chaker, *Imazighen ass-a*; Crawford, "Morocco's Invisible Imazighen"; and Maddy-Weitzman, "Ethno-politics and Globalisation."

10. On the larger question of human rights in Morocco and its relationship to a national and international politics against "Islamic terrorism," see Susan Slyomovics, *The Performance of Human Rights in Morocco* (Philadelphia: University of Pennsylvania Press, 2005).

11. Amale Samie, "Communiqué—28 avril 2005: acharnement judiciare contre l'association et son président," Association pour l'Intégration et le Developpement Durable, http://www.asidd.com/reserve/com28avr.htm.

12. See David Hart, *Dadda 'Atta and His Forty Grandsons: The Socio-Political Organisation of the Ait 'Atta of Southern Morocco* (Boulder, Colo.: Westview Press, 1981).

13. Ilahiane, *Ethnicities, Community Making, and Agrarian Change*, 172–196.

14. Ibid., 195.

15. Paul A. Silverstein, "Islam, Laïcité, and Amazigh Activism in France and North Africa," in *North African Mosaic: A Cultural Reappraisal of Ethnic and Religious Minorities*, ed. Nabil Boudraa and Joseph Krause (Newcastle: Cambridge Scholars Press, 1997), 104–118.

16. See Hoffman, *We Share Walls: Language, Land, and Gender in Berber Morocco* (Malden, Mass.: Wiley-Blackwell, 2008) for an ethnographically nuanced discussion of men and women's construction of territorial homelands through labor, domesticity, and travel.

17. For an analysis of Udayen-t Achour in terms of Amazigh philo-Semitism, see Silverstein, "Islam, Laïcité, and Amazigh Activism in France and North Africa." For a general discussion of Moroccan Berber masquerades, see Abdellah Hammoudi, *The Victim and Its Masks* (Chicago: University of Chicago Press, 1993).

18. Social anthropologists since the colonial period have underlined the tendency of Berber groups to fission into rival parties, sometimes as semi-permanent moieties, sometimes as shifting political alliances. In extreme cases, the resultant factions can come to represent, in the structuralist logic of dual classification systems, two opposed moral universes, often designated with left-hand/right-hand terminology, into which the entire social and natural world is classified. The classical structuralist argument is presented by Claude Lévi-Strauss, "Do Dual Organizations Exist?" in *Structural Anthropology*, vol. 1 (New York: Basic Books, 1963), 132–166. For the Kabyle case, see Pierre Bourdieu, "The Sentiment of Honour in Kabyle Society," in *Honour and Shame*, ed. James Peristiany (London: Weidenfeld and Nicholson, 1965), 191–241; Pierre Bourdieu, "The Kabyle House or the World Inversed," in *Algeria 1960*, trans. Richard Nice (Cambridge: Cambridge University Press, 1979); Mohand Khellil, *La Kabylie ou l'ancêtre sacrifié* (Paris: Harmattan, 1984), 33–34; and Silverstein, "Martyrs and Patriots." For the Moroccan case, see Ernest Gellner, *Saints of the Atlas* (London: Weidenfeld and Nicolson, 1969), 64–68; David M. Hart, "Berber Tribal Alliance Networks in Pre-Colonial North Africa: The Algerian *Saff*, the Moroccan *Liff* and the Chessboard Model of Robert Montagne," *Journal of North African Studies* 1(2): 192–205; and Robert Montagne, *The Berbers: Their Social and Political Organisation* (London: Frank Cass, 1973 [1931]), 27–44 and *Les berbères et le makhzen dans le sud du Maroc: essai sur la transformation politique des Berbères sedentaires (groupe*

chleuh) (Paris: Félix Alcan, 1930), 182–216. For right-hand/left-hand dualism in Morocco, see David Hart, "Right and Left in the Atlas Mountains: Dual Classifications among the Moroccan Berbers," *Journal of North African Studies* 4(3) (1999): 30–44.

19. The focus on the administrative *tampon* as an object of local value and desire was not arbitrary. Given the bureaucratic nature of the Moroccan state, official paperwork and seals have come to mediate all public recognition of personhood and property. See Katherine Hoffman, "Administering Identities: State Decentralisation and Local Identification in Morocco," *Journal of North African Studies* 5(3) (2000): 85–100. If the state monopolizes the regime of officialization for all activities in the political and economic spheres (including commercial transactions, birth registration, rights of dwelling, and voting privileges), cultural, human rights, and development associations have established themselves as parallel forums through which individual and social struggles are rendered public. These associations arm themselves with paperwork and seals that mimic those of the state, deploying them in a fashion that contests state decisions and decries state injustice via communiqués sent to the local, national, and international (electronic) press. Those who carry the *tampon* thus possess powerful symbolic capital, as they are empowered to act on behalf of the institution in a way that precisely parallels the power of *muqaddims* and pashas to act as the local state.

Bibliography

Aourid, Hassan. "Le substrat culturel des mouvements de contestation au Maroc. Analyse des discours islamiste et amazighe." Thèse de Doctorat d'État, Université Mohamed V, Agdal-Rabat, 1999.

Benachir, Bouazza. *Esclavage, diaspora africaine et communautés noires du Maroc.* Paris: Harmattan, 2005.

Bennouna, Mehdi. *Héros sans gloire: Échec d'une révolution, 1963–1973.* Casablanca: Tarik Editions, 2002.

Bourdieu, Pierre. "The Kabyle House or the World Inversed." In *Algeria 1960,* trans. Richard Nice, 133–153. Cambridge: Cambridge University Press, 1979.

———. "The Sentiment of Honour in Kabyle Society. In *Honour and Shame,* ed. James Peristiany. London: Weidenfeld and Nicholson, 1965, 191–241.

Chaker, Salem. *Imazighen ass-a* [Berbers Today]. Algiers: Éditions Bouchène, 1990.

Crawford, David. "Morocco's Invisible Imazighen." *Journal of North African Studies* 7(1) (2002): 53–70.

Ennaji, Mohammed. *Soldats, domestiques et concubines: l'esclavage au Maroc au XIXe siècle.* Casablanca: Eddif, 1994.

Ensel, Remco. *Saints and Servants in Southern Morocco.* Leiden: Brill, 1999.

Gellner, Ernest. *Saints of the Atlas.* London: Weidenfeld and Nicolson, 1969.

Goodman, Jane E. *Berber Culture on the World Stage.* Bloomington: Indiana University Press, 2005.

———. "The Proverbial Bourdieu: Habitus and the Politics of Representation in the Ethnography of Kabylia." *American Anthropologist* 105(4) (2003): 782–793.

———. "Writing Empire, Underwriting Nation: Discursive Histories of Kabyle Berber Oral Texts." *American Ethnologist* 29(1) (2002): 86–122.

Grandguillaume, Gilbert. *Arabisation et politique linguistique au Maghreb.* Paris: Maisonneuve et Larose, 1983.

Hammoudi, Abdellah. *The Victim and Its Masks*. Chicago: University of Chicago Press, 1993.

Hart, David M. "Berber Tribal Alliance Networks in Pre-Colonial North Africa: The Algerian *Saff*, the Moroccan *Liff* and the Chessboard Model of Robert Montagne." *Journal of North African Studies* 1(2) (1996): 192–205.

———. *Dadda 'Atta and His Forty Grandsons: The Socio-Political Organisation of the Ait 'Atta of Southern Morocco*. Boulder, Colo.: Westview Press, 1981.

———. "Right and Left in the Atlas Mountains: Dual Classifications among the Moroccan Berbers." *Journal of North African Studies* 4(3) (1999): 30–44.

Herzfeld, Michael. *Cultural Intimacy*. London: Routledge, 1997.

Hoffman, Katherine E. "Administering Identities: State Decentralisation and Local Identification in Morocco." *Journal of North African Studies* 5(3) (2000): 85–100.

———. "Moving and Dwelling: Building the Moroccan Ashlehi Homeland." *American Ethnologist* 29(4) (2002): 928–962.

———. *We Share Walls: Language, Land, and Gender in Berber Morocco*. Malden, Mass.: Wiley-Blackwell, 2008.

Ilahiane, Hsain. *Ethnicities, Community Making, and Agrarian Change: The Political Ecology of a Moroccan Oasis*. Lanham, Md.: University Press of America, 2004.

Khellil, Mohand. *La Kabylie ou l'ancêtre sacrifié*. Paris: Harmattan, 1984.

Lévi-Strauss, Claude. "Do Dual Organizations Exist?" In *Structural Anthropology*, vol. 1. New York: Basic Books, 1963, 132–166.

Lorcin, Patricia M. E. *Imperial Identities: Stereotyping, Prejudice and Race in Colonial Algeria*. London: I. B. Tauris, 1995.

Maddy-Weitzman, Bruce. "Ethno-politics and Globalisation in North Africa: The Berber Culture Movement." *Journal of North African Studies* 11(1) (2006): 71–83.

McDougall, James. "Myth and Counter-Myth: 'The Berber' as National Signifier in Algerian Historiographies." *Radical History Review* 86 (2003): 66–88.

Miles, Robert. *Racism*. London: Routledge, 1989.

Montagne, Robert. *Les berbères et le makhzen dans le sud du Maroc: essai sur la transformation politique des Berbères sedentaires (groupe Chleuh)*. Paris: Félix Alcan, 1930.

———. *The Berbers: Their Social and Political Organisation*. London: Frank Cass, 1973 [1931].

Omi, Michael, and Howard Winant. *Racial Formation in the United States: From the 1960s to the 1990s*. New York: Routledge, 1994.

Silverstein, Paul A. "Islam, Laïcité, and Amazigh Activism in France and North Africa." In *North African Mosaic: A Cultural Reappraisal of Ethnic and Religious Minorities*, ed. Nabil Boudraa and Joseph Krause. Cambridge: Cambridge Scholars Press, 2007, 104–118.

———. "Martyrs and Patriots: Ethnic, National, and Transnational Dimensions of Kabyle Politics." *Journal of North African Studies* 8(1) (2003): 87–111.

———. "On Rooting and Uprooting: Kabyle *Habitus*, Domesticity, and Structural Nostalgia." *Ethnography* 5(4) (2004): 553–578.

———. "The Kabyle Myth: The Production of Ethnicity in Colonial Algeria." In *From the Margins: Historical Anthropology and Its Futures*, ed. Brian Keith Axel. Durham, N.C.: Duke University Press, 2002, 122–155.

Slyomovics, Susan. "Self-Determination as Self-Definition: The Case of Morocco." In *Negotiating Self-Determination*, ed. Hurst Hannum and Eileen Babbitt. Lanham, Md.: Lexington Books, 2005.

———. *The Performance of Human Rights in Morocco*. Philadelphia: University of Pennsylvania Press, 2005.

Waterbury, John. *The Commander of the Faithful*. New York: Columbia University Press, 1970.

Yacine, Tassadit. "La revendication berbère." *Intersignes* 10 (1995): 95–106.

5

Imazighen on Trial: Human Rights and Berber Identity in Algeria, 1985

Jane E. Goodman

That's the way Justice goes in our country. It's the
privileged site of expression for all the excesses that
erode our society.

—Statement of defendant Said Sadi before the Court of Security of State, December 1985

In mid-December 1985, the Court of State Security (*Cour de surêté de l'état*) in the city of Medéa became a stage for a performance the likes of which had rarely been seen in Algeria. During four long days of testimony, twenty-three political prisoners emerged from the dark cells where they had been held for months and took their places on the stand. Primarily Kabyle Berbers, they had been jailed for creating associations without state authorization—most notably the Algerian League of Human Rights. One after another the defendants spoke, sometimes for as long as two hours at a time, with little interruption from court officials. Their statements formed a lucid, penetrating, and trenchant critique of the Algerian regime while simultaneously reconstituting Berber identity as a global human rights issue.[1] Consider the words of Said Sadi, uttered before the Court on December 17:[2] "When high school students are expelled and even tortured—yes, you heard me, tortured—for writing their names in Berber; when employees—some of whom are here in the witness box—lose their jobs for trying to protect their language and culture; when daily encounters with the state administrative bureaucracy turn into altercations with state security forces for even the most basic of procedures, it should come as no surprise that we wish to defend human rights. Rather, it's a miracle that until now we have responded to this repressive madness by peaceful means."[3] Were Sadi not already behind bars, such remarks surely would have landed him there. Yet during the trial, what could be uttered in no other public forum was given a hearing before not only court officials but also representatives from the international press, human rights agencies, and the Algerian public. Within a year, two accounts of the trial were circulating internationally: the Berber press *Imedyazen* in Paris published the defendants' testimonies as well as a 316-page collection of press reports and related documents.

I shall argue that the Medéa trial introduced the Berber identity project into a new international arena by reconfiguring Berber issues through the lens of "human rights" discourse. This was a compelling achievement given that the trial itself was not ostensibly concerned with Berber matters. None of the charges were specifically Berber-related but were articulated in terms of an attack on the authority of state, distribution of tracts, unarmed gathering, and the constitution of illegal associations. Moreover, at the time, human rights discourse itself was only marginally concerned with ethnolinguistic rights. Sub-national minorities had limited formal access to the international human rights system: many international human rights organizations, beginning with the United Nations, were structured through state membership, and international charters and covenants were ratified by state signatories.[4] Of the various international charters and covenants in force through the 1970s,[5] most had been articulated in universalizing terms that "resulted in the *relative neglect of the protection of minorities.*"[6] The Universal Declaration of Human Rights, for instance, makes only one brief reference to language, which is not constituted as a right per se.[7] A stronger statement appears in Article 27 of the International Covenant on Civil and Political Rights, which states that "ethnic, religious, or linguistic minorities . . . shall not be denied the right . . . to enjoy their own culture . . . or to use their own language."[8]

Even this document, however, issues no call for the active maintenance of minority languages and cultures, let alone their promotion. Likewise, the African Charter on Human and Peoples' Rights,[9] formulated in 1981 but signed by Algeria only in October of 1986 (tellingly, ten months after this trial), makes no mention of minority languages, containing only generalized references to "preserve and strengthen positive African cultural values."[10] Organizations such as Amnesty International likewise provided little overt support for ethno-linguistic rights; Amnesty's mission statement is based directly on "the human rights enshrined in the Universal Declaration of Human Rights and other international human rights standards."[11] Until recently, indigenous rights fared only a little better. In 1982, the United Nations Economic and Social Council established an advisory body called the Working Group on Indigenous Populations, attended by Berbers for the last several years.[12] In 1993, this group completed a draft declaration of the rights of indigenous peoples that has not been passed as of this writing, despite the fact that indigenous peoples have been the beneficiaries of two United Nations "decades": the inaugural International Decade of the World's Indigenous People (1995–2004) was subsequently extended another ten years (2005–2015).[13]

Given the lack of explicit focus on minority rights in both the formal court charges and the human rights documents at that time, how did Berbers manage to transform the 1985 trial into a forum in which ethno-linguistic identity was articulated with human rights discourse? I contend that this was accomplished primarily through the narrative performances of the defendants in the courtroom. In foregrounding narrative performance as an arena where new forms of collective identity can be brought into being, I am inspired by a growing body of scholarship that emphasizes narrative's constitutive and potentially transformative potential.[14] From this perspective, narrative not only represents an existing social reality but can help to configure a new social imagination. As Susan Slyomovics has noted with regard to the narrative performance of human rights discourse in Morocco, "The beginning of a culture of rights is the ability to produce a narrative that moves toward the freedom to practice one's language and culture, [in] which *narrative is itself a practice of that freedom.*"[15] That narrative can accomplish this work is due to its location in a flexible system of verbal genres that speakers can marshal to situate their particular, individualized experiences in relation to wider social discourses[16]—a strategy used to good effect by the Medéa defendants. As I will elaborate, some of the defendants formulated their accounts by drawing on the narrative conventions of genres such as epic folktales or proverbs, which made them instantly recognizable in the Algerian context as speech forms containing a wider moral message.

In crafting courtroom narratives, the defendants also worked explicitly to "potentiate their detachability" so that the accounts could be readily circulated beyond the courtroom.[17] Indeed, the fact that the court testimony is available at all is due to narrative's amenability to being detached from one context and inserted into another. One of the former defendants, Said Doumane, explained to me how the testimonies came to be published when I spoke with him in Paris in 2007. The prisoners agreed before the trial, he told me, to try to get their statements smuggled out of the courtroom to their friends and supporters in Paris, who had in turn agreed to typeset and publish them. To that end, most prisoners drafted statements in prison that they then read in court before trying to hand them over surreptitiously to relatives during prison visits.

According to Doumane, prisoners were supplied with pen and paper in the courtroom, where they were able to take notes on the proceedings, write down questions they were asked, or jot down responses and reactions of court officials. From these notes, the "live" quality of the trial was recreated in the published account. The prisoners' lawyers also took copious notes, which became key documents from which the book was crafted. Not all of the prisoners' statements made it out: Doumane's, for instance, was confiscated by prison authorities, but he later recreated it for publication. Moreover, some prisoners had only minimal schooling and did not draft written statements, providing only oral testimony in the courtroom; those statements do not appear in the book. The published narratives thus do not constitute an official, exact, or complete transcription of what was said during the trial. What they do offer is a record of the kind of discourse the prisoners thought would both resonate in the courtroom and resound beyond courtroom walls.

By transforming the trial into an occasion for political critique, the defendants were engaged in what the renowned French defense lawyer Jacques Vergès has called a "trial of rupture."[18] Unlike in a "trial of complicity [connivence]," where a defendant works within an established legal framework to refute the charges and prove her innocence, in a "trial of rupture" the defendant seeks to demonstrate the injustice of the system that arrested her in the first place. As Vergès put it, the accused becomes a militant, positioning himself in relation to revolutionaries around the world.[19] As in many trials of rupture, the outcome of the Medéa case was virtually a foregone conclusion: both the defendants and their accusers knew that there was little chance of acquittal. All but one would be found guilty of at least some of the charges against them, and would be returned to their cells for another six months to three years. Under these circumstances, the momentary release afforded to defendants during the trial may have seemed to state authorities a small concession. Yet there is a certain paradox in allowing the court to become a forum for the performance of the very discourse that is tolerated in no other public venue. I begin with this paradox.

From one perspective, it could be argued that the state permitted the defendants to speak only to make an example of them by condemning them, thus revealing the limits of the sayable. What this interpretation forecloses, however, is the possibility that the performance of the defendants may exceed the verdict itself, opening new possibilities for political alignment that a "guilty" verdict—no matter how severe the subsequent sentence—failed to entirely close down.

The Algerian Justice System

The twenty-three defendants were not the only political prisoners jailed in Algeria at the time. Just six weeks before this trial started, my friend Muhend (a pseudonym) was arrested at a demonstration in support of these very prisoners. Muhend was unlucky enough to be caught with three pieces of paper folded carefully into his pockets: a flyer about the prisoners' situation; an article on Berber political singer Lounis Ait Menguellet, who had been arrested for voicing his solidarity with the prisoners during one of his concerts; and a short article about the prisoners from the French weekly Le Nouvel Observateur. Following four days of torture ranging from electric shock to battery acid that burned a hole through his jeans, Muhend was handcuffed to a wall outside a door labeled "Juge d'Instruction" (Examining Judge or Magistrate). "There, now you've been before the Judge," he was told. Asking for a lawyer landed him another blow; he then signed a fourteen-page confession. His subsequent sentencing hearing took place at midnight in a courtroom full of armed police but devoid of lawyers. While the defendants for whom he had demonstrated spoke for hours on end in the Medéa courtroom, Muhend languished in a "glacially cold" cell, counting the thirty-seven steps he was allowed to take once a week to go up to the visitors' room.

Yet if what transpired in Medéa was not exactly business as usual in Algeria, neither was it unprecedented. Whereas Muhend was judged in an ordinary criminal court, the Court of State Security in Medéa was the latest in a series of "special" or "exceptional" courts established with the explicit aim of protecting the Algerian patrimoine. In the context of Algeria's one-party populist state, "protection" was construed in both military and ideological terms. Because the interests of the Algerian Revolution were taken as first principles, any critique was understood as a threat to the unity of the nation.[20] Justice, moreover, was formulated in the Algerian Constitution as a "function" rather than as a "power" in its own right. Judges were "to work for the defense and the protection of the socialist revolution."[21] Should they fail to act according to the ideological interests of the single-party state, judges could be relieved of their functions.[22] There was no provision, in other words, for judicial irremovability.

The precedent for both the revolutionary courts and the "trials of rupture" that took place within them had been established nearly a century earlier under French colonial rule. One of the earliest such trials was the Dreyfus Affair (1894, 1898), in which Dreyfus's lawyer Zola turned the courtroom into a forum for "political-judicial warfare"[23] by revealing that Dreyfus had been framed by high-ranking anti-Semitic French officers.[24] Although Zola lost his case, he succeeded in "awakening public opinion"[25] to the anti-Semitism that traversed the highest levels of the French government and military. That this case ultimately effected at least a limited transformation of political consciousness is evidenced in the fact that within less than a decade, Dreyfus received a presidential pardon and was named to the Legion of Honor. Closer to hand, the trials of FLN (Front de libération nationale) militants during the Algerian Revolution became an occasion for the defendants to argue their case "in the name of another legality."[26] Appealing to the international community, these defendants framed their actions in relation to "a collective struggle of all the accused" and used the court to call for "an independent Algerian nationality."[27] The FLN trials were also noteworthy because for the first time, a "collective defense" was put in place.[28] The FLN was able to organize in the prison system itself, coordinating hunger strikes by prisoners in France and Algeria, organizing committees within each prison, and orchestrating a common defense that sought to transcend the activities of particular defendants to foreground the struggle that all were engaged in. As in 1985, the press played a pivotal role: with the trial front-page news for months on end, the United Nations, international organizations, and even the Pope sought to intervene.[29] Ultimately, it was the colonial system itself that was on trial.

Following France's example, the FLN did not wait long to establish its own "special courts" in independent Algeria. In 1964, the country's first President, Ahmed Ben Bella, set up the Criminal Revolutionary Courts (*cours criminelles révolutionnaires*).[30] In the two decades and three presidential regimes that ensued between 1964 and 1985, these "special courts" were periodically renamed and reorganized but remained the ultimate watchdogs for the interests of the state, serving as the sites where perceived "enemies of the people" were supposedly brought to justice.[31] Hocine Ait Ahmed, a revolutionary war hero who came out on the losing side of a bitter power struggle after the war, was tried in one such court in April of 1964 for his role in leading an armed movement opposed to the Ben Bella regime. Along with five other defendants, he was the first "to plead as a political adversary of the government," using the trial to hold the Ben Bella government accountable for its failure to enact the ideals of the Revolution.[32] Ait Ahmed's trial, however, was closed to the public, the international press, and foreign lawyers.[33] When Houari Boumedienne took power in 1965 following a coup d'état, some fifty Ben Bella supporters were arrested, held in the maximum security prison at El Harrach, and tried for attacking the security of state. Before 1985, this may have been the only trial in Algerian history for which defendants' statements were subsequently published, albeit by French intellectuals who supported Ben Bella.[34] In contrast to the Medéa testimonies, the El Harrach accounts are focused almost exclusively on the irregular arrest procedures, torture, and privation to which the prisoners were subjected. Although this trial did attract international attention, these narratives are entirely devoid of political critique of the new regime.

In 1968, Boumedienne reformed the courts, dropping the "criminal" designation and creating a "revolutionary court" made up of a president, eight assessors (all military officers), and two magistrates. This court became the site where any perceived political opposition, no matter how minor, could be tried as an attack on the security of state.[35] Defendants' rights were severely restricted: their lawyers had to be pre-approved by the court president; their property could be confiscated even before they were found guilty; and the court's decisions were not subject to appeal. While in principle open to the public, trials held in the revolutionary courts could be arbitrarily closed to observers without warning. More frequently, the Boumedienne government chose to forego these trials altogether: people simply "disappeared" and were held without trial, to be quietly released months or even years later.[36] These protocols were largely carried forward when Chadli Bendjedid took power in 1978. It was under his regime that the Court of State Security of Medéa was created.

In the 1985 trial in Medéa, however, Chadli broke with precedent: It was the first trial under the Bendjedid regime—and the first in Algeria since 1976—that was open to international observers and the foreign press. Why might that have been the case? When I spoke about this with Said Doumane in 2007, he told me that the Algerian government had been ready to release the prisoners without trial—as it had done on similar occasions—if each prisoner would agree to submit a letter requesting a pardon. The prisoners refused, instead insisting on a public trial that would be open to foreign lawyers and the press. Furthermore, the defendants demanded that they be able to present their testimonies in French. Their rationale, according to Doumane, was that most of them did not master Arabic well enough to be able to clearly and fully express themselves. Only two of the defendants—the two lawyers[37]—had any appreciable fluency in modern standard Arabic, which did not become the sole language of teaching in the Algerian public schools until after many of them had left school. As noted above, some defendants had only limited schooling; if they spoke any Arabic at all, it would have been the Algerian spoken variety, not the official standard Arabic used in the courtroom. In the Kabyle region, for reasons related to both immigration and to the colonial school system, French has long been more of a *lingua franca* than Arabic. (What Doumane did not quite say was that if the publication of the testimonies was to take place in France, the defendants surely had a vested interest in providing their statements in French.)

The fact that the defendants were able to set conditions on their participation is due in no small measure to the nature of the case itself as a human rights trial. Requiring the defendants to use a language they did not master or barring international observers from the courtroom could have been construed as evidence of Algeria's failure to observe internationally accepted human rights protocols. Given that the case had achieved international visibility even before it went to court, and that the International League of Human Rights and Amnesty International were closely monitoring the situation, the Algerian government was under a good deal of pressure to perform for the international community its own adhesion to international human rights practices and protocols.[38] Indeed, one of the government's arguments in the case was that Algeria did not need an independent "League of Human Rights" because the nation already embraced human rights principles. What better way to demonstrate this than to conduct a "human rights" trial under the scrutiny of international organizations?

A further factor may have been the specific kinds of rights defendants are afforded in political trials in the French/Algerian system. Such trials constitute a discrete performance genre that specifically calls for elaborate and often eloquent narratives from defendants. Unlike an ordinary criminal court, where judges and lawyers heavily regiment what can be uttered, in a political trial, defendants are afforded the opportunity to speak with minimal interruption. In this case, the Algerian government appeared to extend that right to the defendants' language choice, so long as that language could be readily understood by court officials and observers (thus, Berber would not have been acceptable even if it were not ideologically problematic). What the government did not apparently reckon for, however, was the degree to which this trial would become an occasion for creating highly public and all-but-irrevocable linkages between the Berber identity project and human rights discourse.

Berbers and Human Rights in Algeria

The trial of 1985 was not the first time that a discourse of human rights had been brought to bear on Berber issues in Algeria. Five years earlier, during the Berber Spring of 1980, the cancellation of a talk on Berber poetry sparked several months of violent street protests as well as a student strike at the University of Tizi Ouzou. Twenty-four Berber activists were jailed between April and June of 1980 (including at least four who were imprisoned again in 1985).[39] In Paris, the Imedyazen collective mobilized the attention of the international press and several human rights organizations, including Amnesty International and the International Federation of Human Rights.[40] When the prisoners were released without trial at the end of June, however, international attention faded. Although "human rights" was one of the vectors through which the Berber Spring was constituted, "Berber culture" occupied the discursive center.[41]

After the events of 1980, Berber cultural activists faced a conundrum: under what conditions could they congregate around issues regarding Berber culture, when Algerian law expressly forbade the constitution of citizen associations without government authorization? As Algerian Law 71–79, repeatedly invoked during the trial, states: "No Association can legally exist or exercise its activities without the agreement of the government."[42] During the Berber Spring, some collective structures were put in place, but these were largely confined to the university. At the national level, it was clear that no association with "Berber" in its title or mission would win approval.[43] In the early 1980s, the Algerian state was still insisting on "one language, one religion, one people" as its founding myth. In this Jacobin context, activists seized upon a way of framing their mission that would be both authoritative and unimpeachable: they created organizations called "Children of Martyrs" (Enfants de chouhada), making explicit reference to those who had given their lives during the Algerian Revolution. Between 1982 and 1985, several "Children of Martyrs" associations were formed, including Tighri ("the cry"), based in Tizi Ouzou; AAHD 54, based in Algiers; and El Badr, based in Chlef. These associations coupled efforts to improve the living conditions of the widows and children of revolutionary martyrs with calls for democracy, cultural pluralism, and freedom of expression. In the Algerian context, this was a coded way of describing the freedom to speak in the Berber language in public contexts.[44]

The members of Children of Martyrs organizations were already in a unique position with regard to the state. As Kamel Chachoua explained, within the context of the "children's" natal villages, their status was ambiguous: they enjoyed relatively greater freedom of movement in the absence of paternal supervision. Many of them benefited from a *prise en charge* by state educational institutions, whether orphanages or boarding schools. They were exempt from military service, which meant that more of them completed advanced educational training. They were among the first to take the baccalaureate exam and enter the university. Yet despite what would seem to be impeccable nationalist credentials, the Children of Martyrs associations were never officially recognized by the state, no doubt because of their roots in the Kabyle region. However, they continued to meet clandestinely. In February of 1985, a number of Children of Martyrs activists tried to attend a government-sponsored seminar on writing the history of the Kabyle *wilaya* (province) of Tizi Ouzou. They were arrested without warrant, jailed for fifty-eight hours (exceeding by ten hours the legal limit for being held without charge), brought before a judge, and accused of "violence and insults to the police" (*violence et outrage à agents*). Released on February 13, they produced a flyer calling for a "state of law," "respect for human rights," "freedom of expression," and "a history [i.e., a historical narrative] worthy of the Algerian people and its martyrs."[45] This "Declaration," as it was titled, would become one of the primary pieces of evidence used against them during the December 1985 trial; in particular, their call for a "state of law" was interpreted as a call for a regime change—a crime punishable in Algeria by death.

If "Children of Martyrs" associations could marshal a certain amount of capital at the national level, their sociological base was perforce limited.[46] Moreover, by using the Algerian Revolution as their founding charter, they had little potential to draw attention beyond Algeria. "Human rights" had far greater currency. In November of 1984, a group of six individuals with diverse affiliations and backgrounds—including Abdennour Ali Yahia, the respected lawyer, former Minister of Agriculture, and founder of the powerful UGTA trade union—met in Algiers to discuss creating a league of human rights.[47] Unable to reconcile their differences, this group splintered, eventually forming three separate human rights groups, with Ali Yahia heading up the group of interest here.[48] In December of 1984, Ali Yahia met with a small group of activists based in Tizi Ouzou, including several members of the Children of Martyrs organizations. This group's members chose the symbolic occasion of the International Day of Human Rights to announce their intention to form their own human rights organization in Algeria, which they called the Algerian League of Human Rights (LADH, League algérienne des droits de l'homme).[49] By June 18, they had drafted a set of bylaws; on June 30, they filed the bylaws with the state, along with an application to create an association, and also sent them to the International Federation of Human Rights (FIDH) in Paris with a request for affiliation. Nowhere in these documents is there any mention of "Berber"; "culture" receives one somewhat buried notation. Instead, the authoritative historical reference is to the United Nations' Universal Declaration of Human Rights of 1948,[50] and in particular, to the right to freely associate.

Five days later, during festivities for Algerian Independence Day on July 5, the arrests began. A number of activists associated with both the Children of Martyrs and the LADH had engaged in a collective action, placing wreaths in cemeteries and at monuments of revolutionary martyrs in the Algerian cities of Algiers, Boumerdes, Chlef, Khenchela, Tipaza, and Tizi-Ouzou. Some two hundred were arrested; of those, twelve were transferred to the infamous Berrouaghia prison. Between July 9 and September

16, another twelve were jailed, including a number of officers of the Children of Martyrs associations. Of the twenty-three prisoners eventually brought to trial, all but two (among them, Ali-Yahia) were known for their activism in Berber matters. Four charges were brought against them: attack on the authority of state by calling for a regime change, making and distributing tracts, unarmed gathering, and creating illegal associations.

Human Rights in the International Context

Global attention soon mobilized around the prisoners. On August 13, Amnesty International's Montreal bureau, acting on a request presumably sent by the Paris-based Collectif contre la répression en Algérie (CCRA), cabled forty-five sections of the organization worldwide. Letter writers were instructed to request information about the prisoners' circumstances and to urge that they be released if they were being "detained solely for their nonviolent expression of political beliefs and freedom of association."[51] On the same day, the International Federation of Human Rights sent to Algeria its representative, the Senegalese lawyer Jean-Gabriel Senghor, on a week-long fact-finding mission. Both of these events were timed to coincide with the initial hearing of the (by then) fourteen prisoners on August 13. In an August 17 audience before Algerian Minister of Justice Boualem Baki, Senghor pointedly reminded the Minister that this case afforded Algeria the opportunity to serve once again as a beacon for all of Africa (as it had during the Revolution), and he urged that foreign observers be allowed to attend the trial.[52] Articles about the situation began to appear in the French press. Amnesty International sent its own delegate to Algeria in late September. On November 27, Amnesty International launched a new letter-writing campaign, contending that the (by then) twenty-two prisoners had been "detained solely for the non-violent exercise of their rights to freedom of expression and association."[53]

Meanwhile, in Paris, "human rights" was the rubric around which a number of groups came together to protest the prisoners' situation. The most significant event took place on September 22 at the Mutualité and included representatives from the International Federation of Human Rights, the French League of Human Rights, and a French workers' union, as well as an observer from Amnesty International. The Kabyle political singers Idir and Djurdjura appeared, alongside the Breton musician Alain Stivell. On November 1, the Algerian national holiday commemorating the start of the Revolution, violence erupted in both Paris and Algeria. In Paris, some one thousand unauthorized protesters showed up at the Place du Trocadéro, despite the last-minute cancellation by French police of what was to have been an official public demonstration in support of human rights. In Algeria, demonstrations took place throughout the Kabyle region, leading police to use tear gas and fire into the air; at least two protesters were injured and dozens were arrested (among them, my friend Muhend). A day later, on November 2, the Algerian League of Human Rights was officially recognized by the International Federation of Human Rights (FIDH). In November and early December, representatives from the FIDH and Amnesty International made additional trips to Algeria to investigate the condition of the prisoners; each visit was accompanied by a flurry of news coverage. By the time of the December trials, this affair had already been subjected to four months of sustained international scrutiny.

The Trial

From the perspective of international human rights agencies and the foreign press, on trial was nothing less than the Algerian regime itself. This surely contributed in no small measure to the state's decision to allow foreign observers into the courtroom. One such observer was *Le Monde* reporter Fréderick Fritscher. As Fritscher describes it, the scene in the small rectangular courtroom was "almost surreal." Despite the high stakes involved (one of the charges, "attack on the security of state," carried a possible death penalty), the atmosphere was characterized by a "somewhat naïve congeniality" (*"une atmosphère bon enfant"*).[54] Fritscher and his colleague Joëlle Stolz, representing France's *Libération*, the Associated Press, and Radio France International, watched the proceedings from ringside seats, their view occasionally obscured by the thick Moorish columns distributed somewhat awkwardly around the room. They were joined by FIDH representative Senghor; by Mohamed Charfi, vice president of the Tunisian League of Human Rights representing the Geneva-based International Commission of Lawyers; by Amnesty International's Peter Duffy; and by at least two French lawyers. The court president, at the room's center, was flanked by two civil assessors on one side and two military officials on the other. The defendants sat on either side of the courtroom in two large witness boxes lined with well-worn wooden benches. Since the trial was also open to the relatives of the defendants, family members and a few friends (who had entered surreptitiously) filled the room: men cloaked in their hand-woven burnouses sat alongside old women decked out in the traditional orange and yellow dress characteristic of the Kabyle region.[55] Despite the extraordinary audience, Algeria's military was hardly absent: armed with Kalashnikovs, members of the security forces stood throughout the room, framing the court physically and symbolically. This was, after all, a military court.

One by one, the defendants took the stand. As each defendant rose, the Court President reiterated the charges: "You are accused of attacking the authority of state, distribution of tracts, unarmed gathering, and constitution of illegal associations. What do you have to say?"[56] Addressed in Arabic, most defendants responded in French.[57] Going well beyond a rebuttal of the specific charges, they crafted hybrid performances that drew various narrative genres into a frame characterized in terms of "human rights." This occurred via specific discursive strategies. Since the trial itself was already oriented to human rights, speakers had to do little narrative work to establish that frame. Many speakers invoked human rights as a framing device at the beginning and/or end of their testimony; in that way, it metapragmatically oriented (that is, made interpretable) the body of their testimony in terms of human rights even as they spoke in depth about their experiences of being Berber in Algeria. Several defendants employed particular speech genres such as Berber proverbs, stories, and even a song fragment; in the courtroom context, such genres took on new meaning as tokens (examples) of Berber culture. The occasional use of the Berber language itself—even if only in a short proverb—was also a clear way of making apparent the connection between speaking Berber and human rights. Finally, some testimony (such as that of Said Sadi, discussed below) was itself explicitly Berberist in nature.

Ali-Fewzi Rebaine, first up, set the tone for the proceedings. In response to the President's invitation ("What do you have to say?"), uttered in Arabic,[58] he responded in French as follows: "Today, I am happy to be before the Court of State Security because for the first time in twenty-three years I can speak."[59] Setting his experiences of torture at the hands of state agents against his own sense of nationalism and patriotism, he gradually wove into his account clear but subtle linkages between human rights and Berber identity. He began with a conventional description of human rights violations, describing for the court the daily torture he had been subjected to over a five-week period during a prior imprisonment: "I couldn't see where the hits were coming from, but I felt them on my skin— some kicked me, some punched me, some beat me with wooden sticks, others with a pipe."[60] He then aligned himself with both revolutionary heroes and human rights: "It is a fundamental right," he contended, "to want to commemorate the memory of our fathers [on national Independence Day] [. . .] If torture is the price to pay to be able to think, speak, and freely associate, I will pay it, as our fathers have already paid it."[61] Rebaine concluded: "I was born a free man in the fullest sense of the term. I will remain that way." In this context, "free man" is a double-voiced utterance: it refers simultaneously to one of the foundational principles of human rights discourse and to "Amazigh," a contemporary Berber term of self-referral, typically glossed as "free man." This term evokes the historical legitimacy and pan-Maghribi rootedness of Berber populations in North Africa even as it also locates Berber culture as a kind of autochthonous domain of freedom. Berbers, in other words, are presented here as quintessential bearers of liberty from time immemorial.

One of the most moving testimonials was that of Amrane Ait Hammouda, son of the renowned war hero Amirouche. Ait Hammouda centered his opening remarks in the generic frame of an epic folktale: "Once upon a time," he began, "there was a warrior people who decided, as a single man, to reconquer its dignity . . ." In the manner of a good storyteller, Ait Hammouda repeated the "once upon a time" framing device four times, the last time locating the current trial in relation to canonical episodes of modern Algerian history: "Once upon a time there were children of martyrs who wanted to honor the memory of the father with flowers. They were put in prison and condemned to death."[62] He then turned from this tale to directly address the President of the Court: "*Monsieur le Président*, I'd like to remind you of some facts." Outlining three general areas—historical, political, and social—about which he wanted to educate the court, he went on to recount specific stories about the plight of the children and widows whose fathers and husbands had sacrificed their lives for the nation, weaving an occasional proverb into his account. For example, he offered a eulogy for Malika Zerouki Belhout, a Kabyle woman who had fought in the *maquis* during the war but was subsequently abandoned by the state during a serious illness. Holding the state accountable for her death, Ait Hammouda lauded Malika as being of that race of warriors who "would rather break than bend." Here, he was evoking the oft-cited Kabyle proverb *axir a nrez wala a neknu* [it is better to break than to bend], which he reportedly stated in Berber and then translated into French.[63] This part of Ait Hammouda's testimony concluded with a personal tale in which his affiliation with the Berber movement was mentioned almost in passing: he recounted his depression as a fatherless child, his difficulty in finding employment, the tremendous hope he experienced upon becoming an FLN party member, and his subsequent sense of outrage when he realized that the FLN had sent him to Tizi Ouzou after the Berber Spring in order to infiltrate and inform on the Children of Martyrs organizations. When he refused, his house was searched, rumors about him were spread, and he was ultimately forced to leave the Party. Ait Hammouda's account peaked with a dramatic tale of betrayal: he told the court of how, in 1982, he discovered that his father's remains had been housed since 1964 in a cell in the basement of the headquarters of the National Guard (Gendarmerie nationale): "Can one imagine a war leader betrayed . . . his body impounded after Independence by the very people who hope to incarnate the revolution and the State? This had for me the effect of an insurmountable shock."[64] He ended his testimony with another string of parallelisms, enumerating nine general areas in which the state had abused its power. Not until his last sentence did he reinvoke human rights, imposing it as a metapragmatic frame to draw together and make interpretable all that had come before: "I will continue," he concluded, "to defend the rights of every man because the defense of human rights is, in my opinion, the key political question at the end of the [twentieth] century."[65]

Whereas Ait Hammouda, Rebaine, and others centered their narratives in personal experience, the two lawyers among the defendants grounded their arguments in textual authority. Ali-Yahia Abdenour and Mokrane Ait Larbi, president and vice president, respectively, of the LADH, performed extended textual analysis of the charges brought against them—in particular, the charge of forming illegal associations (Algerian Law 71–79). Referencing the state's own official texts as well as the UN Charter, the Bandung Conference resolution, and the African Charter of 1981, Ali-Yahia sought to demonstrate that Algerian Law 71–79 violated both international conventions and Algeria's own national charters and constitutions, all of which guaranteed the freedom to associate. Mokrane Ait Larbi opened by listing and thanking the international organizations that supported the LADH, performatively invoking their authority as a discursive frame for his own statement. He then proceeded to outline the specific ways in which his rights had been violated, enumerating a series of errors of fact and logic in the state's case against him. Whereas the statements of Ali-Yahia and Ait Larbi are on the whole more regimented in terms of legal discourse than those of other defendants, Ait Larbi ended with a fragment of an entirely new—and, in this context, highly subversive—genre: political Kabyle song. He recited, in Kabyle Berber, a few lines of a song by the renowned Berber singer Lounis Ait Menguellet, recently condemned to three years in prison for his solidarity with the prisoners:[66] "Let us remind those who forget the past . . . It is in the solid oak that I am rooted, and not in the reed [i.e., that bends with each breeze]."[67] In this context, "those who forget the past" or "bend with each breeze" clearly indexed the state and military officials in the courtroom.

These examples aside, Berber issues hovered as an unspoken subtext for much of the trial. Although the charges carefully avoided any mention of Berber, everyone in the room knew that the founders of the Children of Martyrs Associations and the Algerian League of Human Rights were by and large also active in the Berber Cultural Movement. When Ferhat Mehenni and Said Sadi got up to speak, however, the Berber dimension was brought sharply to the fore. Ferhat Mehenni, a well-known Kabyle political singer who had already been jailed twelve times over the past decade for his participation in Berber activities, told the court of his experience with Algerian Radio & Television (RTA) in 1980. Upon hearing that Ferhat wanted to be interviewed in his maternal language or not at all, the RTA producer was astounded: "You want to speak Kabyle in front of eighteen million Algerians?!"[68] The court president apparently had a similar reaction. In one of the few interjections reproduced in the text, he cried out, "These statements (*propos*) are unacceptable, unacceptable!" "But they are no less authentic, *Monsieur le Président*," Ferhat replied. "I continue."[69] He went on to describe being tortured at the hands of the Algerian regime; decried the absence of Berber in the theater and the cinema as well as in the nation's schools and bureaucracies; and framed his love for the "Berber spirit" as on a par with his "democracy and civic-mindedness."[70]

Said Sadi, speaking on the last day of hearings, set Berber identity in direct relation to human rights: "*Messieurs de la cour* [. . .] You will no doubt be uncomfortable when we bring up certain taboo subjects [. . .] What is the heart of the matter here? It is none other than the 'Berber plot' in whose name all abuses are permissible. It's well known, *Messieurs de la cour*, that Berber is the 'bogey man' (*croque-mitaine*), the ultimate target when the clannish interests of *Le Pouvoir* are threatened."[71] Accusing the state of "Berberophobia," Sadi enumerated a series of events over the past several decades that the state had attempted to construct in terms of a Berber threat to the regime. A day earlier, Kaddour Arrous had been the only defendant directly questioned about his participation in Berber activities (the journal *Tafsut* had been found in his possession). Sadi recontextualized this earlier interaction in his own testimony. "You were quite agitated [when Arrous spoke], *Messieurs de la Cour* [. . .] I was watching in particular the judge on the left [. . .] He literally jumped out of his seat when he heard the word 'Berber.' There was his proof. He was ecstatic. Now, any sentence was possible; neither proof nor verification nor reason would henceforth be required. [. . .] The Inquisition could go forward, collective hysteria would find its preferred target."[72] Accusing *Le Pouvoir* of a "cultural genocide," Sadi—a psychiatrist by training—diagnosed Algeria's ruling clan as suffering from the condition of mimicry, rooted in the *complexe du colonisé*.[73] Sadi ended his lengthy statement by conjoining "cultural repression," "freedom of expression," and the "right of association" under the rubric of human rights: if he had spoken at length about each of them, he argued, it was because "human rights are flouted."[74]

Conclusion

I have argued that the rubric of "human rights" worked to frame this trial for both the state and the defendants. What this meant in each case, however, was somewhat different. From the vantage point of Algerian officials, at stake was the nation's standing in the international arena. They had to demonstrate that the court itself could perform to the standards of the international community, and they did so in part by allowing defendants to speak in French in the manner of a classic "trial of rupture." In that sense, the trial was a mitigated success. *Libération's* Joëlle Stolz described the trial as "a milestone in Algeria's history."[75] Senghor, representing the FIDH, reported that "to Algeria's credit," the hearings themselves had unfolded in an "entirely legitimate" manner.[76] He singled out the government of President Chadli Bendjedid for particular mention: "In the opinion of some of those close to the defendants, this trial would not have taken place in the same conditions under [previous] President Boumedienne."[77] Even Ferhat Mehenni praised the way the trial had been carried out, saying that it was "all to the honor of Algeria."[78]

The state may have hoped that opening the courtroom as a liminal space—that is, as a space in which ordinarily impermissible discourse would be tolerated momentarily—would ultimately work to reinforce its own authority. Here, however, the narrative performances of the defendants exceeded the courtroom, mapping Berber identity onto a discourse of human rights in both subtle and explicit ways. Unlike the more restrictive "Children of Marytrs" affiliation, the "human rights" frame was wide, flexible, and able to accommodate a range of narrative content as well as diverse discourse genres. Mindful of the unusual presence of human rights representatives and foreign reporters in the courtroom, and aware that their statements would no doubt circulate in print before they were released from prison, defendants paid special attention to configuring Berber identity within the context of this globally circulating, authoritative discourse. The prisoners may have been returned to their cells, but their accounts traveled: first, to foreign newspapers, and ultimately to books that would become key documents in the Berber struggle for state recognition.

Yet the transnational dimension of this trial should not obscure the fact that in the mid-1980s, after two decades of fierce repression of Berber culture, Berbers in Algeria were ultimately most interested in achieving national recognition. They sought both acknowledgment of and institutional support for their culture, history and language. Given the state's repeated refusal to recognize its own Berber dimension, Berber activists essentially forced the issue by propelling it into authoritative transnational channels that the state could not easily dismiss.[79] In that sense, the trial should be understood less as a transnational event than as a national forum in which transnational human rights discourse was marshaled to help mediate a new status for Berbers in Algeria.

In the courtroom, the state appeared to have the last word. All but one defendant were found guilty of all charges with the exception of "attack on the security of state." Yet removing this charge gave the defendants the final moral authority. As one observer put it, they had been brought before the highest court in the country for the lowly charge of "associating" with one another. Two years later, this charge would become moot: Algerian law 71–79 was superseded by Law 87–15, which granted citizens the right to create voluntary associations without state approval.[80] By 1990, more than one thousand Berber associations had formed across Kabylia. In the end, it was far more than the defendants' discourse that the state was unable to contain.

Notes

An earlier version of this chapter was presented at the workshop "Berbers and Others: Shifting Parameters of Ethnicity in the Contemporary Maghrib," held at Harvard University on April 28–29, 2006. I am especially grateful for comments by Katherine E. Hoffman, one of the workshop organizers. I also wish to thank participants for their feedback, in particular Susan Slyomovics, Lahouari Addi, and Lisa Bernasek. This chapter has also benefited from discussions with Ilana Gershon. Finally, I am grateful to Said Doumane for agreeing to discuss this trial with me. Any errors of fact or interpretation are entirely mine.

1. The data for this paper come primarily from two accounts, both published by the Collectif contre la répression en Algérie (CCRA) in Paris. (1) *Au nom du peuple* (henceforth NDP) is a reconstituted account of the defendants' statements before the court; see discussion in text below. It also provides the arrest warrant (*arrêt de renvoi*) (translated into French from Arabic); the text of earlier hearings before the examining judge (*juge d'instruction*), held primarily during August 1985; a brief biography for each defendant; and the final report of the lawyer Jean-Gabriel Senghor to the International Federation of Human Rights (CCRA) (Paris: Imedyazen, 1986). The reader should note that this is not an official transcript of the court proceedings. In particular, statements of court officials were selectively included. While press reports mention "numerous interruptions," in this text, only a few especially egregious interactions are recorded. The lawyers' statements do not appear. According to press reports, the lawyers for the defense and prosecution spoke only after all of the defendants had presented their testimony. (2) *Algérie: les droits de l'homme: revue de presse* (henceforth RDP) is a compilation of documents about the affair (CCRA, Paris, 1986). It includes cables from Amnesty International; communications with the FIDH; texts of tracts, flyers and announcements drafted by various committees; texts of the relevant Algerian laws; and hundreds of articles from the national and international press. The material in RDP covers this affair throughout 1985.

2. Said Sadi had long been active in Berberist causes; in 1989, he would become head of the ultrasecular RCD (Rassemblement pour la Culture et la Démocratie) party.

3. NDP, 211.

4. Robert Phillipson, Mart Rannut, and Tove Skutnabb-Kangas. Introduction. In Tove Skutnabb-Kangas and Robert Phillipson, eds. *Linguistic Human Rights: Overcoming Linguistic Discrimination* (Berlin: Mouton de Gruyter, 1994), 1–22.

5. The major charters and covenants are analyzed with respect to their concern for ethno-linguistic rights in Phillipson et al., *Linguistic Human Rights*, 71–110.

6. Ibid., 77.

7. Article 2 declares that "Everyone is entitled to all the rights and freedoms set forth in this Declaration, without distinction of any kind, such as race, colour, sex, language . . ." Charter of the United Nations and Statute of the International Court of Justice. United Nations 2009. http://www.un.org/en/documents/charter/index.shtml (accessed Sept. 28, 2009).

8. Ibid. The Covenant was signed in 1966 to go into effect in 1976.

9. The African Charter on Human and Peoples' Rights had been formulated in 1981 but went into effect only in 1986.

10. Article 28.7, cited in Phillipson et al., *Linguistic Human Rights*, 84.

11. A Guide to the African Charter on Human and Peoples' Rights. Amnesty International, 2006. http://www.amnesty.org/en/library/info/IOR63/005/2006 (accessed Sept. 28, 2009).

12. United Nations Permanent Forum on Indigenous Issues. http://www.un.org/esa/socdev/unpfii/index.html (accessed Sept. 28, 2009).

13. Ibid.

14. For a sampling of works related to narrative testimony and identity construction, see Nancy K. Miller and Jason Tougaw, eds., *Trauma, Testimony, and Community* (Urbana: University of Illinois Press, 1998); Susan F. Hirsch, *Pronouncing and Persevering: Gender and the Discourses of Disputing in an African Islamic Court* (Chicago: University of Chicago Press, 1998); Susan Slyomovics, *The Performance of Human Rights in Morocco* (Philadelphia: University of Pennsylvania Press, 2005); Richard A. Wilson, ed., *Human Rights, Culture and Context: Anthropological Perspectives* (London: Pluto Press, 1997); and Richard A. Wilson, *The Politics of Truth and Reconciliation in South Africa: Legitimizing the Post-Apartheid State* (Cambridge: Cambridge University Press, 2001).

15. Susan Slyomovics, "Self-Determination as Self-Definition: The Case of Morocco," in Hurst Hannum and Eileen F. Babbit, eds., *Negotiating Self-Determination* (Lanham, Md.: Lexington Books, 2006), 153, emphasis added.

16. Patricia Ewick and Susan S. Silbey, "Subversive Stories and Hegemonic Tales: Toward a Sociology of Narrative," *Law & Society Review* 29(2) (1995): 200. See also Richard Bauman, *A World of Others' Words: Cross-Cultural Perspectives on Intertextuality* (Malden, Mass.: Blackwell, 2004).

17. Richard Bauman and Charles Briggs, "Poetics and Performance as Critical Perspectives on Language and Social Life," *Annual Review of Anthropology* 19 (1990): 74.

18. Jacques Vergès, *De la stratégie judiciaire* (Paris: Éditions de Minuit, 1968). During the Algerian Revolution, Vergès had been involved in the defense of Djamila Bouhired, imprisoned for her role in planting bombs in the Algerian capital on behalf of the National Liberation Front. For more on Vergès, see Barbet Schroeder, *L'Avocat de la terreur* (Magnolia Pictures: Wild Bunch/Yalla Films, 2007), 137 min.

19. Jacques Vergès, *De la stratégie judiciaire*, 104, 117.

20. See Lahouari Addi, *L'impasse du populisme. L'Algérie: Collectivité politique et état en construction* (Algiers: Entreprise Nationale du Livre, 1990), and Jean Leca,

"Paradoxes de la démocratisation: L'Algérie au chevet de la science politique," *Pouvoirs: Revue française d'études constitutionnelles et politiques* (1998): 7–27.

21. Front de libération nationale, *Constitution* (Algiers: République algérienne démocratique et populaire, 1976), 59.

22. Tabrizi Bensalah, *La République algérienne* (Paris: Librairie Générale de Droit et de Jurisprudence, 1979), 246.

23. Vergès, *De la stratégie judiciaire*, 175.

24. Ibid., 162–176. The Dreyfus Affair unfolded over several trials, with different lawyers adopting different judicial strategies. Whereas Zola used a defense of rupture, other lawyers used the more classic defense of complicity.

25. Ibid., 171.

26. Ibid., 184.

27. Ibid., 185, 187.

28. Ibid., 192.

29. Ibid., 198.

30. See *Journal Officiel de la République Algérienne* (henceforth JORA) 64(2) (Jan. 8, 1964): 17–18. See also Tabrizi Bensalah, *La République algérienne*, 243ff., and Étienne-Jean LaPassat, *La justice en Algérie 1962–1968* (Paris: Fondation Nationale des Sciences Politiques, 1969), 115. Following a coup d'état, President Houari Boumedienne (1965–1978) changed the name to simply "Revolutionary Court" (*cour révolutionnaire*) (JORA 68–609). The special courts were sanctioned by Article 59 of the 1964 Algerian Constitution. See *La Constitution* (Algiers: Front de libération nationale, 1964) and Article 166 of the 1976 Constitution, *La Constitution* (Algiers: Front de libération nationale, 1976).

31. LaPassat, *Justice en Algérie*, 11.

32. Ibid., 116.

33. Ibid., 118.

34. *Les torturés d'El Harrach* (Paris: Éditions de Minuit, 1966).

35. Bensalah, *République algérienne*, 258.

36. LaPassat, *Justice en Algérie*, 121.

37. The two lawyers were Mohand Arezki Ait Larbi and Ali Yahia Abdennour.

38. Salem Chaker speculates that the Bendjedid regime was already weak and subject to internal dissension in its ranks. From this perspective, even the arrest of Ali Yahia—politically isolated, old, and ill, with impeccable nationalist and symbolic credentials—could be linked to a series of uncoordinated individual decisions rather than an explicit strategy on the part of the regime. See Salem Chaker, "Les droits de l'homme sont-ils mûrs en Algérie? Réflexions d'un acteur sur la Ligue Algérienne des Droits de l'Homme," *Annuaire de l'Afrique du Nord* 24 (1985): 489–503.

39. Said Sadi, Ferhat Mehenni, Mohand Arezki Ait Larbi, Arezki Abboute.

40. Imedyazen, *Tafsut Imazighen (Printemps berbère)* (Paris: Imedyazen, 1981).

41. For an extended analysis of the Berber Spring, see Jane E. Goodman, "Reinterpreting the Berber Spring: From Rite of Reversal to Site of Convergence," *Journal of North African Studies* 9(3) (2004): 60–82.

42. NDP, 30. According to Kevin Dwyer, Morocco, Egypt, and Tunisia had similar laws; see his *Arab Voices: The Human Rights Debate in the Middle East* (Berkeley: University of California Press, 1991).

43. Algeria was hardly the only newly ex-colonized state to refuse to recognize associations based on ethnic criteria. See Sten Hagberg, "Ethnic Identification in

Voluntary Associations: The Politics of Development and Culture in Burkina Faso," in Harri Englund and Francis B. Nyamnjoh, eds., *Rights and the Politics of Recognition in Africa* (London: Zed Books, 2004), 195–218.

44. Kamel Chachoua, "Les enfants de chuhada: fils de veuves ou fils de martyrs?" *Monde Arabe Maghreb-Machrek* 154 (1996): 31–39.

45. RDP, 291.

46. Chaker, "Droits de l'homme," 490.

47. Susan E. Waltz, *Human Rights and Reform: Changing the Face of North African Politics* (Berkeley: University of California Press, 1995), 140.

48. See Waltz, *Human Rights*, for an account of these three groups. Salem Chaker provides a somewhat different chronology of the initial meetings in "Droits de l'homme." See also Saïd Sadi, *Algérie: l'échec recommencé?* (Algiers: Éditions Parenthèses, 1991) and RDP, 40–44.

49. RDP, 32–33. When a government-backed "Algerian League of Human Rights" was created, Ali-Yahia's organization changed its name to "Algerian League for the Defense of Human Rights (LADDH)." On the schism between the two organizations, see Ramdane Babadji, "Le phénomène associatif en Algérie: génèse et perspectives," *Annuaire de l'Afrique du Nord* 28 (1989): 229–242.

50. RDP, 27–30.

51. Ibid., 68.

52. Ibid., 51.

53. Ibid., 71.

54. Ibid., 296.

55. Ibid., 306.

56. The specific charges slightly varied for each defendant; whereas all faced "attack on the security of state" and "illegal association," not all were accused of the lesser charges of illegal gathering and distributions of tracts.

57. This was not the case for the lawyers; two French lawyers were unable to take the floor because they were required to speak in Arabic (NDP, 232).

58. I was not able to find the specific Arabic text; the one ex-prisoner with whom I spoke told me that he did not speak Arabic well enough to provide it.

59. NDP, 195.

60. Ibid.

61. Ibid., 197.

62. Ibid., 63–64.

63. Ibid., 66. The information on translation comes from Said Doumane.

64. Ibid., 69.

65. Ibid., 71.

66. Ait Menguellet was arrested on September 5 on a trumped-up charge of illegal arms possession (he had a collection of traditional firearms mounted on his wall). This arrest came after he had dedicated a song in his concert to fellow singer Ferhat Mehenni, one of the twenty-three prisoners.

67. NDP, 87. Of course, this recalls the proverb cited in earlier testimony ("It is better to break than bend").

68. In the end, the interview did not take place.

69. NDP, 167.

70. Ibid., 166.

71. Ibid., 202–203.

72. Ibid., 209.

73. Ibid., 213–214. Sadi was surely familiar with the work of Frantz Fanon, who had worked as a psychiatrist in a French military hospital during the Algerian Revolution before aligning himself with the Front de libération nationale in its war against France.

74. Ibid., 221.

75. RDP, 300.

76. NDP, 240.

77. Ibid., 241.

78. RDP, 305.

79. See Greg Urban, *Metaculture: How Culture Moves Through the World* (Minneapolis: Minnesota University Press, 2001).

80. Law 89–15 of July 21, 1987, granted the right to form locally based non-political associations without prior governmental authorization. Law 90–31 of December 4, 1990, extended this right to national organizations.

Bibliography

Addi, Lahouari. *L'impasse du populisme: l'Algérie, collectivité politique et état en construction.* Algiers: Entreprise Nationale du Livre, 1990.

Bauman, Richard, and Charles Briggs. "Poetics and Performance as Critical Perspectives on Language and Social Life." *Annual Review of Anthropology* 19 (1990): 59–88.

Bensalah, Tabrizi. *La République algérienne.* Paris: Librairie Générale de Droit et de Jurisprudence, 1979.

Chachoua, Kamel. "Les enfants de chuhada: fils de veuves ou fils de martyrs?" *Monde Arabe Maghreb-Machrek* 154 (1996): 31–39.

Chaker, Salem. "Les droits de l'homme sont-ils mûrs en Algérie? Réflexions d'un acteur sur la Ligue Algérienne des Droits de l'Homme." *Annuaire de l'Afrique du Nord* 24 (1985): 489–503.

Collectif Contre la Répression en Algérie (CCRA). *Algérie: Les Droits de l'homme. Revue de Presse.* Paris: CCRA, 1986.

———. *Au Nom du peuple.* Paris: Imedyazen, 1986.

Dwyer, Kevin. *Arab Voices: The Human Rights Debate in the Middle East.* Berkeley: University of California Press, 1991.

Front de libération nationale. *La Constitution.* Algiers: Front de Libération Nationale, 1964.

———. *La Constitution.* Algiers: République algérienne démocratique et populaire, 1976.

Goodman, Jane E. *Berber Culture on the World Stage: From Village to Video.* Bloomington: Indiana University Press, 2005.

———. "Reinterpreting the Berber Spring: From Rite of Reversal to Site of Convergence." *Journal of North African Studies* 9(3) (2004): 60–82.

Hagberg, Sten. "Ethnic Identification in Voluntary Associations: The Politics of Development and Culture in Burkina Faso." In *Rights and the Politics of Recognition in Africa,* ed. Harri Englund and Francis B. Nyamnjoh. London: Zed Books, 2004, 195–218.

Hirsch, Susan F. *Pronouncing and Persevering: Gender and the Discourses of Disputing in an African Islamic Court.* Chicago: University of Chicago Press, 1998.

Imedyazen. *Tafsut Imazighen (Printemps berbère).* Paris: Imedyazen, 1981.

Kapil, Arun. "L'évolution du régime autoritaire en Algérie: le 5 octobre et les réformes politiques de 1988–1989." *Annuaire de l'Afrique du Nord* 23 (1990): 499–534.

LaPassat, Étienne-Jean. *La justice en Algérie 1962–1968.* Paris: Fondation Nationale des Sciences Politiques, 1969.

Leca, Jean. "Paradoxes de la démocratisation: l'Algérie au chevet de la science politique." *Pouvoirs: Revue française d'études constitutionnelles et politique* (1998): 7–27.

Les torturés d'El Harrach. Preface by Henri Alleg. Paris: Éditions de Minuit, 1966.

Miller, Nancy K., and Jason Tougaw, eds. *Trauma, Testimony, and Community.* Urbana: University of Illinois Press, 2002.

Slyomovics, Susan. "Self-Determination as Self-Definition: The Case of Morocco." In *Negotiating Self-Determination,* ed. Hurst Hannum and Eileen F. Babbitt. Oxford: Lexington Books, 2006, 135–157.

———. *The Performance of Human Rights in Morocco.* Philadelphia: University of Pennsylvania Press, 2005.

Urban, Greg. *Metaculture: How Culture Moves Through the World.* Minneapolis: Minnesota University Press, 2001.

Vergès, Jaques. *De la stratégie judiciaire.* Paris: Éditions de Minuit, 1968.

Waltz, Susan E. *Human Rights and Reform: Changing the Face of North African Politics.* Berkeley: University of California Press, 1995.

Wilson, Richard A., ed. *Human Rights, Culture and Context: Anthropological Perspectives.* London: Pluto Press, 1997.

———. *The Politics of Truth and Reconciliation in South Africa: Legitimizing the Post-Apartheid State.* Cambridge: Cambridge University Press, 2001.

6

Globalization Begins at Home: Children's Wage Labor and the High Atlas Household

David Crawford

Nearly forty years ago, Jacques Berque wrote that forms of Berber social organization "provide a vigorous safeguard for one of the Maghreb's most hopeful features, its communal solidarity."[1] Now, between an accelerating neo-liberal reconstruction of the Moroccan economy and the increasing potency of international political Islam, between race riots in France and bread riots in Casablanca, it might seem a curious time to examine what "vigorous safeguards" for communal solidarity are still available. It might seem even more curious to examine this "hope" in the context of the rising incidence of rural children migrating for urban wage labor, a phenomenon that has elicited visceral horror and bureaucratic exasperation in Morocco far more than optimism.

While I do not intend to excuse the exploitation of children, I will contend that rural children's urban wage labor demonstrates, if not hope, then *what can be hoped for* in today's Morocco. I will suggest that our discomfort with working children, and in particular what are in Morocco called *petites bonnes* (child-maids), can be read as a contemporary manifestation of much older debates about "social solidarity"; that is, the means and meanings used to forge individuals into functioning social bodies. The majority of *petites bonnes* work in the cities to support their rural households, suggesting that their situation is not the result of a "failure of solidarity," as many urbanites assume, but rather is a testament to the continuing resiliency of rural communities and their key constituent social form, the household.

Amazigh/Berber Social Organization

Social solidarity is an old concern among Europeans. How we take care of one another in an atomized, anonymous economy grounded in the material fecundity of institutionalized selfishness remains a core problem in social theory, not to mention political practice. Cosmopolitans are still working abstractly on the question, and, I will suggest, High Atlas farmers are actively grappling with it, too.

To cite farmers here is not simple mischief. Rural Imazighen, and rural North Africans more generally, have provided key evidence for contemplation of social solidarity. From Ibn Khaldun's dialectical 'asabiya to Tocqueville's musings on Algeria, from Durkheim's theories of mechanical and organic solidarity to Gellner's segmentary schema, how Berbers and other North Africans have organized their struggles has long fascinated thinkers. This has been especially true of rural Berbers. The material lives of Berber farmers and pastoralists have been and continue to be productive of a wide variety of discourses that work far beyond the context of rural Morocco.

For instance, Jane Goodman has written, "The Berber village has been 'good to think' across three discursive traditions—colonial, anthropological, and activist—for well over a century," and she makes a solid case for her assertion.[2] She cites Hanoteau and Letourneux's confident statement in 1872 that "to make known the [Kabyle] village is to make known the whole society," and along with others she points out that the Berberness of the iconic village played an important role in the French colonial imagination. It seems clear that "the village" continues to function in many versions of the Berber social imaginary, not least in terms of the "structural nostalgia" so important to transnational Amazigh/Berber consciousness.[3]

It is hardly villages only that have served farmers, thinkers, and theorists. "Tribes," too, have been "good to think" for many people, and have been even more celebrated in Morocco, along with the genealogical, segmentary means of organizing them. Here again, it is not the brute facts of social organization but specific and widely abstracted implications about social solidarity that have captivated the minds of intellectuals. For example, Ernest Gellner writes of the saintly lineages of Ait 'Atta Berbers, "Here, a separation of powers is not merely a check on tyranny, as intended in classical political theory, but also a check on inequality. The inegalitarian potential of society is as it were drained by the saints. Here, at least, equality and liberty go together."[4] In fact, Gellner's saints do (or did) live in villages rather than roaming the conceptual ether in evanescent tribes, but for Gellner, villages are not so good to think. We read little about how villagers organize irrigation, harvest, or thresh; we hear almost nothing about women, children, or non-saintly men. This is, after all, a book about saints, and saintly significance inheres in saintly litigation, *baraka*-suffused maneuverings that serve to construct and define the contentious terrain of tribal borders. Gellner favors tribal dynamics, in other words, which are important to him not for their Berber essence or North African location, but because they illuminate the limitations of "classical political theory," the means by which Berbers organize themselves beyond the purview of the state.

There are, of course, other ways to think about Berber social solidarity. From Montagne's *lfuf* and *sfuf* moieties to overdrawn assertions of a general Berber *siba* standing in contradistinction to an Arab *bled al-makhzan*, there has been no shortage of discursive frames that have served to put Berbers to work in understanding social processes, philosophical positions, historical trajectories, academic tyrannies, and political conundrums.[5] The overwhelming diversity of actual Berber social life is probably one reason for this abounding service to academic humanity, a diversity that we find subtly articulated in Berque's own definitively plural *Structures sociales du Haut-Atlas* and in contemporary work by Ali Amahan and Hassan Rachik.[6] It is, I think, the resiliency of this diversity that gives Berque his hope, and if we want to essentialize this as Berber, then the widely noted, continual, creative reorganization of Berber life may be related to a range of contemporary phenomena, from the proliferation of "cultural associations" in the Moroccan countryside all the way up to the new, national Institut Royal de la Culture Amazighe (IRCAM).

My intervention here is to suggest more attention to the political economy of these social modalities. Pre-eminently, to my mind, this means attention to household dynamics, the social form Berbers call *tikatin* (sing. *takat*). A *takat* is the most basic economic association in the mountains, but it is also literally a bread oven, and thus resonates well with the French *foyer* or the English "hearth." I would not contend that households are more important than other levels of rural social organization (for instance, lineages, tribes, villages, political parties or newly arising associations of all sorts), but rather that understanding household dynamics is vital to understanding these other social forms and how they operate in the broader political economy of wage labor and state power. I argue that what Nicolas

Michel calls *l'économie de subsistances,* or a subsistence economy, is fundamentally a household affair, and I agree with him that it represents not only an economic mode, but a set of values.[7]

Perhaps this is an artifact of the place where I do my research—a very poor, very labor-intensive mountain agricultural community—where households are the fundamental institution of labor organization, production, and consumption. Contra Bernard Hoffman's classic statement on the matter, households are not "nuclear families."[8] They are instead economic entities, a defined group of people who share labor and divide its rewards. *Tikatin* are generally organized around the production of children, as children are key to rural production, but not all households contain children or even married adults, and thus households should not be reduced to, or saddled with, the Western notion of a "nuclear family." Households contain many differently related people whose distinguishing characteristic is that they pool resources, work together, and divide the rewards. I do not suggest by this a radical empiricism where households exist "out there" for inspection, but as a "theoretical apparatus," households are very "good to think."[9] They have the distinct advantage of being cross-culturally identifiable, and they are obviously important to the rural Berbers I know.

The bad news about this is that our economic understanding of households is rudimentary. Amartya Sen, winner of the 1998 Nobel Prize in economics, writes that "Inequality inside the household is one of resource-use and of the transformation of the used resources into capability to function, and neither class of information is well captured by any devised notion of 'income distribution' within the family."[10] While the focus on "resource use" may be more apposite for non-agricultural, non-subsistence-oriented households, the basic idea that within households people have motivations that cannot be reduced to self-interest confounds liberal economic theory at its core. Economist Deidre McCloskey makes this case in a discussion of free trade. She writes, "Suppose a big part of the economy— say the household—is, as the economists put it, 'distorted' (e.g., suppose people in households do things for love: you can see that the economists have a somewhat peculiar idea of 'distortion'). Then it follows rigorously (that is to say, mathematically) that free trade in *other* sectors (e.g., manufacturing) will *not* be the best thing."[11] Simply put, people do things for their household members that they would not do for strangers. General theories of the reasons strangers exchange goods and labor are irrelevant to the exchanges among household members.[12]

In the Moroccan mountains, households are not "a big part" of the economy, they are the very basis of it. Thus, without taking up the "free trade" part of McCloskey's argument, we can still say that because the rural economy is based in and on households, economic theories devised to understand the changing rural economy are of little use in understanding village-level dynamics. The typically long-term exchanges between different households (within lineages, for instance) amplify the confusion wrought by intra-household exchanges.

This failure to understand the economy of household affection is problematic on many levels, not least because "globalization" happens in villages, that is, villagers live in the places to which the world economy is expanding.[13] While we know perfectly well why international capital seeks new opportunities (profits are motivating), we know very little about why farmers do or do not become workers, why they choose or choose not to become embroiled in the larger economic schema. Part of the answer is surely demographic, and crudely economic; the mountains have for millennia produced more people than the land can support, ensuring that a steady stream of labor flows out of the hills along with the melting snow.

For cultural, agricultural, and economic reasons, the High Atlas is and has long been a demographic pump. But how people flow, who exactly migrates and why, and what sorts of connections migrants retain with the rural economy are much less well understood. This is partly because migration decisions occur in the household context. Thus, because economists do not well understand the curiously tangled, long-term combination of affection and exploitation inherent in household production, and because households are key to demographic growth and migration (among other things), it would seem we have few theoretical tools to understand the articulation between the rural household economy and the larger wage-labor sector.

In this section, I have tried to make the case that Berber social solidarity is grounded fundamentally in the bundle of intimate economic exchanges contained within households. It is households that comprise lineages, villages and tribes, cantons, and notional homelands (*timizar*),[14] households that reproduce the material and cultural order, households that constitute the human bodies on which and through which so much discursive labor is expended. Why households have been relatively ignored in Moroccan scholarship in favor of other social forms is an interesting topic in its own right, but if we are going to assess "hope" for Berbers, or for the Maghrib more generally, if we are going to ponder what can be hoped for in Morocco in the face of global capital expansion, it makes good sense to start by examining how rural households are coping, and how they struggle with the perils and potential of the wage-labor economy and its associated political regimes. One way they cope is by sending their children to the city to work.

Child Labor in Morocco

One cannot deny the horrors associated with child labor in urban Morocco. Droves of homeless children wander Casablanca, many of them runaways from tyrannical bosses and abusive foster families, sniffing tattered rags soaked with industrial glue. As political scientist Abdeslam Maghraoui notes, "in Casablanca, a city of three million people, some 10,000 homeless children fall prey to drug and prostitution rings. By comparison, São Paulo, Brazil, a city of more than 10 million people, has 5,000 homeless children."[15] Many thousands of other "non-homeless" Moroccan children work as beggars, shoeshine boys, touts, carpet makers, agricultural laborers on large farms, and other menial workers. Among the most emotionally wrenching of all child laborers, however, are the girls sent to work in urban households. While difficult to estimate, the practice of hiring child-maids is widespread. There are perhaps 60,000 to 100,000 Moroccan girls between seven and fifteen years old working in households that are not their own.[16] The fact that this work occurs in the affectively charged confines of "the home," the sense of innocence betrayed, and the terrible gulf between servant and served all jolt our sense of justice and familial normalcy and hint at a dark underside to Morocco that few of us wish to contemplate.

BBC reporters mince no words in their report on the topic, painting a picture of endemic social despair reminiscent of Dickens' London:

> "Parents are raising their children for sale," says Bashir Nzaggi, news editor with the respected Moroccan newspaper, *Libération.* "They send them to work in the towns, and never see them except to collect their pay-packets." . . . According to a recent government survey, 2.5 million children aged under 15 drop out of school, and more than half a million work. Many pursue the tradition of toil in the fields. But in exchange for $30 a month (about 15% of a teacher's salary), tens of thousands of parents are now contracting their children to urban families to work as domestic servants in conditions of near slavery. Dealers earn up to $200 per child. It's so institutionalized that kitchens are designed with low counters for child-maids to wash and cut vegetables.[17]

If the BBC writes indignantly about parents colluding with "dealers," industrial child-production, and "near slavery," the Human Rights Internet (which is linked to the United Nations Human Rights System) gives the parents of working girls more credit, suggesting a system that is broken rather than one deliberately promulgating evil. They summarize their report on labor conditions in Morocco with less bombast than the BBC, but with equally clear condemnation:

General points made under the heading "economic exploitation" included the following: The widespread abuse of young girls working as household maids, or *petites bonnes*, is among the most serious problems confronting children; in most cases, these girls—50 percent of whom are below the age of 10—are sent by their families from rural areas to work as maids in houses in the cities; often the parents genuinely believe that they are doing the best for their child; other parents see their daughters as a lucrative source of revenue; often an agreement will have been reached with the future employer that the child will receive a certain number of hours of education each week. The results of various studies of the situation of these girls, however, showed that, for example: in most cases, the work involved is cleaning and general housework, looking after the children and doing the cooking for the whole family; the working day often began before 7:00 AM and did not end until after 11:00 PM; the child's salary was usually US$30/month and was sent directly to the parents; in some cases, parents were not allowed to visit their daughters; others were allowed only one visit per month with parents; some parents only visited their daughter to collect her salary; up to 70 percent of the girls did not receive any education, regardless of the agreements made before the child left her parents; up to 50 percent had no access to medical care.[18]

It is difficult to remain unmoved by such accounts. Even the U.S. Department of Labor concurs, noting that "the Government of Morocco is taking steps to address the country's child labor problem" in a report connected with the establishment of a free trade agreement between the United States and Morocco.[19] This report is an attempt to adhere to the spirit of U.S. laws concerning trade pacts that depend upon the "elimination of the worst forms of child labor."[20] This report mentions "child labor" in the Moroccan context no less than thirty-eight times in twenty-six pages and is deeply depressing to read.

A parallel U.S. Department of Labor Report (also from July 2004), "Laws Governing Exploitative Labor Report—Morocco," is much shorter. It admits there is no "universal definition of exploitative child labor" and seeks only to comment on the "worst forms of child labor" as defined by the International Labor Organization. These include "all forms of slavery," "procuring a child for prostitution," using children for the "production and trafficking in drugs," and work which "by its nature or the circumstances in which it is carried out is likely to harm the health, safety or morals of children."[21] This report is concerned only to make clear that there are relevant laws in Morocco against such outrages, and that the free trade agreement between the United States and Morocco does not transgress norms of the International Labor Organization. Others, including human rights groups and the Moroccan government, take up the task of assessing why these laws are ineffective.[22]

Human rights activists, and specifically child rights groups like Save the Children, place some of the blame on the adoption or foster-parenting of girls, which is seen as a way to lock children into conditions of domestic servitude. Save the Children notes, for instance, that 5.3 percent of girls in urban households were living in situations without any kin present, the presumption being that these girls may be *petites bonnes*.[23] The report suggests that survey methods undercount such situations, however, as unrelated household members are often ignored by the persons completing questionnaires. Overall in this report, the work of the girls in urban homes is explicitly understood as an alternative to education by all parties involved; maids do not expect to be treated as members of the household in which they work.[24]

It would seem that one main difficulty in making sense of child labor is a matter of clarifying the category. Children doing household chores is obviously a different issue than children forced into prostitution or treated as household slaves. However, it is unclear what percentage of child laborers in Morocco, or specifically child-maids, are working under these conditions, how many are suffering extreme forms of degradation, and how many are working under conditions that are actually better than those in the rural world they have left behind. Anglophone anthropology, my own discipline, has made a cottage industry of studying Morocco, but we have not judged or even studied the treatment of children there. We have been very interested in Morocco, but relatively uninterested in the less palatable political or economic features of Moroccan life. Only recently have anthropologists begun to assess human rights travesties and other sensitive issues.[25]

The Moroccan government seems, in fact, ahead of most U.S. scholars. One academic working for the Ministry of Planning produced a report that calls child labor a "taboo topic" and cites work by the Ligue marocaine pour la protection de l'enfance to say that a total of 16 percent of all *petites bonnes* had a deceased father, 5 percent a deceased mother, but fully 72 percent still had living (but presumably impoverished) parents.[26] In other words, according to some accounts, the majority of maids cite their family's poverty as a main reason they are working in the city, but they do not typically refer to the breakdown of their family unit or community. This suggests that the majority of child-maids remain economically embedded in, and even vital to, rural households. Clearly we must look to the dynamics of rural households to understand children's urban wage labor.[27]

Down to the Cemetery, Down to the City

In the village where I have done most of my research, there is a morbid vein of humor that involves a play on the word "city" (medina or *lmdint*), which is also sometimes used for "cemetery."[28] There is, in other words, a certain death in the city, as you leave the living body of the natal community and exist among strangers in a social vacuum. Still, the city is attractive to some. Young men explain to me that they would not mind spending part of the year in the city (especially the cold winter months), and many young women would be very happy to find an employed urban husband who could deliver them from the drudgery of rural labor. Some claim they would prefer to work in urban households than in their own rural setting. The sentiments held by the rural young are relatively unimportant, however. A young person does not decide to go to the city any more than she decides when it is time to die; young people go to the city when they are sent to the city: when fate, or their father, decrees.

Whether a young person is sent to the city depends upon the decision of the household patriarch, and this decision is based on the condition of the household economy. Surely everyone who sends a daughter out of the mountains to work is "poor" by Western standards, but rural poverty is more complicated than urbanites tend to assume. An example of the migrant girls in two households should make this clear.

We should note at the outset that it is quite normal for children to move between villages through networks of female kin. As most girls marry out of their natal lineages and villages, women come to have relations spread across the rural landscape. In summers, women especially go home to visit, or move through the mountains to vacation with their mothers' relatives, married sisters, and so forth. Children commonly accompany their mothers, and sometimes children are left behind, exchanged between households for periods of time. Since rural children (and especially girls) work for whatever household they live in, we can say that prior to integration with the wage labor economy, rural children are already quite frequently "economic migrants." Yet the crucial role of women and children in the village economy, and specifically the role of women's social networks, is strikingly absent from the classic Moroccan anthropological literature, especially the debates on social solidarity.[29]

Household #1

Omar and Khadija are unusual in the village of Tadrar in that they maintain their own household even though Omar's father is still alive.[30] Normally, because sons do not inherit land until the death of the patriarch and women receive half the land that their brothers do, couples cannot form independent households until the death of a patriarch and the subsequent division of land. Couples may live in a different house, but they remain part of the extended patriarchal household, an economic unit grounded (literally) in rights to irrigated land. Boys and men owe their fathers labor so long as the father is alive, and married women, through their husbands, owe their labor to this same household.

However, Omar has managed to circumvent this in part by working in the city out of season (and returning to work with his brother for his father during peak agricultural periods) and by sending his daughters to work in the city. He has built his own house and is largely separated from his father's support and from economic obligations to him.

Omar's oldest daughter, Fatim, works in Casablanca as a maid and previously worked in Agadir. The next oldest, Naima, remains in the village to assist her mother with the younger children and to help with the household. The next oldest daughter, Mina, began work in Marrakesh as a maid in 1999, and her younger sister Fatima began working in Marrakesh in 2002. Malika, Najat, and the youngest boy, Lahcen, all live in the village.

It was very difficult for me (as a male, an outsider, and a nominal Christian) to interview these women. During my research in 1998–1999, I was single and understood to be wealthy, and this made me a frequent object of marriage negotiations and made interviews with unmarried women awkward. Compounding the difficulty was the sensitive nature of the topic of sending young girls to the city. Omar was certainly not proud of sending his children away. When visiting, the girls seemed to have visibly warm relationships with their family. It has to be a tough decision to send a child away to work, but the reason is not a blanket state of "poverty" or disregard for children. Instead, the long-term dynamics of households (Omar's father still being alive) and demographics (Omar's household has too many girls for the needs of the household) shape who migrates, when, and why. The most sensible way in which the girls can contribute to Omar's household is to work for wages. Contributing to the household is utterly sensible to these girls.

The normalcy of rural girls accepting work in the city is borne out in other studies. In a study of migration, Sommerfelt writes, "in surprisingly many cases . . . girls not only claimed to want to go working in town, but also pushed their parents or siblings to find them a job as a maid in town . . ."[31] These researchers spoke with a young woman who had returned from the city (she worked in Tangier from age six to age seventeen) who decided to return to the village because she wished to help her ailing mother. The timing of the return was facilitated by the fact that three other younger sisters had found work in the city and were sending wages home. Households are built of long-term exchanges of obligation and labor, and short-term wage labor is integrated into these longer cycles.

Household #2

Culturally valued fidelity to a household does not prevent girls from breaking away, however. Young women do not typically pursue "independence" like young men do, by heading off to work and then establishing their own households. Instead, girls seek to find work in the city and thereby to arrange their own marriages, to link themselves to a male wage laborer and establish a household where they can raise children of their own. Young women typically accomplish this with the help of other (usually female) relatives in the city. Again, I am privy to only bits of these transactions as they tend to take place outside the village (where I did almost no research) and among women (with whom my interactions were limited, especially in the case of unmarried women).

The case of Muhammed is illustrative. He has one of the largest families in the village—nine girls and five boys in my 1999 census—at least partly because he has more land than anyone else. As the sole heir of one of the main sub-lineages of the most powerful *ikhs*, or "bone" in the village, Muhammed is, on paper at least, one of the wealthiest men in the community. He is ranked second of twenty-nine households in the village in terms of the amount of irrigation time he controls, with three times the village median irrigation time, and six times that of the poorest households. Access to irrigation water is not the only important economic factor, but it is well correlated with land ownership and thus to general economic well-being.[32]

Muhammed has not been blessed with easy demographics, however. His five oldest children are all girls, and cannot be used for male agricultural work. While this is a good household in which to be a woman (i.e., there are many women to share the labor), it is hard to find a way to put so much female labor to work in the village context, even with a surfeit of agricultural land. By 1999 Muhammed had sent three of his girls to work in the city: Fatima to Casablanca, Kabira and Zahra to Marrakesh. All wages returned to the rural household. I only spoke to one of these young women when she visited the village, but she seemed happy enough. She was an eager participant in water fights with the village boys, and evinced little passion over her urban work, positive or negative.

However, by 2004 this young woman and her two urbanized sisters were all married to men in the city, depriving Muhammed of income even as the new brides extended their family's social network out in space. Muhammed then sent another daughter to the city to work, Zaina, and sent his oldest son to study in the city, specifically to live with the oldest daughter and her new husband (both now living in Marrakesh). Muhammed is thus continuing to put his "extra" daughters to work, and is depriving himself of male agricultural labor (a son finally old enough to help with irrigation) in order to better prepare someone in the household for the future. It is clear that Muhammed thinks of girls' labor differently than boys': girls work for their mother on women's chores, while boys work directly for Muhammed. The fact that Muhammed is willing to make his daily life more difficult by sending away an able-bodied boy is evidence that Muhammed is not lazy or selfish. At least from his perspective, he is preparing his household for the future by educating one member of it and putting the rest of the household labor resources to use as best he can. At the same time, the children, too, are doing their part to work for more secure futures. Five of Muhammed's children now live in Marrakesh, forming a kind of urban network of rural-born offspring who provide support for one another and for their rural household.

Importantly, Muhammed's children are not in the city because they are "poor" by village standards. Most of the girls were sent for demographic reasons—there was nothing for so many girls to do despite the material resources the household controlled. The girls quickly found husbands and established connections for others to follow. They even made it possible for their brother to get an urban education, ensuring that someone in their family might garner some literacy that could help the rest of them cope with the expanding bureaucracy of the state. These two cases serve to illustrate the point that "poverty" is not a simple cause of migration and child labor in the cities and that rural households creatively engage with the changing economic landscape of Morocco.

The World That Would Be Left Behind

To better make sense of these two cases, and of the trauma and potential of wage labor for girls, it is necessary to understand the lives girls might want to escape, the working lives of rural Berber women today. For this I turn to the words of Rqia and her husband Brahim as they describe work in the village of Tadrar. Rqia was born outside of Tadrar, like 80 percent of the women in this village, and moved to Tadrar to live with her husband upon marriage. At the time of the interview, the couple had one married daughter living in Rabat and two married in the village. Their oldest son was not married, and their youngest son was but a small boy. This means that Brahim had at least one older boy to help him (and even the little boy could do some things), while Rqia was left alone to handle the feminine labor of the household. Brahim has reached "old age," when he can begin to relax and let his son work for him; Rqia is not quite there, still waiting for her husband to bring her son a wife, a young woman in the household to relieve Rqia of some of the more arduous labor. We taped the interview in October of 1998.[33]

David: What's your name?

Rqia: Rqia. Rqia Hussein Ait O. from A.

David: From A [her natal village]?

Rqia: A.

David: Your *aṣl* [origins] are in A?

Rqia: A.

David: Do you want to talk about women's lives?

Rqia: Yeah. Women. You want to speak about women's lives in [Tadrar]. Yes. We go to the mountains to bring wood and fodder. We come back and light the ovens, we make bread and put it in the ovens, we milk cows. We make lunch. We do everything like that. We go to fetch water. We go to the river and wash clothes. Everything like this we do. And we prepare wool. We wash wool and card it. We put it on the loom and work on it. Like this women work. They bring fodder for the cows, and give it to them. We milk them and if there is a calf we take him to his mother for some milk. We give them food. We wash dishes, sweep, and shake out the blankets. We fold up the carpets and take them out in the sun to get rid of the bedbugs, if there are any. We feed the chickens and rabbits, if we have any. That's all we do. We go up there, and come back. They spend their whole day moving.

David: Moving.

Rqia: Yeah, moving around. To the mountains for wood and fodder for the animals. They bring *aouri* (shrub) and they give it to cows to eat. They prepare something to eat for themselves, they eat it . . . They go to the fields to bring the cows something to eat, so we can milk her. Because if you don't give them any fodder, they won't give you any milk. They come back and prepare dinner. They churn buttermilk . . .

[Her small son chimes in: they churn buttermilk . . .]

Rqia: They eat a little butter and a little buttermilk. They stir a little *tagoula* (a soupy curdled milk porridge). They prepare *bddaz* (corn flour porridge). They prepare couscous, bread, press it in the ovens when they're hot. They sweep the kitchen, wash the pots, wash the serving dishes, and they take the refuse from the cooking area and throw it out. They carry it in bags and take it far from the house, so that it won't come back in. Everything they do is like this.

David: Is the life of women harder than men's life, or easier?

Rqia: Oh no, women's lives are harder than men's [laughter]. Their activities (*tizla*, "rushing about") are harder. They go to the mountains for wood and bring food for the cows. When they come in the late afternoon, they light the ovens and prepare food. Men, when they come back from the fields, they "take off their belts" and go to pray. After prayers, they say to women, "what have you done, have you prepared lunch or something to eat? You haven't prepared anything?" [laughter]. You have not prepared anything!? I am rushing around, but I have not done anything! The oven does not want to light. The wood does not want to light. Like this . . . men, their job is easy and nearby. Women, it's hard. They spend the whole day rushing, from morning to night.

David: Until afternoon? Until night?

Rqia: Until night, then they can rest. At first light they get up again, and they start hurrying around. And men, they have a little job. They don't have lots to do. Right?

David: Yeah . . . [addressing her husband] Do you know it's like this?

Brahim: Huh?

Rqia: He said to you, do you know that this is true or not?

Brahim: Oh yes!

Rqia: [To David] Have you seen? [laughter]

Brahim: Women of the mountains are always like this, always, always. They bring kindling from the forest. *Aouri* from the forest. They carry it on their backs. Then they take their sickle to the fields, and they gather fodder. They bundle it . . .

Rqia: We put it here [indicating on her back]

Brahim: They carry it on their backs . . .

Rqia: *Hba* (things carried on the back, whether babies, fodder, or wood) . . . here [indicating her back].

Brahim: . . . when they arrive, they parcel it out to the cows, and they go to see if there is any *asskif* (barley porridge) to drink. If there is none, they light the oven. This is what they do until ten at night. At ten they go to bed. And she gets up at four and goes to the oven. She makes coffee, she makes *asskif.* She prepares food for the children, and they eat it. She takes her rope [to carry the bundles of wood] to the mountains. To bring wood to make fire. After, when she brings the wood, she comes down and eats a little. She takes her basket to the river to bring fodder for the cows. She feeds the cows, and she makes lunch. She feeds the children and she takes grain to grind in the river. [There was at this time a water-powered mill wheel in the river.] She makes *tagoula* for the children.

David: Phew . . .

Brahim: That's all. She does not rest. Never, never.

David: Never.

Brahim: When she finishes one thing, another thing comes . . . Men, no. When they irrigate and plough the plots, they go up to the fields. They come back and sit. That's all their job. That's all.

David: That's all?

Brahim: That's all their job.

Ten days before this, I had interviewed Brahim and Rqia's daughter Fatima. Fatima had moved to the city after she divorced her first husband, her patrilateral parallel cousin. She lived with her sister for some time in Rabat before returning to Tadrar to marry her present husband. Like her mother, Fatima gave a long, passionate, and gruelingly detailed iteration of the difficulties of women's labor, how it changed from season to season, including everything from the leaking mud roofs to the agonies of child-birth and the all too common death of babies and infants. Part of the inter-view repeated Rqia's recounting of the unequal sexual division of labor, but Fatima seemed to take great pride in being able to do more work than a man, in being able to carry more on her back and work more hours, in being able care for her family in the harsh conditions of a mountain agri-cultural community. Then I asked her:

David: Do you think life in the city is easier?
Fatima: Life in the city is easy, because I have seen it. Life in the city, you find a job, you will work there and your children will go to school. Women work, and men. Some might work in a factory. Men, God knows, in whatever he finds he can work in the city. But in the mountains, there is no work. Only wood, fields, that's all. That's all the [paying] work in the mountains. But life in the city is nice (tshwa).

From these interviews it might seem that any woman would want to move to the city, and any man would be reluctant to do so. This is not en-tirely accurate, however. Rqia, Brahim, and Fatima deemphasized the ben-efits of village life (the safety and security of living among people you have known a lifetime, making a living in ways that are difficult but at least reli-able) and expounded on the benefits of urban life. But Fatima came back to the village, and Brahim has never discussed taking his household to the city no matter how vehemently Rqia drives home the unfairness of women's fate. These interviews were done at a time when Brahim had one grown son at home, a son who did most of the family's male-gendered labor and left his father to "take off his belt" and just sit, as Rqia said. It is not surpris-ing that Brahim found mountain life agreeable; he was a leisured, proper-tied patriarch. By 2004, when his son had married and the new bride was brought into the household, Rqia's life eased some. Rqia became more in-volved with raising her granddaughter while her teenage daughter-in-law took over some of the heavy labor of wood, fodder, and grain transport.

Fatima's opinion of city life is based on the situation of her sister, who is married to a man with a job and whose children are in school. This is ob-viously "nice" compared to the women's labor in the village. Fatima did not suggest that she wanted to go look for a job, however, or that she could find one, or that her husband should; only that a good life could be had in the city, that city life was "nice." Years later, Fatima tried sending her oldest son to the city to live with her sister so that he could go to school. The ex-periment failed, however, as the boy became homesick and did not easily learn Arabic. He did poorly in school, and wanted to come home. Fatima mused that some of her younger children might some day go to live in the city and tap into some of the resources available there. However, in order to support their parents, some children must stay in the village and endure the hardships of rural life. Others will necessarily go down to the city, to the "cemetery." It is unclear which is preferable.

Conclusion

Child abuse is obviously and rightfully upsetting, but child labor is not necessarily child abuse. In rural Morocco all children work from a very young age. Girls as young as four can be depended upon to care for younger children, carry wood and water, and clean house; boys will start to irrigate and tend goats well before they are teenagers. This is common throughout the continent, indeed throughout the Global South.[34] It should not be surprising to us that as rural Morocco becomes increasingly articulated with the urban, wage labor economy, different values and understandings of child labor come into conflict. Urban scholars and bureaucrats studying labor sometimes choose to ignore children's work, but most dwell on it as a moral wrong that can and ought to be ameliorated. I am sympathetic to this position, but it is not without logical as well as practical problems.[35]

In the mountains the alternative to working in the city is not usually school, but working in the village. Girls are sent to the city when their labor cannot be put to productive use in their household, or in a related household. It is true that many rural parents do not value education in the same way that urban, middle-class parents do, but this is not necessarily shortsighted. It is not obvious that rural girls stand a better chance of long-term personal fulfillment or improved employment options by going to school than they do by working. While education is obviously desirable for many people for many reasons, the opportunity costs of education are easily overlooked. Education for all is a worthy ideal, but from the perspective of rural Moroccans it is not a pragmatic alternative for many children today.

A survey of the literature suggests two main ways that scholars explain the migration of children in Morocco: they are victimized by "bad" parents who selfishly exploit them, or they suffer because they have "poor" parents who are forced to forsake parental love for some small amount of money. I have made the case that this is too simple. High Atlas children all "work" in the village—within and outside the home—and this does not make parents ignorant, bad, or even especially poor. The many years of grueling education suffered by middle-class children around the world might be seen as at least as cruel by some mountain observers. The precariousness of a mountain farming life is indeed the primary issue, but the "poverty" of such lives is more complicated than simple lack of income. Poverty relates as much to demography and the gendered dynamics of labor as it does to a paucity of property and the vagaries of the weather.

Today, one of the primary terms rural Moroccans use to understand their condition is *maskin* (poor), even in cases where material conditions have evidently improved. Rural poverty is thus both an absolute condition (no medicine, no money, no shoes, no potable water) and a comparative assessment born of an understanding of what other (urban) people have. Rural people attempt to deal with their poverty as households, employing the cultural values inherent in the household economy. They are not socially atomized by the fissiparous allure of Capital, but sustain themselves by incorporating wages into their household bodies; they continue to reproduce these fundamental units through larger lineage and village forms of community, through inter-household and village-wide labor exchanges.[36] The clearheaded grasp rural Berbers have of their position at the bottom of the global economy, and the institutional organization of households as a way of dealing with that position, are key to making sense of child labor and to making ironic sense of it as somehow "hopeful."

Crucially, girls slaving away for long hours and little money are working for someone else, not themselves. Sometimes, of course, these working children are evidence of a breakdown in social solidarity, the kind of anomie Durkheim feared. Some girls are indeed exploited by people who have no interest in the girl, and in whom the girl has no interest. One urban woman who claims to have hired over a hundred rural girls says explicitly of the parents, "They are not *so poor*, these people have lost their sense of family solidarity."[37] Clearly, this woman sees the child labor problem as a problem of greedy parents, as evidence of a breakdown in social solidarity, an erosion of traditional values.

This may be so. Many girls have evidently suffered a "loss of solidarity," though the evidence suggests they are typically orphans or others whose kin networks have frayed or dissolved.[38] The middle-class employer's understanding of "solidarity" focuses on parents providing for children; in the mountains, however, family solidarity involves children providing for parents. All of the children I know from Tadrar who work in the city do so precisely because powerful forms of social solidarity remain intact. In other words, working children can be a product of a breakdown of solidarity, but they can just as well be working because of an intense loyalty to others, loyalty to forms of solidarity like the patriarchal household. The latter case, it seems to me, is the kind of "solidarity" we can hope for in the contemporary Maghrib, and it suggests we rethink the "romance of community" as something outside and opposing Capital, to something integral to it. Following Miranda Joseph, scholars might profitably ask: Why do we believe solidarity to be necessarily a good thing, and exactly what kinds of solidarity are worth admiring?[39]

Our discomfort with working children is an artifact of our discomfort with the increasingly polarized nature of our contemporary world economy.[40] I want to make clear that I am absolutely in favor of all children receiving an education, and on principle I am opposed to drudgery, but I also want to make clear that such framings of the nightmare of child wage labor emerge from my own comfortable urban existence. Those Berbers actually engaged in the contemporary rural economy and who endure the physical hardship of agricultural life see things differently. To "drop out of school" one would have to go to school (and many rural children do not), for school to be beneficial it would have to pay off in some way (and it often does not), to have a discrete "working day" requires some distinction between work life and home life (there is none for rural girls), and "toiling" in the fields is what all rural boys do all their lives, day in and day out. Everyone agrees rural life is "hard" (*ishqa*), but that does not mean it is miserable or abusive.

Berber households—now sustained through wage labor of every imaginable kind—continue to form the bedrock of thriving, or at least surviving, rural communities. Berber children remain loyal to social modalities geared to the long-term, terminal trajectory of human life. Household solidarity allows for the modest hope that at the end of long lives of unremitting and sometimes brutal labor, one can rest and die among family, in relative comfort. Whether this is hopeful solidarity, or simply the best that can be hoped for, remains a troubling and open question.

Notes

I take the first part of the chapter title from Homi Bhabha, *The Location of Culture* (London: Routeledge, 1994), xxv. I should acknowledge the incisive comments I received on earlier drafts of this paper from members of the colloquium organized at Harvard University by Katherine Hoffman and Susan Gilson Miller. In addition to the conference organizers, I am particularly indebted to Susan Slyomovics and Hillary Haldane.

1. Jacques Berque, *French North Africa: The Maghrib between Two World Wars*, trans. Jean Stewart (New York: Praeger, 1967), 218.

2. Jane E. Goodman, *Berber Culture on the World Stage: From Village to Video* (Bloomington: Indiana University Press, 2005), 69.

3. Paul A. Silverstein, *Algeria in France: Transpolitics, Race, and Nation* (Bloomington: Indiana University Press, 2004).

4. Ernest Gellner, *Saints of the Atlas* (London: Weidenfeld and Nicholson, 1969), 64.

5. Robert Montagne, *The Berbers*, trans. David Seddon (London: Frank Cass., 1973).

6. Ali Amahan, *Mutations sociales dans le Haut Atlas: les Ghoujdama* (Paris: Éditions de la maison des sciences de l'homme, 1998); Hassan Rachik, *Sacré et sacrifice dans le Haut Atlas marocain* (Casablanca: Afrique Orient, 1990); and Rachik, *Le sultan des autres: rituel et politique dans le Haut Atlas* (Casablanca: Afrique Orient, 1992). I make a general case for regional variation in "Berber" social organization in David Crawford, "Royal Interest in Local Culture: The Politics and Potential of Morocco's Imazighen" in *Nationalism and Minority Identities in Islamic Societies*, ed. Maya Shatzmiller (Montreal: McGill-Queens Press, 2005), 164–194.

7. Nicolas Michel, *Une économie de subsistances: le Maroc précolonial* (Cairo: Institut français d'archéologie orientale, 1997), 3.

8. Bernard G. Hoffman, *The Structure of Traditional Moroccan Society* (Paris and The Hague: Mouton and Co., 1967), 46.

9. Michel-Rolph Trouillot, "The Anthropology of the State in the Age of Globalization," *Current Anthropology* 42(1) (2001): 125–138.

10. Amartya Sen, *Inequality Reexamined*, 6th ed. (Cambridge: Harvard University Press, 1992), 122–123.

11. Deirdre McCloskey, *The Secret Sins of Economics* (Chicago: Prickly Paradigm Press, 2002), 17. Emphasis in the original.

12. For a few recent examples, see Homa Hoodfar, *Between Marriage and the Market: Intimate Politics and Survival in Cairo* (Berkeley: University of California Press, 1997); Martha Mundy, *Domestic Government: Kinship, Community and Polity in North Yemen* (London: I.B. Tauris, 1995); and Diane Singerman and Homa Hoodfar, *Development, Change, and Gender in Cairo: A View from the Household* (Bloomington: Indiana University Press, 1996).

13. For a critical understanding of the term "globalization," see Michel-Rolph Trouillot, "The Anthropology of the State in the Age of Globalization: Close Encounters of the Deceptive Kind," *Current Anthropology* 42(1) (2001): 125–138. I do not mean a "world without boundaries," but a world where new sorts of connections are impacting rural Moroccan life in new ways. Primarily, here, we are talking about circular migration for low-paid wage labor.

14. Katherine Hoffman, "Moving and Dwelling: Building the Moroccan Ashelhi Homeland," *American Ethnologist* 29(4) (2002): 928–962.

15. Abdeslam Maghraoui, "Political Authority in Crisis," *Middle East Report* no. 218 (2001): 16.

16. Mehdi Lahlou, "Child Labour in Morocco: The Socio-economic Background of the 'Little Maids' Phenomenon." http://www.araburban.org/childcity/Papers/English/Lahlou%20Morocco.pdf, 6 (accessed Nov. 10, 2005).

17. Nick Pelham, "Street Life," BBC World Service, Jul. 1, 2000. http://www.bbc.co.uk/worldservice/people/highlights/streetlife.shtml (accessed Oct. 18, 2005).

18. Human Rights Internet/The United Nations Human Rights System, "Thematic Reports: Morocco." http://www.hri.ca/fortherecord2001/engtext/vol2eng/moroccotr.htm (accessed Nov. 11, 2005).

19. U.S. Department of Labor, Bureau of International Labor Affairs, "Morocco Labor Rights Report," 2004: 19.

20. Lahlou, "Child Labour in Morocco," 3.

21. U.S. Department of Labor, Bureau of International Labor Affairs, "Laws Governing Exploitative Child Labor Report," 2004, 3–4.

22. Lahlou, "Child Labour in Morocco." In his related report, Lahlou writes that the existing labor laws in Morocco are not adhered to and do not give strong protection. See Tone Sommerfelt, ed., *Domestic Child Labour in Morocco* (Norway: FAFO Institute for Applied Social Science, 2001), 78.

23. Jon Pedersen, "The Demography of *Petites Bonnes* in Morocco," in *Domestic Child Labour in Morocco*, ed. Tone Sommerfelt (Norway: FAFO Institute for Applied Social Science, 2001), 17.

24. Sommerfelt, *Domestic Child Labour in Morocco*, 38.

25. Susan Slyomovics, *The Performance of Human Rights in Morocco* (Philadelphia: University of Pennsylvania Press, 2005).

26. Lahlou, "Child Labour." The author of this report is located in the "Ministry of Planning," presumably of Morocco, and this report provides much of the basis for Sommerfelt, *Domestic Child Labour in Morocco*.

27. Chakib Guessous, *L'exploitation de l'innocence: le travail des enfants au Maroc* (Casablanca: Éditions EDDIF, 2002). The statistical dimensions of rural children's urban labor remain poorly understood, and even basic causes of the phenomenon need more sociological research. Here I rely on anecdotal evidence, interviews in one particular village, and government statistics. Further research is in progress.

28. See Hoffman, "Moving and Dwelling," for another example.

29. This depends on what parts of the vast corpus of writing on Morocco one considers "classic." There has been important recent work on the significance of women and households in Moroccan society. See Aïcha Belarbi, *Femmes rurales* (Casablanca: Fennec, 1996); Mounira Charrad, Rahma Bourqia, and Nancy Gallagher, *Femmes, culture et société au Maghreb*, 2 vols. (Casablanca: Afrique Orient, 1996); David Crawford, "Making Imazighen: Rural Berber Women, Household Organization, and the Production of Free Men," in *North African Mosaic*, ed. Nabil Boudraa and Joseph Kraus (Cambridge: Cambridge Scholars Press, 2007), 329–346; Monique Gadant and Michèle Kasriel, eds., *Femmes du Maghreb au présent: la dot, le travail, l'identité*, 2nd ed. (Paris: Éditions CNRS, 1992); Hoffman, "Moving and Dwelling"; Deborah A. Kapchan, *Gender on the Market: Moroccan Women and the Revoicing of Tradition* (Philadelphia: University of Pennsylvania Press, 1996); Michèle Kasriel, *Libres femmes du Haut Atlas? Dynamique d'une micro-société au Maroc* (Paris: L'Harmattan, 1989); and Tourya Temsamani, "La femme rurale au Maroc: une bibliographie annotée," in *Femmes rurales*, ed. Aïcha Belarbi (Casablanca: Fennec, 1996), 25–43.

30. All names herein are pseudonyms.

31. Sommerfelt, *Domestic Child Labour in Morocco*, 43.

32. David Crawford, "Work and Identity in the Moroccan High Atlas" (Ph.D. diss., University of California, Santa Barbara, 2001), 293.

33. Translations of these taped interviews were done by Latifa Asseffar, whom I thank for this, as well as for her insightful commentaries on all things Ashelhi.

34. Anne Kielland and Maurizia C. Tovo, *Children at Work: Child Labor Practices in Africa* (Boulder, Colo.: Lynne Rienner, 2006).

35. Global Workforce in Transition (GWIT) Indefinite Quantity Contract, "Morocco Workforce Development Assessment," USAID contract GDG-1-00-02-00003-00, May 20, 2003. This study was intended to assess the impact of the now-completed free trade agreement between the United States and Morocco. It mentions child labor exactly once. A "professional training official" interviewed for the report refused to take children in his program because he "will be accused of encouraging child labor" (p. 25). Beyond this, we read nothing about the topic. Child labor evidently did not fit any

of the sub-headings, including sections on "Analysis of Morocco's Skills and Labor Markets," "Analysis of Morocco's Education and Training System," and a "USAID/ Morocco Workforce Development Strategy."

36. David Crawford, "Arranging the Bones: Culture, Time, and In/equality in Berber Labor Organization," *Ethnos* 68(4) (2003): 463–486.

37. Sommerfelt, *Domestic Child Labour in Morocco*, 48. Emphasis in the original.

38. Work on homelessness in the United States suggests that a breakdown of kin networks is universally a precursor to social ills like homelessness (in New York City) or the *petites bonnes* phenomenon in Morocco. See Kim Hopper, *Reckoning with Homelessness* (Ithaca, N.Y.: Cornell University Press, 2002).

39. Miranda Joseph, *Against the Romance of Community* (Minneapolis: University of Minnesota Press, 2002).

40. See Bernard Rosenberger, *Société, pouvoir et alimentation: nourriture et précarité au Maroc précolonial* (Rabat: Alizés, 2001); Michel, *Une économie de subsistances*; and B. A. Mojuetan, *History and Underdevelopment in Morocco: The Structural Roots of Conjuncture* (London: International African Institute, 1995). Rosenberger and Michel give some idea how precarious the rural economy is and has been, at least since the nineteenth century. Mojuetan and Rosenberger both discuss the interlocking trajectories of Morocco and Europe, with the former sliding into penury, and the latter rising to become economically dominant.

Bibliography

Amahan, Ali. *Mutations sociales dans le Haut Atlas: les Ghourjdama*. Paris: Éditions de la maison des sciences de l'homme, 1998.

Belarbi, Aïcha. *Femmes rurales*. Casablanca: Fennec, 1996.

Berque, Jacques. *French North Africa: The Maghrib between Two World Wars*, trans. Jean Stewart. New York: Praeger, 1967.

Bhabha, Homi. *The Location of Culture*. London: Routledge, 1994.

Charrad, Mounira, Rahma Bourqia, and Nancy Gallagher. *Femmes, culture et société au Maghreb*. 2 vols. Casablanca: Afrique Orient, 1996.

Crawford, David. "Arranging the Bones: Culture, Time, and In/equality in Berber Labor Organization." *Ethnos* 68(4) (2003): 463–486.

——. "Making Imazighen: Rural Berber Women, Household Organization, and the Production of Free Men." In *North African Mosaic*, ed. Nabil Boudraa and Joseph Kraus. Cambridge: Cambridge Scholars Press, 2007.

——. "Royal Interest in Local Culture: The Politics and Potential of Morocco's Imazighen." In *Nationalism and Minority Identities in Islamic Societies*, ed. Maya Shatzmiller. Montreal: McGill-Queens Press, 2005.

Gadant, Monique, and Michèle Kasriel, eds. *Femmes du Maghreb au présent: la dot, le travail, l'identité*. Paris: Éditions du Centre nationale de la recherche scientifique, 1992.

Gellner, Ernest. *Saints of the Atlas*. London: Weidenfeld and Nicholson, 1969.

Global Workforce in Transition (GWIT) IQC, "Morocco Workforce Development Assessment," USAID contract GDG-1-00-02-00003-00, May 20, 2003.

Goodman, Jane E. *Berber Culture on the World Stage: From Village to Video*. Bloomington: Indiana University Press, 2005.

Guessous, Chakib. *L'exploitation de l'innocence: le travail des enfants au Maroc*. Casablanca: Éditions EDDIF, 2002.

Hoffman, Bernard G. *The Structure of Traditional Moroccan Society.* Paris and The Hague: Mouton and Co., 1967.

Hoffman, Katherine. "Moving and Dwelling: Building the Moroccan Ashelhi Homeland." *American Ethnologist* 29(4) (2002): 928–962.

Hoodfar, Homa. *Between Marriage and the Market: Intimate Politics and Survival in Cairo.* Berkeley: University of California Press, 1997.

Hopper, Kim. *Reckoning with Homelessness.* Ithaca, N.Y.: Cornell University Press, 2002.

Human Rights Internet/The United Nations Human Rights System, "Thematic Reports: Morocco." http://www.hri.ca/fortherecord2001/engtext/vol2eng/moroccotr .htm (accessed Nov. 11, 2005).

Joseph, Miranda. *Against the Romance of Community.* Minneapolis: University of Minnesota Press, 2002.

Kapchan, Deborah A. *Gender on the Market: Moroccan Women and the Revoicing of Tradition.* Philadelphia: University of Pennsylvania Press, 1996.

Kasriel, Michèle. *Libres femmes du Haut Atlas? Dynamique d'une micro-société au Maroc.* Paris: L'Harmattan, 1989.

Kielland, Anne, and Maurizia C. Tovo. *Children at Work: Child Labor Practices in Africa.* Boulder, Colo.: Lynne Rienner, 2006.

Lahlou, Mehdi. "Child Labour in Morocco: The Socio-economic Background of the 'Little Maids' Phenomenon." http://www.araburban.org/childcity/Papers/English/ Lahlou%20Morocco.pdf (accessed Nov. 10, 2005).

Maghraoui, Abdeslam. "Political Authority in Crisis." *Middle East Report* no. 218 (2001): 16.

McCloskey, Deirdre. *The Secret Sins of Economics.* Chicago: Prickly Paradigm Press, 2002.

Michel, Nicolas. *Une économie de subsistances: le Maroc précolonial.* Cairo: Institut français d'archéologie orientale, 1997.

Mojuetan, B. A. *History and Underdevelopment in Morocco: The Structural Roots of Conjuncture.* London: International African Institute, 1995.

Montagne, Robert. *The Berbers,* trans. David Seddon. London: Frank Cass, 1973.

Mundy, Martha. *Domestic Government: Kinship, Community and Polity in North Yemen.* London: I.B. Tauris, 1995.

Pedersen, Jon. "The Demography of *Petites Bonnes* in Morocco." In *Domestic Child Labour in Morocco,* ed. Tone Sommerfelt. Norway: FAFO Institute for Applied Social Science, 2001.

Pelham, Nick. "Street Life." BBC World Service, Jul. 1, 2000. http://www.bbc.co.uk/ worldservice/people/highlights/streetlife.shtml (accessed Oct. 18, 2005).

Rachik, Hassan. *Le sultan des autres: rituel et politique dans le Haut Atlas.* Casablanca: Afrique Orient, 1992.

———. *Sacré et sacrifice dans le Haut Atlas marocain.* Casablanca: Afrique Orient, 1990.

Rosenberger, Bernard. *Société, pouvoir et alimentation: nourriture et précarité au Maroc précolonial.* Rabat: Alizés, 2001.

Sen, Amartya. *Inequality Reexamined.* Cambridge: Harvard University Press, 1992.

Silverstein, Paul A. *Algeria in France: Transpolitics, Race, and Nation.* Bloomington: Indiana University Press, 2004.

Singerman, Diane, and Homa Hoodfar. *Development, Change, and Gender in Cairo: A View from the Household.* Bloomington: Indiana University Press, 1996.

Slyomovics, Susan. *The Performance of Human Rights in Morocco.* Philadelphia: University of Pennsylvania Press, 2005.

Sommerfelt, Tone. *Domestic Child Labour in Morocco.* Norway: FAFO Institute for Applied Social Science, 2001.

Temsamani, Tourya. "La femme rurale au Maroc: une bibliographie annotée." In *Femmes rurales*, ed. Aïcha Belarbi. Casablanca: Fennec, 1996.

Trouillot, Michel-Rolph. "The Anthropology of the State in the Age of Globalization." *Current Anthropology* 42(1) (2001): 125–138.

U.S. Department of Labor, Bureau of International Labor Affairs. "Laws Governing Exploitative Child Labor Report," 2004.

U.S. Department of Labor, Bureau of International Labor Affairs. "Morocco Labor Rights Report," 2004.

PART 3

VARIETIES OF

REPRESENTATION

7

The "Numidian" Origins of North Africa

Mokhtar Ghambou

The so-called "Berber Renaissance" of the early 1990s inspired Berber scholars and activists to write their own history, regardless of whether they were professional historians. After all, a cultural revival is a collective project whereby every active member of the marginalized community becomes engaged with the basic issues of origins, history, and memory. For Berber advocates, the problem is less about expertise than about sources. How can Berbers reconstruct their history without relying upon the very texts that deny their existence as a distinct cultural group? The challenge is typical for all minority groups with no textual legacy they can claim as their own. Part of the solution can be found in orality, whose referential power is valorized by many postcolonial theorists.[1] But in Islamic North Africa, the reliance on oral sources might be a poor strategy if the main purpose is to contest the dominant discourse from within. Islamic scholars as well as Arab nationalists still hold the written word (*al-maktub*) as too sacred to be seduced by oral sources.

The solution offered by Berber scholars develops as a compromise: they fully respect the rules of *al-maktub* although the texts they use to rewrite their history are alien to North African traditions. More explicitly, they turn to Greek and Roman texts of antiquity to secure material "venerable" enough to challenge the "holiness" of Islamic or Arab hermeneutics. But what do these alien texts, made accessible through French translations,[2] actually tell us about pre-Islamic North Africa? How and why do Berber scholars read them? I will address the second question, as it allows us to understand the modern context within which Berber scholars have resurrected ancient texts and used them as valid sources for writing the pre-Islamic past of North Africa.

Retrieving the Pre-Islamic Past through Greek and Roman Texts

Even if the wide circulation of texts across time and space is no longer an issue in our global age, one is still puzzled to see Herodotus, Polybius, Strabo, or Pliny enjoy a growing popularity in Berber history books, magazines, articles, and conference papers. Specialists and non-specialists alike turn to these authors to exhume names of Berber kings, places, and heroic battles thought to be buried forever. Their archeological influence goes beyond the confines of academic circles. Families in Kabylia, the Atlas Mountains, and the Rif are naming their children "Masinissa," "Yuba," "Yugarthen," or "Numidia." Confirmed by Greek and Roman sources on the one hand, and hardly acknowledged by North African history books on the other, these names continue to spread despite the strong resistance from imams, religious scholars, Arab nationalists, and political authorities.

In fact, the resurrection of ancient foreign texts in North Africa appears less puzzling when the modern reasons provoking the act are understood. By appropriating Greek and Roman texts, critics intend to send a strong message to the dominant discourse shared by French and Arab texts. They hold up Greek and Roman authors as witnesses against the French colonial and Arab national(ist) historiographies that have either absorbed Berber cultural specificity or ideologically manipulated it.[3] French and Arab historians were too preoccupied with their own binary conflict to leave room for Berber self-expression. Moreover, both parties are considered responsible for the erasure of Berber memory, or "popular" North African culture, as a prominent Algerian intellectual puts it. "Contemporary Arab and Islamic thought," says Mohammed Arkoun, "uses for its own sake, without being able to admit it, the very positivism so much deplored in colonial scholarship."[4] The complicity of national-colonial historiography becomes much more visible in the presence of a third textual agency considered distant, disinterested, or neutral. At the very least, the intrusion of a third agency helps Berber critics to shift the study of North African history from a national-colonial binary conflict to a heterogeneous debate open to new voices and experiences.

Participating in the debate as a fresh competing voice, Berber critics insist on taking us back to what they consider a major turning point in the history of North Africa: the Islamic conquest of the late seventh century. The "Muslim conquest," asserts the Moroccan historian Ali Sidqi Azayko, "not only concerns the future of Imazighen, but also condemns their past to a complete darkness."[5] Mosques and schools in North Africa perpetuate the stereotype of pre-Islamic darkness through the derogatory expression of *jahiliyya* (ignorance). Once Greek and Roman sources are ready to offer archival assistance, the concept of *jahiliyya* no longer makes sense. Readers can quickly turn to Herodotus, Polybius, Strabo, or Pliny to learn about the Punic wars, Masinissa's heroic resistance to Rome, Yuba's kingdom, the splendor of Carthage, and many other important events erased or simply forgotten by official history books. New generations recover these historical events as moments of a rich Berber past to reiterate that the history of North Africa does not begin with Islam. The islamization of North Africa, they would argue, constitutes a historical discontinuity, not a "happy" beginning as the Arabic word *futuhat* (conquest) implies.

Since history always implies geography, Greek and Roman texts enable their users to recuperate the Mediterranean as one of the fundamental dimensions of North African civilization. The relocation of North Africa in the Mediterranean sphere gives Berbers a cultural autonomy that is more visible in a South-North relationship than in the traditional geopolitics of East and West. Alhocein Iskan reaches this conclusion after he sets out to illustrate a significant concept he borrows from Roman sources: "The historical sources of the Roman era indicate that Berber communities were called 'Gentes' or 'Nations', but not tribes." One of the distinct characteristics of the Berber "nation" lies in its social and political organization. The Berber "social system," stresses Iskan, "was different from its Eastern and European counterparts"; the division of political power among Berbers was "non-despotic" in comparison to the "Eastern tribal system" which gives full power to "sheikhs and caliphates." Iskan concludes that the Berber political system "contained a form of secularism, as it is called today, because the political and the religious were kept separate."[6] Although Iskan's references are to ancient texts, the context within which he interprets them is alive enough to satisfy urgent concerns and excite modern projections.[7] His special political vocabulary—secularism, nation, non-despotism, tribe— betrays an obvious critique of the *mashriq-maghrib* (East-West) dichotomy, where North Africa, the Maghrib, has historically occupied a subordinate position.

It is wrong to interpret, as some Arab nationalists do, the Berber appropriation of Greek and Roman texts as an expression of an anti-Islamic or anti-Arab sentiment.[8] Rather, the Berber narrative, still in its formative stage, cannot draw attention to itself as a distinct voice without practicing some kind of strategic essentialism. The *kulshi kifkif* (we are all the same) rhetoric of the nationalists is not a convincing argument in an environment that has yet to appreciate the value of difference. The Berber narrative, like any minor narrative seeking to protect itself from an absorbing sameness, must highlight its distinct characteristics on the one hand and dim those it shares with the dominant discourse on the other. At the same time, it is mainly the latter that determines the strategies and the thematic priorities of the minor narrative. For example, white racism forces African Americans to invest in black color just as religious repression in Egypt incites the Copts to capitalize on their Christian identity. In all cases, the basic concepts sustaining the minor narrative—color, religion, or language—look essentialist because the writer traces them back in time to a distant topos lying safely outside the historical and geographical scope of the dominant group. The topos is imagined as Africa for African Americans, Pharaonic Egypt for Copts, and pre-Islamic North Africa—Numidia, Libya, or Africa in antiquity—for Berbers. Each of these ethnic groups revisits its utopian world whenever it feels compelled to identify its origins, history, or collective memory.

If Utopia is indeed the right word to describe pre-Islamic North Africa in the Berber imagination, it must be understood as a trope of resistance, not a sign of essentialism. The trope will continue to be used as long as the dominant discourse in North Africa refuses to recognize the importance of pre-Islamic history, a central issue in the Berbers' struggle for cultural and linguistic rights. However, the legitimacy of the cultural struggle is undermined by the very sources employed to support it. The normative approach Berber scholars adopt in their reading of Greek and Roman texts defeats their purpose. Their desperate need for the written word to support their critique of the modern dominant discourse prevents them from being alert to the authority their Greek and Roman references are increasingly gaining in their narrative.

Ironically, almost every historical, geographic, cultural, or linguistic feature of Berber identity has to have a definition in Greek or Roman sources to become intelligible. As an imam routinely quotes from the Qur'an or Hadith (sayings of the Prophet Muhammad) to make his point powerful, the Berber writer feels obliged to cite ancient authors even if the point he or she wants to make is self-evident. Not even "Amazigh," the term all Berbers agree is their own, is spared. To convince us that "Amazigh" is truly our own term, Mohamed Chafiq feels constrained to validate its etymological roots in the Greek and Latin dictionary. Notice the long confusing detour he takes: "In the fifth century BC, Herodotus referred to them [Berbers] as 'Maxyes', and the Latin historians used the same name slightly modified into 'Mazax' or 'Mazaces' or 'Mazikes', all of which are collective names given to the 'Numidian people'."[9] Historian Ali Wahidi goes to another source to justify, not critique, why Berbers were called "Numidians": "according to Salistius, 'Numidian' derives from the Latin word 'nomad'."[10]

Surprisingly, no one is curious enough to ask why Greek and Roman authors identified North Africans with the names of Numidian and Nomad. On the contrary, for Chafiq, Wahidi, and Azaykou, Numidia represents a perfect match between the signifier and the signified: North Africa was called Numidia because its Berber inhabitants were, as a matter of fact, nomads. Applying the same semiotic rule to Berber language, Azaykou suggests that the nomadic essence of the Berber people is still redeemable in the tribes that have kept their original Berber names. For example, Iznaten have to be "sheep raisers" because "history reports that they were nomads in their majority."[11] Though vaguely identified, his "history" refers to Herodotus and Strabo whom he quotes in his book to confirm the nomadic lifestyle of pre-Islamic North Africa. The closest Azaykou gets to looking critically at his sources is when he defines the relation between nomadic and sedentary peoples as a complementary one: "In this sense, nomads always represented in North Africa a sort of human reserve which ensured the occupation of fertile lands whenever natural calamities decreased the number of peasantry."[12]

Azaykou's conclusion is the kind of reading to which the unquestioned belief in Numidia/Nomad would lead: a native confirmation of an imperial Greco-Roman trope whose main purpose is identifying a territory and positing the intellectual means to rationalize its occupation. As I will argue in the next section, the sedentary and the nomad are not complementary, but diametrically opposed. The former is the civilized Greek or Roman who possesses the art of agriculture (the root of the word "culture"); the latter is the uncivilized Berber wanderer who has neither the capacity nor the wish to cultivate his land. What Berber scholars and activists consider sacred texts for retrieving facts relating to their pre-Islamic origins, I reinterpret as the oldest manifestations of an imperial metaphor that has served colonial powers since Greco-Roman antiquity.[13]

Greco-Roman Sedentarization versus North African Nomadism

As Franz Boas said, "to understand a phenomenon we have not only to know what it is, but also how it came into being."[14] Nomadism came into textual being with Herodotus, in whose imagination Greece is mapped like an urban island surrounded by dangerous nomads. In his classic *The Histories*, most of the nations and tribes living in Asia and Africa are described as "wanderers," "shepherds," "pastoralists," or "nomads." North

Africa, known to the Greeks as Libya, enters Herodotus's text as a fertile region whose colonization was ordained by an oracle and established by Battus, one of the leaders of Thera. Battus's political ambition was undermined by a speech impediment. He begged the goddess Pythia to fix his stammer but was granted a colonial mission overseas instead:

> Battus, you came for a voice, but the Lord Phoebus Apollo has a Mission for you:
>> You are to go to sheep-breeding Libya and found a colony there.[15]

Battus's colonial mission is important to Herodotus because it allows him to argue that North Africa owes the foundation of its cities to Athens. In fact, the only cities visible on his North African map are Barqa and Cyrene, both founded by Battus and other Greek colonists. The rest is nomadic, at least the part of North Africa with which Herodotus is familiar: "All the way from Egypt to Lake Tritonis, then, the Libyans are nomads who eat meat and drink milk."[16] Nomadism is defined here as geography and identity. As mentioned above, North Africa was known to Greek and Roman authors by the various names of Libya, Numidia, or simply Africa. For Herodotus, the entire coastal stretch from Egypt to eastern Tunisia (Lake Tritonis) is inhabited by nomads who live on meat and milk regardless of whether their land is fertile or arid. The possibility of finding pastoralists among the Greeks is ruled out, although ancient texts, like Homer's *Odyssey*, which Herodotus cites on numerous occasions, are full of Greek pastoralists who supply the *polis* with livestock and cheese.[17] His emphasis on North African pastoralism allows him to maintain a strict dichotomy between the Greek colonists and the natives. Hardly named in the text, the latter are what they do—pastoralists or nomads.

Even when Herodotus stretches his map further west, from Tunisia to the Pillars of Heracles (Morocco), he has nothing important to say about North Africa outside the context of nomadism. The practice of nomadism might stop at a certain line in his imaginative map but not his urge to bring it back: "That is the way of things in this part of the world. The nomadic life stops at Lake Tritonis, and west of there the Libyans live quite differently. In particular, there is something the nomadic tribes do to their children which is not done west of the lake."[18] As the reader is more curious to hear about the differences west of the lake, Herodotus switches back to the east to provide us with details about the nomads' good health, sacrifice, and religious rituals. A few passages later, he seems to finally admit that some tribes have names and are capable of building houses and farming the land: "West of the Triton River, next to the Ausees, is a Libyan tribe called the Maxys who cultivate the land and whose custom is to have houses." The "Maxys" is the same word Mohamed Chafiq explains as the etymological root of the name "Amazigh." Still, Herodotus is too uncomfortable to give away the sedentary-nomad dichotomy and imagine the Libyans to be fit for agrarian civilization. Therefore, he quickly finds new ethnic origins to the Maxys who, Herodotus states, "claim to be descendants of Troy."[19]

The wider the author's North African map stretches, the more his ignorance of the world he is set to describe betrays him. Beyond the nomadic coast, Herodotus continues, North Africa becomes a land "infested by wild animals," "a sandy ridge that runs all the ways from Thebes in Egypt to the Pillars of Heracles."[20] His map reaches its farthest point in the south, where the land is "sheer desert, without water, wildlife, rain or vegetation."[21] Wildlife and desert are symptoms of Herodotus' own empirical limits disguised as geographical facts. Ancient or modern, the imperial narrative hardly admits its ignorance; when the author is stuck, he simply transfers his rhetorical limits (wilderness, darkness) to his object of inquiry. At the same time, the pieces of ethnographic information Herodotus possesses are expanded to represent all of North Africa. Stephen Greenblatt makes a similar argument in his critique of Columbus' description of the New World: "The discoverer sees only a fragment and then imagines the rest in the act of appropriation. The supplement that imagination brings to vision expands the perceptual field, encompassing the distant hills and valleys or the whole of an island or an entire continent, and the bit that has actually been seen becomes by metonymy a representation of the whole."[22] In our context, the metonymy implies that the part of North Africa with which Herodotus is familiar is introduced to the uninformed Greek reader as a nomadic space that speaks for the whole region, from Egypt in the East to Morocco in the West. This imperial metonymy is one of the many examples demonstrating that Herodotus, as Yves Lacoste puts it, needs to be criticized as "the agent of Athenian imperialism" rather than celebrated as "the father of history."[23]

The nomadic metonymy would continue to be useful for generations to come. By the second century BCE, when Rome began to extend its imperial hegemony throughout the Mediterranean, Greek and Roman geographers and historians had difficulty describing North Africa without automatically associating it with nomads. Polybius is the distinguished representative of this historical era. In his attempt to correct previous stereotypes of Libya as "arid" and "sandy," Polybius writes: "The excellence of the soil of Libya must excite our admiration . . . The supply of horses, oxen, sheep, and goats in it is beyond anything to be found in any other part of the world; because many of the tribes in Libya do not use cultivated crops, but live on and with their flocks and herds."[24] Polybius rejects the views defining the nomadic on the basis of natural and climatic conditions such as droughts and desertification. For him, nomadism is essentially an economy which privileges animal-breeding over farming. His definition establishes a significant discrepancy between the natives and their land. On the one hand, Libya possesses excellent agricultural resources; on the other, Libyans make no use of them and prefer to live on pastoralism instead.

Pastoralism and farming form the two extremities of ancient economics. Their co-existence is, however, only a matter of time: the nomad's rudimentary or inappropriate exploitation of his environment can, at any moment, degenerate into chaos to threaten the harmony of the ecosystem. As modern theorists of nomadism show, the relationship between pastoralism and agriculture is constantly marked by antagonism and conflict of interests. In his 1938 classic, *The Empire of the Steppes*, René Grousset notes that the nomad of ancient times, "the typical nomad," had no "taste for cultivated land as such; when he took possession of it, he instinctively allowed it to relapse into a fallow, unproductive state, and fields reverted to steppe, to yield grass for his sheep and horses."[25]

Inspired by Herodotus, Polybius depicts North Africa as a virgin land wasted in the absence of the civilized Roman farmer to colonize it and save it from the ignorance of its shepherds. Of course, the evidence that North Africa was the object of ancient imperialism because of its agricultural resources is not lacking. For several centuries, North Africa had the reputation of being the "bread basket" of Rome.[26] The Moroccan historian Abdallah Laroui notes that the North African province "interested the Romans only as a producer of wheat." "Agricultural settlements," Laroui clarifies, "were in existence well before the first millenium, and the development of hydraulic installations owes no more to the Phoenicians than to the Romans."[27] Referring to Polybius's accounts, Gabriel Camps notes that Africans lived on agriculture long before the reign of Masinissa: "Agriculture developed at the same time as the organization of Berber society."[28]

How did this obvious fact escape Polybius, whose reputation as the great historian of his time is established on the basis of his extensive travels and thorough knowledge? In his introduction to *The Histories*, F. W. Walbank states that Polybius's "reputation as a historian rests partly on the magnitude of his theme, and partly on the seriousness and competence with which he approached it." He adds that Polybius is the "spokesman" of the rise of the Roman empire just as Gibbon is the spokesman of its fall.[29] It is in this political perspective that Polybius's accounts of North Africa reveal much of their significance. By describing Libya as an admirable and unexploited land, Polybius at once masks and legitimizes Rome's imperial desire for territory.

Toward the end of his narrative, Polybius begins to acknowledge that an important evolution is taking place in Libya, which now assumes the double name of Africa and Numidia. At the center of this economic evolution is Masinissa, "the King of Numidians in Africa." The ninety-year-old king strikes him as the "the most powerful man physically of all his contemporaries."[30] Particularly important for Polybius are the king's successful economic policies:

> But his greatest and most divine achievement was this: Numidia had been before his time universally unproductive, and was looked upon as incapable of producing any cultivated fruits. He was the first and only man who showed that it could produce cultivated fruits just as well as any other country.[31]

Initially explained by Polybius as an economic mode of living which privileges animal-breeding over cultivation, here the pastoral is redefined as the failure to "produce cultivated fruits." Masinissa, the Berber king of the second century BCE, deserves special recognition for being able to overcome this failure and lead his Numidian subjects from the nomadic to the agricultural stage.

But Polybius's description is problematic if we recall the meanings of Numidian. As mentioned above, even Berber scholars agree that Numidian is a synonym for nomad. According to the French linguist Emmanuel Laroche, Greek and Roman authors used "Numidian" as an emphatic synonym for nomad: "the Numidians were the perfect type of nomads; the term is at any rate very old."[32] He adds that Polybius is one of the first Greek writers to use the term Numidian in his writings. One might add a central point to Laroche's statement: not only is Polybius the first to write down the term Numidian, most importantly, he is the first author to convert the word "nomad" into a proper name (Numidian). His linguistic gesture paves the way for his successors to use nomad and Numidian interchangeably and in exclusive connection to the Berbers of North Africa.

Polybius's switch from the name Libyan to the name Numidian is less indicative of a geographical or a cultural identity than of a nomadic hierarchy within which the natives are classified. On the one hand, Masinissa and his people deserve special recognition for progressing out of their nomadic lifestyle; on the other, the name Numidian, under which they are placed, relegates them back to nomadism. What Polybius drops in content he recuperates through terminology. Moreover, their new name makes them even more nomadic than they used to be, for, as Laroche explains, the "perfect type of nomads" means pastoralists who have absolutely no contact with agricultural or urban communities.[33] How is it possible, then, for Masinissa and his people to lead both nomadic and agricultural life-styles, knowing that the two activities are defined as binary opposites in Greco-Roman thought? Why should the concept of the nomadic still designate that which already departs from it?

While Polybius does not need to explain the pastoral significance in the word/name Numidian, his historical account of North Africa is one of the first texts in which nomadism begins to include in its meaning violence and warfare. Throughout his text, Numidians show neither signs of political stability nor tribal and social organization. The nomadic arts of violence and warfare are exemplified by the Numidian's special attachment to his horse and weapons. In addition to the Libyan who embodies the pastoral, the Numidian combines the roles of the horseman, raider, and warrior. Polybius attributes Masinissa's political genius to his physical qualities, above all to his extraordinary capacity to "remain in the saddle day and night continuously."[34] As a precursor of the modern cowboy, Masinissa owes his political power less to the communities which crowned him king than to horse riding and speed.[35] The saddle functions as a wandering throne for a wandering nation.

In case readers forget the nomadic essence of the Numidian identity, Polybius constantly reminds them of its supplements: "Numidian cavalry," "Numidian horse," "Numidian raid," "Numidian terror," and "Numidian speed." He exults in the Numidian war machine, vividly delineated in the battles taking place between Carthage and Rome. His praise of the Numidians is manifest when they are fighting on the side of the Romans. But when the two sides are engaged in fighting one another, Polybius underscores that Numidians represent "even more damage to their [own] country than the Romans. The terror which they inspired drove the country to flock for safety into the city."[36] The heroic qualities of the nomad are transformed into terror, violence, and pillage because they make no sense in the context of peace and outside the framework of the battlefield. Polybius's exaggeration of Numidian violence recalls his description of Libyan pastoralism: just as Libyan pastoralists misuse the natural properties of their fertile land, Numidians represent a danger to the political stability of their own environment. By emphasizing the violent nature of the natives, Polybius enacts the purpose of the colonial presence of Rome in Africa as a pacifying mission whose moral duty consists of saving native communities from their self-destruction.

The story of Masinissa's conversion of his men into farmers is restated in Strabo's geographical accounts of the first century BCE. Strabo is equally fascinated by the King Masinissa. In the seventeenth book of his *Geography*, Strabo praises Masinissa as a strong leader who "turned the Numidians into citizens and farmers, and taught them to be soldiers instead of bandits."[37] Like Polybius, Strabo is surprised that despite their "fertile region," Numidians made no use of it, "leaving it to the wild beasts." He adds that natives preferred to fight each other rather than destroy the beasts and to "work the land in peace."[38] Strabo's imagery posits Numidia as frontier territory, waiting for the civilized outsider to clear it, exploit its economic potential, and save it from its political chaos. His appeal to the Roman colonizer needs no further explanation. What one expects from Strabo's historical accounts instead is the answer to the following important question: what was the state of Numidia during the century that separates the two Greek authors, and how successful were Masinissa's social and political reforms?

This question is provoked by the distinction Strabo makes between the past and the present of the Numidians. By Strabo's time, Masinissa is credited with another historical transition: he turns his men into "citizens" and "soldiers." Numidian identity is not only dissociated from pastoralism, but also from banditry and anarchism, the political characteristics on which Polybius's definition of nomadism was mainly based. But surprisingly, Strabo, in the same paragraph, switches to the present tense to arrest what he himself has extolled as the Numidian economic and political evolution: "Thus they lead a wandering, migrant life, no different from those who are driven to it by barren lands and inclement weather. Hence the Masaesyli are just called Nomads or Numidians. Of necessity their food is poor: they eat roots as often as meat, and are nourished with milk and cheese."[39] Once again, the Masaesyli, a tribe located in the east of present day Algeria, is constructed as the part that represents the nomadic whole. In several respects, Polybius's statement can be read as a comment on his earlier description of the Numidians' transition to agricultural civilization. Strabo's account reveals how the correlation between the terms Nomad and Numidian was being gradually strengthened. It also shows that whether the land is fertile or infertile makes no difference to the natives. For Strabo, the natives' devotion to mobility supersedes every other aspect of their life.

Still, Strabo is forced to return to the argument of fertility to nomadize another Berber group and automatically link it to the Numidians. In addition to the Africans, the Libyans, and the Masaesyli (all of whom are subsumed under the general heading of Numidians), Strabo states: "most of the rest of the Moors, although they live in a region largely fertile, up to this time have wandered about with no fixed settlements."[40] Despite Strabo's reference to "the rest of the Moors," all Berbers who come under his gaze are nomadic, either because their land is no good for farming or because they are unqualified to take advantage of its fertility. However, as the example of Masinissa illustrates, the transition of the natives to the agrarian stage does not make them appear less nomadic in the eyes of Strabo, Polybius, and their successors.

The urbanization of the Berbers does not make them less nomadic, either. The most explicit account in which the Berber sedentarization is distorted and nomadized is provided by Pliny, the Roman historian of the first century CE. In his famous text, *Natural History*, the nomadic territory and its inhabitants are mapped as follows:

> East of the Amsaga is Numidia, famous for the name of Masinissa, called Metagonites by the Greeks, and its people Numidians—really nomads—from their habit of changing their pasture they go around with "mapalia" [straw huts], their houses on wagons. The towns are Chollo, Rusicade from which forty-eight miles to the south is the colony of Cirta of *sittii* and further inland Sicca and the free town of Bulla Regia.[41]

For all its names and topographic details, Pliny's account amounts to little more than a recapitulation of previous conjectures about nomadism. Pliny evokes the heterogeneity of North African ethnic nations to display the ways in which they rotate in the nomadic role. With the passage of time, the nomadic connotations of the name Numidian become fixed and irreversible. North Africans are known to the Greeks as authentic nomads not because of their migrancy and pastoralism but because of the name—Numidian—that designates them.

Pliny, like all his predecessors, fails to carry his geographical descriptions further without contradicting his own statement. He concludes the passage above with a long list of Numidian cities inhabited by the very people he identifies as "real nomads."[42] How can one be a city dweller and a roving nomad at the same time? The confusion is caused by Pliny's choice to be practical rather than scientific in his historical accounts. As he complains elsewhere, "the names of these people [North Africans] and these cities are extremely difficult to pronounce, except in their own language."[43] Of course, "nomad" is practical to use not only as a Greek-Latin name but also as a trope that obviates the curiosity to engage with the natives' language and other aspects on which their identity is normally founded.

From Herodotus through Strabo to Pliny, definitions of nomadism have come full circle, ranging from pastoralism and violence to mobility and speed. Yet, the flexibility of meaning is always contained within the act of naming. As the example of Masinissa clearly illustrates, when Greek and Roman authors are challenged by evidence proving the natives' agriculture or urbanity, they deliberately switch to the name Numidian, underscoring its nomadic essence in order to override those elements that do not fit the prejudiced picture drawn about North Africans. Indeed, as Laroui points out, the conflation of nomad and Numidian was practiced by Roman writers and colonial administrators to reject the political significance of the natives' resistance to occupation; their armed struggle was seen as an instinctive expression of their Numidian/nomadic identity, not as resistance to colonial violence. Laroui writes:

> The numerous revolts of the Libyans (396, 379, etc.), the war of the mercenaries in 240, the conflict with Masinissa which from 207 to 148 erupted every ten years—all these disturbances have been characterized (with the help of the dubious pun Numidian-nomad) as opposition to forced settlement; but they can equally well be interpreted as revolts of a conquered, mistreated and exploited population of longtime farmers.[44]

The French conquest of Algeria in the early 1830s provided the modern context within which Greek and Roman accounts of North Africa were resurrected to serve comparative imperial purposes. Nineteenth- and twentieth-century French historians retrieved "Numidia" in order to rewrite native resistance to foreign occupation as nothing more than a natural antagonism between pastoralism and agriculture. E. F. Gautier, for one, argues in his book, *Le Passé de l'Afrique du Nord*, that the (then) French-occupied Numidia represents a "special terrain, an eternal battlefield between two economic systems, the pastoral and the agricultural."[45] He cites Pliny to remind the modern reader that "Numidians mean real nomads," a group of wandering tribes "controlled by powerful princes, Masinissa, Syphax, Jugurtha."[46] Gautier cautions against understanding the meaning of "Numidia" only in strict relation to the Roman civilizing mission in North Africa, lest the name suggest that Gautier's Roman ancestors failed to sedentarize their nomadic subjects.

This point is made clearer when he historicizes the most important event in North Africa after the fall of the Roman empire: the Arab conquest of the seventh century. Gautier argues that while Berbers were successfully converted into farmers and citizens under the Roman administration, their embrace of Islam forced them back into nomadism. The challenging task awaiting the French conqueror was to rescue Berber North Africa from its Arab nomadism and bring it back to sedentary civilization. Gautier demonstrates that it is irrational to expect Arabs to defeat the very political and social system (nomadism) to which they owe their existence: "Organizing nomadism is not impossible; Rome did it in Numidia, France in Algeria. But to organize nomadism is also to kill it; its profound virtues, at least its warfare instincts, cannot resist administrative organization. For the Arab conqueror, to organize nomadism is to commit suicide."[47]

If religion and nomadism are normally incompatible—the Arabic words *madaniyya* (urbanity) and *madina* (the city) derive from *din* (religion)—French historians express a different opinion when it comes to Islam. On the wide historical screen of the Maghrib and Islamic Spain, all they see are Arab Bedouins from the East conquering and plundering the Berber cities and villages of North Africa.[48] Charles André Julien describes the eleventh-century migration of the Beni Hilal tribe to North Africa as an "invasion" led by a "torrent of nomadic peoples who destroyed the beginnings of Berber organization—which might very well have developed in its own way—and put nothing whatsoever in its place."[49] Julien's lament is a polished paraphrase of Gautier's statement that the pre-Islamic Numidia was ready to reap the fruits of the Roman civilization when the Arabs suddenly emerged and killed the sedentary process in its infancy. Thus the game is still the same: nomadism played with a new figure, the medieval Arab Bedouin within whose cultural sphere, it is assumed, the classical Numidian has been fatally absorbed. The sedentary identity of the latter is stressed, both retrospectively and negatively, to exaggerate the nomadic threat that Arabs or Muslims have posed from the fall of the Roman empire to the rise of the French empire in Algeria.

Putting their lamentation over the past aside, Gautier, Julien, and others provide no solid evidence to justify their claim that Arab nomadism poses a threat to the French presence in North Africa, any more than Greek and Roman authors did before them. On the contrary, the myth of the nomad turned out to be so useful to the French colonial discourse that it was kept alive by all possible means. According to de Tocqueville, native nomadism could even be tolerated, not to say invented, to satisfy the exigencies of colonial pragmatism. Unless Algerian nomads were prepared to settle down, he warned, the French colonial administration should not "let a single one emerge among them, and all the [French] expeditions whose aim is to occupy or to destroy the old towns and the nascent ones . . . [were] useful."[50] Recalling the stereotypical definition of nomadism as aversion to "agriculture" and "culture," Tocqueville recommends that Berbers or Arabs should be left to roam on their own "because the wandering life they lead prevents them from cultivating even coarsely the sciences and arts that are indispensable even to the least advanced civilization."[51] Why should one bother to settle the nomads when they continue to provide the French empire with the rhetoric needed to assert itself as the inheritor of the Roman empire in North Africa, to legitimize its land acquisitions, to attract new settlers to the colonies, and to reinforce its divide-and-rule colonial policy?

A closer investigation of Greek and Roman texts, as well as of the French historiography that appropriated them, suggests that their representations of North Africa are historically too suspect to shed light on Berber (or Arab) origins. Still, this is no reason to ignore these texts or reject them as relics of a bygone era; rather, they remain instructive for understanding how North African identities have been subject to negotiation over the course of history. In fact, it is a lack of serious academic interest in these texts that must to be blamed for the current popularity of "Numidia" and the controversy this awkward name has raised in the Maghrib. Visiting a Berber city or village, one may encounter "Numidia" as a fancy name for young girls, musical bands, albums, cafes, boutiques, and cultural associations. How can the average person question the term when Berber historians have already authorized it as a native name? By preventing families from naming their daughters "Numidia," religious and civil authorities add the missing element that makes "Numidia" a cause worth fighting for, rather than a longstanding stereotype worth fighting against. The comedy will continue as long as the colonial foundations of "Numidia" remain hidden from their North African detractors and advocates alike.

Notes

1. See in particular Ngugi wa Thiongo, *Decolonising the Mind: The Politics of Language in African Literature* (London: Heineman, 1986).

2. Berber scholars gained access to Greek and Roman texts by reading twentieth-century French texts by William Marçais, Robert Montagne, Stephane Gsell, and Charles André Julien.

3. The issue of Berber origins is a controversial one. Just as French colonial authors seek to trace the origins of Berbers to ancient Europe, Arab nationalists believe that Berbers came originally from Yemen. Both theories are considered ideologically oriented; their real intention is to blur the historical gap between "natives" and "foreigners" and between "conquered" and "conquerors." Most Berber critics see no particular reason why Berbers must have an origin outside North Africa.

4. Mohammed Arkoun, "Les Fondements arabo-islamiques de la culture maghrébine," in *Französisch heute* 15 (1984): 178. Unless otherwise indicated, all translations from French and Arabic are mine.

5. Ali Sidqi Azaykou, *Histoire du Maroc, ou les interprétations possibles* (Rabat: Centre Tariq Ibn Ziyad, 2002), 6.

6. Alhocein Iskan, "Istimrar al-tanzimat al-ijtima'iya wa as-siyasiya al-amazighiya bil-maghrib khilala al-'asr al-wasit wa atharuha fi tashkil al-thaqafa al-maghribiya," in *Le substrat amazigh de la culture marocaine*, ed. Moha Ennaji (Fez: Université Sidi Mohamed Ben Abdellah, 2006), 50, 52.

7. For an analysis of how the discourse of nationalism projects its modern political needs on the deep past, see Benedict Anderson, *Imagined Communities* (London: Verso, 1990)

8. The simple fact that Berber writers use French, Greek, or Roman references exposes them to harsh criticism. For example, the Moroccan intellectual Mohamed Ghnaim attacks the Berber cultural movement as a "derivative" discourse informed

by "pre-Christian, pre-Islamic, as well as Orientalist references." See Mohamed Ghnaim, "Azmat matn at-tayar al-barbari," *Almassae* (Oct. 17, 2006): 21.

9. Mohamed Chafiq, *Lamha ʿan thalatha wa-thalathina qarnan min tarikh al-amazighiyin* (Rabat: Isdarat infobrant, 2003), 7.

10. Ali Wahidi, "Nadra tarikhiya an al-mamalik al-amazighiya," in Ennaji, *Le substrat*, 56.

11. Azakyou, *Histoire du Maroc*, 16.

12. Ibid., 13.

13. As Hayden White argues, the historical narrative "can be judged solely in terms of the richness of the metaphors which govern its sequence of articulation." See his *Tropics of Discourse* (Baltimore, Md.: Johns Hopkins University Press, 1978), 46.

14. Franz Boas, *Race, Language, and Culture* (New York: Macmillan, 1940), 305.

15. Herodotus, *The Histories*, trans. Robin Waterfield (Oxford: Oxford University Press, 1998), 4, 155, and 287.

16. Ibid., 4, 186, and 297.

17. Homer, *The Odyssey*, trans. Robert Fagles (New York: Penguin, 1997).

18. Herodotus, *The Histories*, 4, 187, and 298.

19. Ibid., 4, 191, and 299.

20. Ibid., 4, 181, and 296.

21. Ibid., 4, 185, and 297.

22. Stephen Greenblatt, *Marvelous Possessions: The Wonder of the New World* (Chicago: University of Chicago Press, 1991), 122.

23. Yves Lacoste, "Pourquoi Herodote? Crise de la géographie et géographie de la crise." *Hérodote* 1 (1976), 59. For a detailed analysis of imperialism in Greek and Roman texts, see Jean Bergevin, *Déterminisme et géographie: Hérodote, Strabon, Albert le Grand et Sebastien Munster* (Saint-Foy: Les Presses de l'Université Laval, 1992).

24. Polybius, *The Histories of Polybius*, trans. Evelyn S. Shuckburgh (Bloomington: Indiana University Press, 1962), 12, 3.

25. René Grousset, *The Empire of the Steppes*, trans. Naomi Walford (New Brunswick, N.J.: Rutgers University Press, 1970), xxvi.

26. Charles Picard, "Neron et le blé d'Afrique," *Cahiers de Tunisie* 14 (1956): 168.

27. Abdallah Laroui, *The History of the Maghrib: An Interpretive Essay*, trans. Ralph Manheim (Chicago: University of Chicago Press, 1977), 33, 43.

28. Gabriel Camps, "Massinissa ou les débuts de l'histoire," *Libyca* (Série Archéologie-épigraphie), vol. 8 (1960), 88.

29. Polybius, *Histories*, vii, viii.

30. Ibid., 37, 10.

31. Ibid.

32. Emmanuel Laroche, *Histoire de la racine nem-en grec ancien (nemō, nemesis, nomos, nomizō)* (Paris: Klincksieck, 1949), 121.

33. Ibid., 122.

34. Polybius, *Histories*, 32, 10.

35. Ibid., 25, 12.

36. Ibid., 1, 31.

37. Strabo, *The Geography of Strabo*, trans. Horace Leonard Jones (London: William Heineman, 1930), 17, 3, and 5.

38. Ibid.

39. Ibid.

40. Ibid., 17, 3, and 7.

41. Pliny, *Natural History*, trans. Harris Rackham (London: Loeb Text, 1950), 5, 1, and 22.

42. According to many historians, the names of Chollo, Rusicade, Cirta, Sicca, and Bulla Regia correspond to cities and towns founded by the natives of North Africa between the first and tenth centuries CE. In addition to Laroui's *History of the Maghrib*, see Charles André Julien, *Histoire de l'Afrique du Nord. Tunisie-Algerie-Maroc. Des origines à la conquête arabe* (Paris: Payot, 1956), chaps. 2 and 3; and Marcel Benabou, *La Résistance africaine à la Romanisation* (Paris: L'Harmattan, 1976), chaps. 1 and 2.

43. Cited in Azayko, *Le substrat*, 25.

44. Laroui, *The History of the Maghrib*, 44.

45. E. F. Gautier, *Le Passé de l'Afrique du Nord* (Paris: Petite Bibliothèque Payot, 1952), 245.

46. Ibid., 242.

47. Ibid., 269.

48. In his critical study of the representation of the Maghrib in French historiography, Yves Lacoste writes: "The Arab invasions may not, as has so often been claimed, be the 'decisive event' in the history of the Barbary states, but they certainly became the main theme of North African historiography from the nineteenth century onward." See Yves Lacoste, *Ibn Khaldun: The Birth of History and the Past of the Third World*, trans. David Macey (London: Verso, 1984), 68.

49. Charles André Julien, *History of North Africa: From the Arab Conquest to 1830*, trans. J. Petrie, C. Stewart (New York: Praeger, 1970), 73.

50. Alexis de Tocqueville, *Writing on Empire and Slavery*, trans. Jennifer Pitts (Baltimore, Md.: Johns Hopkins University Press, 2001), 73.

51. Ibid.

Bibliography

Anderson, Benedict. *Imagined Communities: Reflections on the Origin and Spread of Nationalism*. New York: Verso, 1983.

Arkoun, Mohammed. "Les Fondements arabo-islamiques de la culture maghrébine." *Französisch heute* 15 (1984): 176–190.

Azaykou, Ali Sidqi. *Histoire du Maroc ou les interpretations possibles*. Rabat: Centre Tariq Ibn Ziyad, 2002.

Benabou, Marcel. *La Résistance africaine à la Romanisation*. Paris: L'Harmattan, 1976.

Bergevin, Jean. *Determinisme et géographie: Hérodote, Strabon, Albert le Grand et Sebastien Munster*. Saint-Foy: Université Laval, 1992.

Boas, Franz. *Race, Language, and Culture*. New York: Macmillan, 1940.

Camps, Gabriel. "Massinissa ou les débuts de l'histoire." In *Libyca*. Série Archéologie-épigraphie 8, 1960.

Chafiq, Mohamed. *Lamha 'an thalatha wa-thalathina qarnan min tarikh al-amazighiyin*. Rabat: Isdarat infobrant, 2003.

de Tocqueville, Alexis. *Writing on Empire and Slavery*, trans. Jennifer Pitts. Baltimore, Md.: Johns Hopkins University Press, 2001.

Ghanaim, Mohamed. "Azmat matn at-tayar al-barbari." In *Almassae*, Oct. 17, 2006.

Greenblatt, Stephen. *Marvelous Possessions: The Wonder of the New World*. Chicago: University of Chicago Press, 1991.

Grousset, René. *The Empire of the Steppes*, trans. Naomi Walford. New Brunswick, N. J.: Rutgers University Press, 1970.

Herodotus. *The Histories*, trans. Robin Waterfield. Oxford: Oxford University Press, 1998.

Homer. *The Odyssey*, trans. Robert Fagles. New York: Penguin, 1997.

Iskan, Alhocein. "Istimrar al-tanzimat al-ijtima'iyya wa as-siyasiyya al-amazighiyya bil-maghrib khilala al-'asr al-wasit wa atharuha fi tashkil al-thaqafa al-maghribiyya." In *Le substrat amazigh de la culture marocaine*, ed. Moha Ennaji. Fez: Université Sidi Mohamed Ben Abdellah, 2006.

Julien, Charles-André. *Histoire de l'Afrique du Nord. Tunisie-Algérie-Maroc. Des origines à la conquête arabe*. Paris: Payot, 1956.

———, *History of North Africa: From the Arab Conquest to 1830*, trans. J. Petrie, C. Stewart. New York: Praeger, 1970.

Lacoste, Yves. "Pourquoi Hérodote? Crise de la géographie et géographie de la crise." *Hérodote* 1 (1976): 8–62.

Laroche, Emmanuel. *Histoire de la racine nem-en grec ancien (nemō, nemesis, nomos, nomizō)*. Paris: Librairie C. Klincksieck, 1949.

Laroui, Abdallah. *The History of the Maghrib: An Interpretive Essay*, trans. Ralph Manheim. Chicago: Chicago University Press, 1977.

Picard, Charles. "Neron et le blé d'Afrique." *Cahiers de Tunisie* 14 (1956).

Pliny, *Natural History*, trans. Harris Rackham. London: Loeb Text, 1950.

Polybius. *The Histories of Polybius*, trans. Evelyn S. Shuckburgh. Bloomington: Indiana University Press, 1962.

Strabo. *The Geography of Strabo*, trans. Horace Leonard Jones. London: Heineman, 1930.

Virgil. *The Aeneid*, trans. Allen Mandelbaum. New York: Bantam Books, 1971.

Wa Thiongo, Ngugi. *Decolonizing the Mind: The Politics of Language in African Literature*. London: Heineman, 1986.

Wahidi, Ali. "Nadra tarikhiya 'an al-mamalik al-amazighiya." In *Le substrat amazigh de la culture marocaine*, ed. Moha Ennaji. Fez: University Sidi Mohamed Ben Abdellah, 2006.

8

"First Arts" of the Maghrib: Exhibiting Berber Culture at the Musée du quai Branly

Lisa Bernasek

Behind glass at the Musée du quai Branly, France's new museum for the arts and civilizations of Africa, Asia, Oceania, and the Americas, is a mask from the Tabelbala oasis in southwestern Algeria. It is a small rectangular piece of wood, narrower at the chin than at the forehead, with holes carved out for the eyes and mouth and a ridge running down the center in the shape of a nose. It is painted white and decorated with tufts of goat hair to represent eyebrows, eyelashes, a mustache, and a beard. Small pieces of goat bone have been inserted in the open mouth as teeth. This mask was used as part of an ʿashura masquerade in Tabelbala. A similar masquerade in a village in the Draa Valley in southwestern Morocco is depicted on a small video screen on the side of the exhibit case. In a museum that houses carved and painted masks from all over the world, including many that are considered "masterpieces" by collectors of African and Oceanic art, this small white wooden rectangle is easily overlooked. Its presence in the exhibition halls of the new museum is significant, however, and indicative of the new interpretations being given to objects from North Africa, particularly from Berber regions, in the context of a vast new state museum project.

Berber art and material culture[1]—textiles, pottery, jewelry, weaponry, and other objects of everyday life—have been collected and exhibited by French museums since the early twentieth century. These objects, originally manufactured to serve as integral parts of Berber life, were given new meanings when they were transported to France, where they were reinterpreted according to the categories and conventions of the institutions in which they were housed. Today, Berber material culture is again being reinterpreted, this time in the context of a new museum project that brings together ethnographic collections from around the world in a €232 million-complex along the Seine in the shadow of the Eiffel Tower. Objects that were once framed as "artifacts," "art," or "decorative arts" are now being reclassified as *arts premiers*, or "first arts,"[2] and interpreted as material evidence of an ancient, pre-Islamic past. Here we shall examine the specific processes of collection and exhibition that have shaped these categories and the interpretation of Berber objects in French museums, both historically and today.

State museums are not the only place for the exhibition or circulation of Berber material culture in France. Objects similar to those exhibited at the Musée du quai Branly can be found on display at Berber cultural associations, used as decoration in people's homes, for sale at shops and galleries, or worn by people of North African origin to cultural events or family festivities. As I have argued elsewhere, in each of these contexts objects may take on new meanings or be associated with different narratives than those used in the context of state museum projects.[3] But these museums, and the specific practices of collection and exhibition they employ, have played an important role in shaping the interpretation of Berber material culture for scholars and the general public from the colonial era to the present day. I examine these practices—from collection and donation patterns in the late nineteenth and early twentieth centuries to the use of architecture, museography, and interpretive texts at the new Musée du quai Branly—to investigate what Pierre Bourdieu calls the "symbolic production" of these objects as they move through different museum settings.[4] I begin by examining the collection and exhibition practices that shaped the collections now housed at the Musée du quai Branly, exploring the way these practices helped to establish categories like (Islamic) art and (Berber) ethnography that are still used to define the material culture of North Africa today. I then explore a new category, *arts premiers* or "first arts," that has become central to the interpretation of non-Western art at the Musée du quai Branly. Finally, I discuss the processes through which the Musée du quai Branly has transformed Berber material culture from ethnographic "evidence" to "first arts." I shall argue that elements like architecture and museography, as well as curatorial choices about object selection and interpretive texts, have resulted in an argument that Berber art provides evidence of an ancient, pre-Islamic past. This argument supports a portrayal of North African art and culture that ignores important aspects of post-Islamic Berber history and contemporary life.

The Collections and Their Origins: Scientists and Connoisseurs

The Musée du quai Branly was officially opened by French president Jacques Chirac, the project's most important proponent, on June 20, 2006. The new museum is now home to most of the French state's ethnographic collections, drawn from two museums originally founded in the 1930s. The largest collection (236,509 objects from Africa, Asia, Oceania, and the Americas) comes from the Musée de l'homme (Museum of Man); the rest of the collection (22,740 objects) is from the former Musée des arts d'Afrique et d'Océanie (Museum of African and Oceanic Art, MAAO).[5] Over the past seven years the museum has also acquired over 8,000 pieces through purchases and donations. The Musée du quai Branly's collections from North Africa are made up of approximately 25,000 objects, mostly from Morocco, Algeria, and Tunisia, although the section also includes objects from Libya, Egypt, Mauritania, and the Saharan regions. The majority of these collections (20,400 objects) come from the Musée de l'homme; the remainder are from the MAAO plus a small number (80 objects) of recent acquisitions. Just under 200 objects are now on display in the 200 m² section devoted to Northern Africa (*Afrique septentrionale*), the first part of the 1700 m² exhibit space devoted to the African continent. Despite the preponderance of objects from the Musée de l'homme in the museum's collections, only about one-third of the objects on display come from that museum. Why this is the case becomes clear in an analysis of the collection practices associated with these two museums. This history also reveals how Berber art has been collected and defined through French museum practice since the early twentieth century.

The categories that shape our understanding of the arts of North Africa today—Islamic or Arab versus Berber, urban versus rural, art versus ethnography—were established in the context of collection and exhibition practices in the late nineteenth and early twentieth centuries. The museums whose collections are now housed at the Musée du quai Branly played a central role in this process, and the collections themselves both reflected and helped to constitute these categories. As Stephen Vernoit has shown for the history of Islamic art, the complex connections between scholarship, the art market, museums, collectors, and specific historical and cultural configurations have all shaped the interpretation of Berber art.[6] In North Africa an important factor in this dynamic was the attitude of the different colonial administrations to the collection, documentation, and preservation of indigenous art forms;[7] these policies, combined with colonial-era assumptions about the history and culture of North Africa, had a direct impact on the constitution of the collections now housed at the Musée du quai Branly.

In the early twentieth century when most of these objects were collected, North African material culture was integrated into three very different museums in France: the Musée de l'homme, France's main ethnographic museum; the Musée des colonies (Museum of the Colonies, precursor to the MAAO) which began as a celebration of France's colonial power; and the Musée des arts décoratifs (Museum of Decorative Arts), which focused on "industrial" or decorative arts. At the same time, the Louvre was establishing its collection of Islamic art, but its collection focused more on manuscripts and painting, both genres that were not extensively collected in North Africa. Instead, French collectors in Algeria, Morocco and Tunisia focused on "indigenous" or "ethnographic" arts, categories that overlapped significantly with their interest in Berber ethnography, an interest connected to colonial-era ethnic policies.[8] As Nadia Erzini argues, even in their study of what were labeled "Islamic" monuments, French scholars in North Africa tended to focus on the medieval Berber dynasties rather than later Arab ones and interpreted later arts in terms of "decadence" and "decline," an interpretation that was central to the colonial ideology.[9] Thus the category "Islamic art" was used only for a small portion of the arts of North Africa, referring mainly to architectural monuments and their decoration.

The "decorative arts" housed at the Musée des arts décoratifs occupied a symbolic place somewhere between the "fine" Islamic art found at the Louvre and the ethnographic objects of the Musée de l'homme. At this museum, as at museums of industrial art elsewhere in Europe, collections from the Muslim world were used as examples of design and technique that were meant to serve as an inspiration to French designers and manufacturers. They were also exhibited as art objects to be appreciated in their own right, and exhibits like the 1917 Exposition des arts marocains at the Musée des arts décoratifs played an important role in exposing the Parisian public to the craft industries of the French colonies in North Africa. The collections of the Musée des arts décoratifs included ceramics, woodwork, metalwork and textiles from both Berber and Arabic-speaking regions, and from both urban and rural settings, but all of them were framed in terms of "decorative" or "industrial" arts. Although this process is beyond our scope here, these collections are now being redistributed to different state museums, including the Louvre, the Musée du quai Branly, and the Museum of European and Mediterranean Civilizations in Marseilles, in a similar process of redefinition as described here.

At the opposite end of the aesthetic hierarchy from the Islamic art housed at the Louvre were the ethnographic collections of the Musée de l'homme, which officially opened its doors as part of the International Exposition of 1937. The Musée de l'homme was created as a scientific institution devoted to the study of humankind from prehistoric times to the present.[10] The museum's original ethnographic collections from around the world were largely inherited from its precursor, the Musée d'ethnographie du Trocadéro, founded in 1878. These collections were significantly expanded in the 1920s and 1930s through intensive collecting missions in France's regions of colonial influence, including Morocco, Algeria, and Tunisia. Museum directors Paul Rivet and Georges-Henri Rivière worked with trained anthropologists as well as colonial administrators and officers, guiding them to collect objects that would serve as "witnesses" (*témoins*), evidence of social practices that formed part of in-depth village or regional studies.[11] At the Musée de l'homme, an object was not to be judged on aesthetic criteria, but in relation to the information it could provide. Of the over 20,000 objects from North Africa formerly housed there, many are items related to processes of manufacture (primary materials, samples of objects in different phases of production) or objects of daily life now deemed too "ethnographic" for exhibition at the Musée du quai Branly.

These objects originated among both Arabic and Berber-speaking populations and from both rural and urban settings. However, especially in museum-sponsored collecting missions, there was a bias toward the less-accessible Berber regions, as they were perceived to be both more "pure," meaning less influenced by urban life and French colonization, and at the same time under constant threat of "disappearing" as that influence spread further into the countryside. The Musée de l'homme was thus fully implicated in the typical salvage paradigm of late nineteenth and early twentieth century anthropology and its museums, whose collections generally reflect efforts to catalogue traditional cultures, freezing them in a "pure" state while obscuring any evidence of the changes occurring within these societies.[12] At the Musée de l'homme, Berber materials were used primarily as artifacts of indigenous life, and the objects collected were directly related to the demands of anthropological scholarship.

In contrast, the collections of the Musée des arts d'Afrique et d'Océanie were largely gathered by people who saw themselves above all as art collectors or connoisseurs, not as anthropologists embarking on an in-depth study of a particular region or society. The MAAO began its life as the Musée des colonies, founded as part of the International Colonial Exposition in 1931.[13] Before its reconceptualization in the 1960s, the museum was an explicit tool of colonial propaganda, using indigenous arts, historical objects, and other documentation to celebrate the accomplishments of French colonial influence. In the 1950s, with growing independence movements in the colonies and sharpened critique of colonialism at home in France, the museum's clear colonial message became increasingly problematic. In 1960, under Minister of Culture André Malraux (1958–1969), the museum was recast as a museum of African and Oceanic art. Instead of celebrating the history and progress of French colonization, the museum halls displayed the objects of these soon-to-be-former colonial regions as art. At this time, the museum also began to expand greatly its collections, benefiting from the donations of many important collectors of North African arts.

Although most of the major donations and acquisitions at the MAAO were made after 1960, the objects were actually collected in the late nineteenth and early twentieth centuries by Europeans living in Morocco, Algeria, and Tunisia. Many of these collectors had worked with the French colonial administrations in North Africa, and some of the more important and systematic collections were made or guided by people like Prosper Ricard, director of the Moroccan Service des arts indigènes (Native Arts Service). Ricard and his collaborators encouraged the collection of eighteenth and early nineteenth century textiles, ceramics, jewelry, and embroidery as part of their efforts to catalogue, preserve, and ultimately modernize Moroccan artisanal production.[14] Following this model, many of the collectors whose objects eventually entered the MAAO focused on specific object types and collected broadly within the genre, producing collections that covered a large number of regional variations.[15] Like the collections of the Musée de l'homme, those of the MAAO were formed in the context of a discourse that prioritized "pure," "authentic" examples of specific styles, often ascribed to an individual tribe. However, at the MAAO these objects were framed as a specifically North African art, and as aesthetically interesting objects rather than ethnographic data. These collections, formed by "connoisseurs" rather than "scientists," fit more easily within the aesthetic paradigm of the Musée du quai Branly, and many of these objects, especially the museum's well-known collections of textiles and jewelry, are now the highlights of the new museum's North African section.

Late nineteenth and early twentieth century practices of collection defined Berber art in terms such as "ethnographic artifact," "decorative art," or "art object." In these museums and in colonial-era scholarship, Berber art was often opposed to categories like "Islamic," "urban," or

"Hispano-Mauresque." Scholars of North African arts in the early twentieth century maintained a strict division between these categories, arguing, for example, that "[d]ecorative arts in Morocco derive from two sources and follow two parallel paths which, except on rare occasions, never meet."[16] The exact nature and content of these categories varied: in their work on Moroccan arts, Terrasse and Hainaut (1925) drew a distinction between "Berber arts" and the "Hispano-Mauresque" tradition, while in a narrative catalogue accompanying an exhibit held in Alger in 1924, the arts of Algeria were divided into "Urban arts," "Berber arts," and "Saharan arts."[17] These divisions have had lasting effects. Instead of being called into question by recent scholarship that problematizes ideas of culture areas linked to specific bounded territories,[18] the reconceptualization of collections at the Musée du quai Branly has resulted in the further ossification of many of these categories.

From Ethnographic Evidence to *Arts Premiers*

The process taking place at the Musée du quai Branly can be read as belonging to the French state's response to dilemmas that have recently plagued ethnographic museums around the world. Many of these institutions, founded in the late nineteenth and early twentieth centuries, are now struggling to make their collections more relevant to changing social contexts and new publics, many of whom come from the very communities who originally created the works on display. These changes have taken different forms, from attempts to draw community members more closely into the curatorial process, to exhibits that expose and deconstruct the processes of collection and exhibition.[19] In France, a series of museum projects, including a center devoted to the history of immigration in Paris and a museum of European and Mediterranean civilizations in Marseilles, will tackle different aspects of these issues.[20] These projects and others, like the redistribution of collections at the Museum of Decorative Arts, and the renovation of the Louvre's Islamic Art department, will all have an impact on the way Berber art and material culture are exhibited and interpreted. However, the most important project of this nature (not least because it is the one with the strongest presidential backing) is the Musée du quai Branly, where the state's colonial-era collections from North Africa and elsewhere have been recast as "first arts."

James Clifford's description of the "art-culture" system that has shaped how non-Western material culture is classified and given meaning is useful for understanding the radical reconceptualizations taking place through the Musée du quai Branly project.[21] Clifford describes a system based on two sets of oppositions, between "masterpiece" and "artifact" and between "authentic" and "inauthentic," that result in four "zones" of meaning for material objects. Two of these zones, the zone of "authentic masterpieces" (embodied in the art museum) and the zone of "authentic artifacts" (embodied in the ethnographic museum), are particularly relevant to the program at the Musée du quai Branly.[22] It is important to note that the placement of objects within these zones is not static, and in fact the movement of objects—from artifact to masterpiece, from tourist art to artifact, or from mass culture to masterpiece—is at the heart of Clifford's discussion. Through exhibition and interpretation practices, for example, ethnographic objects may be transformed into "art," using lighting, glass cases, and a focus on individual objects in order to emphasize their aesthetic aspects rather than their social meanings or uses.[23]

In their initial plan for the museum, the directors of the Musée du quai Branly called into question this dichotomy between an aesthetic approach and an ethnographic one, writing, for example, that "the opposition between the approach called 'aesthetic' and the ethnographic approach does not make sense if the museology is respectful of the works, the cultures and the public."[24] Their project was to create a museum where these oppositions would no longer apply, and through architecture, museography, and object selection, the new museum locates itself in a liminal zone between the traditional art museum and the ethnographic one. This new zone is best characterized as the realm of "first arts," or *arts premiers*, a French neologism meant to replace outdated terms like "primitive" or "tribal" art. These terms, as well as the term *arts premiers*, have been criticized by scholars who point out the evolutionary assumptions and the sense of spatial and temporal distance embedded within them.[25] The term *arts premiers* descends from other French terms used to describe non-Western arts (*art nègre*, *arts lointains*, *arts primitifs*, and André Malraux's *arts primordiaux*); it was used by Jacques Kerchache, one of the main proponents of the Musée du quai Branly project, in his publications on African art.[26] Nélia Dias argues that the term is not easily translated into other languages, as it refers not only to a sense of temporal distance from the present, but also to a sense of the origins of art, making *arts premiers* "above all the vestigial arts of extinct cultures."[27]

While the term *arts premiers* may not be as clearly evolutionist as "primitive art," the sense of primordialism it evokes masks the connections between the societies that produced these objects and the global political economy, both historically and today. Also, as Dias points out, it implies that these cultures have "disappeared" in the mists of time, an implication that people from these cultures today would certainly dispute. I use "first arts" to refer to the concept as invoked by those involved in the Musée du quai Branly project, and keep it in quotation marks (or in French) to indicate my own dissatisfaction with the term. Although the Musée du quai Branly was first conceived of explicitly as a museum for *arts premiers*, the use of this term was criticized early on, and it is no longer part of the museum's official name.[28] However, among the general public the museum is still widely perceived as a museum of *arts premiers* or primitive art, and it is commonly referred to as such in the press.[29] In fact, the original "first arts" paradigm has had an important influence on both architecture and museography, shaping object choice and thematic selection across the museum.

A Home for *Arts Premiers*: Architecture and Museography at the Musée du quai Branly

The transformation of objects from ethnographic evidence to "first arts" has been accomplished largely through architectural and design decisions that have a direct impact on the visitor's perception of the objects on display. Through architecture that explicitly evokes a sense of a distant, "primitive" world and museography that attempts to strike a balance between the aesthetic appreciation of objects and their contextualization, the directors of the museum project have created a home for *arts premiers*. The museum building was designed by French architect Jean Nouvel, perhaps best known for his design of the Institut du Monde Arabe (Arab World Institute) in Paris, where he took elements of Middle Eastern architecture—most notably *mashrabiya* latticework windows—and incorporated them into an ultra-modern steel and glass building. He seems to have followed a similar process of inspiration for the Musée du quai Branly by drawing on notions of the "primitive," "natural," or "sacred" world from which the collections supposedly originated. The building is separated from the busy quai Branly by a tall glass wall and is surrounded by a garden of wild grasses, creating a separation between the museum and the bustling urban world outside. The front of the building is punctuated by brightly colored "boxes" whose colors were inspired by those of the collections housed within; between these boxes a glass wall printed with a thick, green forest of vegetation sets the stage for the visitor's "journey of discovery."[30] At one end of the building parts of the exterior wall have been made into a living "vertical garden" (*mur vegetal*), further emphasizing the idea of a wild, overgrown natural habitat as the proper home for these collections from exotic parts of the world. Jean Nouvel himself has described the building as "a place marked by the symbols of the forest, the river, and obsessions with death and oblivion . . . a place that is laden, lived in, where the ancestral spirits of the people who, discovering the human condition, invented gods and beliefs, converse . . ."[31]

Inside the darkened halls of the exhibition space, the museography is somewhere between the singularizing aesthetic of a museum of art and the more heavily contextualized presentation typical of an ethnographic one. The beauty of individual objects is emphasized through cases that often contain only a few pieces, accessible to view from all sides. Each case has object labels offering basic information about the objects (name, place of origin, population or tribe, date, materials, collector or donor, inventory number), and some cases also have brief texts that provide further insights into the uses and meanings of these objects in their places of origin. These texts range from 250 to 600 characters, and, along with the object labels, are often placed on the sides of the exhibit cases so as not to obstruct the visitor's view of the objects. In the North Africa section, most of the exhibit cases are devoted to single genres of artistic production, emphasizing these objects' aesthetic aspects rather than their societal uses and meanings. The cases contain a small number of objects displayed against a black or white background, giving little idea how these pieces were used in daily life. This encourages the visitor to see the pieces—everyday objects like pottery, carpets, clothing, and utensils—primarily as art.

Small screens installed in the cases or on nearby walls are another source of information about the objects on display, giving the visitor a sense of these objects in their original contexts through photographic or video presentations. These representations are often rather outdated, however, going back to a time when the objects were still made and used in their "traditional" contexts, at least through the curious lens of the ethnographer. In the North Africa section, for example, one small screen shows photographs of women in different styles of jewelry taken by Jean Besancenot in Morocco between 1934 and 1938; the other depicts an 'ashura masquerade in a village in the Draa Valley in 1968–1969.[32] Although meant to add an element of contemporaneity to the exhibit displays, these presentations actually tend to freeze the societies depicted in a timeless traditional past.

Additional information about the objects is provided in contexts of increasing specialization and decreasing accessibility. These include multimedia stations in the main exhibit space devoted to broader themes relevant to each region; computers that provide additional interactive programs; and the museum's *médiathèque*, which houses more specialized publications, photographs, films, and audio collections. The interactive multimedia programs, prepared by anthropologists and other area specialists, present a more complex picture of many of the societies depicted in the permanent exhibit and include a sense of contemporary life. This type of hierarchized contextualization means that the motivated visitor can find more information about a specific object, region, or practice; but for the average visitor, it means that the aesthetic experience of the pieces on display is the main information to be gathered.

The architecture and museography described here help to place the objects exhibited at the Musée du quai Branly somewhere between the two extremes of Clifford's "art-culture" system. The collections are not exhibited purely as art objects behind glass and needing no further interpretation, but their aesthetic aspects are emphasized by exhibit cases that highlight individual objects while placing contextualizing information out of the visitor's direct line of vision. The different types of information provided about the objects and their societies are more typical of an ethnographic museum, but it is difficult for the visitor to obtain the in-depth contextualization that is usually present in such a museum. The result is a presentation that satisfies neither the art collector nor the ethnographer, but instead creates a new type of exhibition space considered appropriate for *arts premiers*.

A Voyage to North Africa

This new type of museography has had a clear impact on the interpretation of Berber material culture presented at the museum. Curatorial decisions regarding object and thematic selection have also served to place these objects firmly within the realm of "first arts," a category not generally associated with the arts of North Africa. During the planning stages for the Musée du quai Branly, the museum curators and directors decided to organize the permanent exhibit into four large geographical regions: Africa, Asia, Oceania, and the Americas. Faced with this division, the curators in charge of developing the museography for the North African collections, Marie-France Vivier of the MAAO and Jean Lambert of the Musée de l'homme, argued that the Maghrib should be placed within the Africa section. They wrote in one of their first reports, "In the Maghrib, like everywhere in Africa, themes of identity, rites of passage, fertility, and protection are conveyed through signs which are inscribed on the body and on everyday objects."[33] This decision reversed the practice at the Musée de l'homme, where the North African collections were part of a department for North Africa and the Near East. Its effect is to emphasize the African origins of the Maghrib's original inhabitants, placing Berber pottery, jewelry and textiles alongside the African masks and statuary more generally associated with a "first arts" paradigm.

The curatorial focus on Berber art, and its implications for the museum's portrayal of North Africa in general, is made clear in an analysis of the content of the North Africa exhibit. The North Africa section is divided into eleven exhibit cases and three of the "boxes" seen from the exterior of the building. Devoted to different themes, the "boxes" are small rooms that serve as extensions of the main exhibition space. In an arrangement that reproduces the colonial-era categories described above, the main part of the exhibit is organized around three "poles" of artistic production—urban, rural, and nomadic—that tend to slip into ethnic divisions—Arab, Berber, and Saharan—in museum texts and curators' reports. In addition to exhibit cases that focus on each of these "poles," the exhibit includes cases that address three main thematic topics: Prehistory and History; Expressions of the Sacred; and Rituals.

Throughout the exhibit, the emphasis is on the Berber elements of North African art and culture. Urban arts are found primarily in a box containing gold jewelry, embroidery, woven silk, painted ceramics and a carved and painted wooden door representing "this refined art [that] has inherited a tradition combining Arabo-Andalusian and Ottoman influences with the pre-Islamic Berber foundation."[34] Urban craftsmanship is also found in a small case on the history of North Africa at the beginning of the exhibition space, where, in a direct echo of Terrasse and Hainaut, objects like an astrolabe and carved fragments from the *minbars* (pulpits) of North African mosques are described as part of the "Hispano-Mauresque" style.

The remainder of the exhibit is devoted to the rural and nomadic arts, with most cases organized around a single object type or artistic genre (arms, pottery, jewelry, textiles). These cases contain primarily, though not solely, objects made in Berber-speaking regions. However, a number of texts referring to different genres of Berber art—Berber Arms, Berber Jewelry, Berber Crockery—give the impression that all of these objects were produced by Berber communities. In the one major example where this is not the case, the largest exhibit box containing a selection of carpets made in both Arabic and Berber-speaking regions, the exhibit text is simply "Rural Art: Carpets." However, as the Berber-rural connection is so tightly drawn in other parts of the exhibit, it is likely to extend to the visitor's understanding of this collection as well. A similar connection is drawn between the Berber-speaking Tuareg and "nomadic" art.[35] Although the exhibit cases devoted to Saharan regions contain some objects from Arabic-speaking populations, the emphasis is on the Berber-speaking Tuareg, who remain the iconic Saharan population in the French collective imagination.[36] The focus on the Tuareg again reinforces the priority given to objects from Berber-speaking populations in the museum's permanent exhibit.

This emphasis is partially the result of the main curator's desire, stated repeatedly in interviews, to "valorize" Berber art for a public who may not be as familiar with it as with the urban or Islamic art displayed at the Louvre or the Institut du monde arabe. Marie-France Vivier also described the focus on Berber material culture as fitting the museum's mission to exhibit art from five continents with "very ancient cultures." Although the Berbers had converted to Islam, they had also kept "all their older culture," their myths and beliefs in spirits, nature, and ancestors, beliefs she described as part of cultures everywhere.[37] The choice to focus on Berber art, and specifically objects that can be interpreted as evidence of these "ancient beliefs," has meant the exclusion of many objects in the museum's collections deemed more appropriate for the Louvre's Islamic Art department, where they are placed on semi-permanent loan. It has also meant a lack of attention to the long history of connections between the Maghrib and Mashriq, a history that is only vaguely hinted at by the placement of the North Africa section adjacent to the section of the exhibit devoted to the Middle East. These decisions have resulted in an argument that equates the Maghrib with (pre-Islamic) Berber culture and transforms Berber material culture into *arts premiers*.

"First Arts" of the Maghrib

The transformation of Berber material culture into the "first arts" of the Maghrib has been achieved through different strategies of framing and interpretation. In museographic techniques and exhibit texts, the curators have employed strategies of both "exoticizing" and "assimilating," to use Ivan Karp's terminology. Karp describes the display of ethnographic objects as art as an assimilating strategy, done to "emphasize the similarities between the aesthetic that is involved in appreciating the object in a museum and the aesthetic assumed to have been involved in its making."[38] At the Musée du quai Branly, many pieces that were formerly used as ethnographic "evidence" have been reframed as "art" through the museographic techniques described above.

Other objects, however, need a more heavily interpretive context to make the transition from ethnographic object to "first arts." For these pieces, their status as *arts premiers* is directly linked to their interpretation as exhibiting elements of the pre-Islamic past. The two displays organized around societal themes rather than genres of artistic production—"Expressions of the Sacred" and "Rituals"—are the most explicit examples of the curators' use of North African objects to portray pre-Islamic or "animist" beliefs and practices, thereby making the argument that the Maghrib is culturally closer to sub-Saharan Africa than to the Middle East. This strategy is a clear example of exoticizing, as objects are taken from cultures that are actually quite familiar to a French audience and de-familiarized through the trope of "animism." Karp cites the reference to African religious practice as "animism" as a common strategy of exoticization that casts non-Western practices as inverting familiar beliefs—in this case, anthropocentric Western religions.[39] Although these two displays form a small part of the exhibit in comparison to the cases that focus on North African artistic genres, their use of objects from Berber regions to convey a sense of the primacy of pre-Islamic practices is important to the transformation of Berber art into the "first arts" of the Maghrib.

The exhibit box "Expressions of the Sacred: Religions and Beliefs" discusses the presence of Islam and Judaism as well as the influence of "pagan" and "animist" beliefs on religious practice in North Africa.[40] It contains two cases—"Writing" and "Religions and Beliefs." The Writing theme includes objects that bear examples of the Arabic, Hebrew, and Tifinagh alphabets, though there is a preponderance of objects in Arabic, including a group of Koran tablets from the original Musée des colonies collection. In the Religions and Beliefs case, however, objects related to formal religion—a decorated Koran box, a Torah shield and a Hanukkah lamp—are outnumbered by objects related to more popular beliefs or rituals, such as amulets, protective ornaments, and objects used by religious brotherhoods. The text associated with this box discusses Islam and Judaism along with pre-Islamic beliefs and post-Islamic practices that are presented as forms of those beliefs, stating that "popular Islam integrated a number of pagan survivals" and that "animist rites for fertility and fecundity are found in Muslim festivals."[41] This treatment de-emphasizes the centrality of orthodox Islam in North African life, focusing instead on practices that are interpreted as pre-dating its arrival and therefore linked to a somewhat mythical originary Berber culture. This emphasis, while it may reflect the importance of popular religious practice in the Maghrib, is presented in terms that exoticize and defamiliarize these practices.

A similar emphasis is found in the case devoted to "Rituals: Marriage, Myths and Games."[42] Orthodox Islam is completely absent here, and the focus is on the survival of pre-Islamic practices in Berber regions. The case includes a wedding costume from the Siwa oasis as well as a decorated ostrich egg and a Kabyle pottery lamp, both used as symbols of fertility and good luck in wedding ceremonies. A text placed on the side of the case describes some of the marriage rituals that have been "inherited from the Berber animist past and reinterpreted by Islam."[43] The rest of the case focuses primarily on "Myths," and the brief accompanying text describes how "ceremonies that accompany life cycles such as marriage and Muslim festivals contain echoes of the animist rites of fertility and fecundity."[44] This theme is evoked by three main objects: a figurine from the Middle Atlas used in a form of community justice;[45] a doll called a *telghunja* or "bride of the rain"; and the mask used in the celebration of 'ashura described at the beginning of this chapter. These last two objects were collected in the oasis of Tabelbala in southwestern Algeria in the 1950s by Dominique Champault, an anthropologist who later served as head of the North Africa and Near East division at the Musée de l'homme. Although the oasis is not Berber-speaking or of exclusively Berber ethnic origin (the inhabitants speak a Songhay language specific to the oasis called Korandje), these objects are similar to those used in practices once widespread across North Africa.[46]

The *telghunja* is a doll made from a wooden stick with two wooden spoons attached as arms, clothed in bits of cloth and pieces of jewelry. In Tabelbala, and in many parts of the Berber world, similar dolls were used as part of a rain ritual in which young women paraded the doll through the village, symbolically offering it as a bride to Anzar, the rain personified. Anzar is sometimes referred to as an ancient Berber god of rain.[47] The mask was used as part of a masquerade in the celebration of 'ashura, the tenth day of *Muharram*, the first month of the Muslim calendar. For Shi'ite Muslims, 'ashura is a day of mourning in commemoration of the battle of Karbala and the death of the prophet Muhammad's grandson Husayn, considered by Shi'ites to be the third Imam.[48] In the Sunni Maghrib, the celebration of 'ashura is related to the prophet Muhammad's designation of this day as a day of fasting, and it incorporates pre-Islamic practices related to agrarian festivals. In some regions one aspect of these practices is a masquerade, in which the young men of a community disguise themselves with masks and proceed through the village, visiting individual houses or performing in a public square. These carnavalesque performances are often sexually explicit, linking the practice to ancient agrarian or fertility rituals. Similar practices, such as the masquerade known as *Bilmawn*, take place at the time of the festival of *al-'id al-kabir*.[49]

The presence of these objects in one of the few exhibit cases meant to depict North African social life serves to underline the curators' argument that Berber material culture should be interpreted in terms of pre-Islamic practices and ideas. Using descriptive texts that evoke "animism" and "ancient" practices, this interpretation serves to exoticize and defamiliarize, distancing the societies that produced them from the museum visitor. In addition, the displaying of the two very rare North African examples of objects that can be fitted into the primitive art genres of masks and statuary indicates the strenuous interpretive work needed to make Berber art into the *arts premiers* of the Maghrib.

Conclusion

French museums have housed significant collections of Berber material culture since the late nineteenth century, when Berber objects began to be collected by both anthropologists and art collectors. The connections between individuals, state institutions, academic scholarship, and colonial arts policies have shaped our understanding of Berber arts, and the categories (art versus ethnography, Arab/urban versus Berber/rural) established early on continue to organize the production of knowledge about these arts today. The largest collection of Berber material culture owned by the French state has now entered the new Musée du quai Branly, making it the single most important museum portrayal of Berber art and culture in France. While many objects deemed too "ethnographic" or too "Islamic" have been excluded from the permanent exhibit halls of the new museum, other examples of Berber artistic production have been transformed from ethnographic objects and colonial arts into the "first arts" of the Maghrib.

This transformation has been accomplished largely by framing Berber art in terms of an ancient, pre-Islamic past. This selective portrayal gives scant attention to the multiple influences—Roman, Arab, Muslim, Mediterranean, and European—that have shaped Berber life over the centuries. It also ignores important aspects of Berber dynastic history as well as contemporary life, and glosses over the dynamics that make the categories urban-rural and Arab-Berber often very difficult to compartmentalize. In addition, because the vast majority of the objects being used to represent these "ancient" practices and beliefs originated in the late nineteenth or early twentieth centuries, the portrayal and the term "first arts" are somewhat contradictory.[50]

The new Musée du quai Branly displays a number of beautiful objects that attest to the skill and aesthetic sensitivity of artisans and craftspeople from different parts of the Berber-speaking world. Despite the effort to reconceptualize these collections, the museum has largely reproduced colonial-era categories and assumptions, resulting in a portrayal of Berber arts as caught in a supposedly timeless realm of "traditional" culture. The fact that Paris is home to a large population of Berber descent, and is itself a center for creative production and performance for that population, has had little impact on the work of curators and other museum personnel. Unlike other recent museum projects that have made an effort to portray contemporary life alongside "traditional" objects and practices, the Musée du quai Branly has chosen to transform its collections into *arts premiers*. This transformation, while granting a degree of recognition to what a recent museum publication calls "the very unrecognized Berber culture,"[51] leaves little room for contemporary stories, voices, or reinterpretations that might originate beyond the museum walls.

Notes

I am grateful to Susan Miller, Jane Goodman, Katherine Hoffman, Rubie Watson, Suzanne Blier, and Christopher Stone for their insightful comments on earlier drafts of this paper. Research was funded by dissertation research fellowships from the German Marshall Fund and the Krupp Foundation, travel grants from the Centers for Middle Eastern and European Studies at Harvard University, and a P.E.O. Scholar Award.

1. I use the term "Berber art" in a broad anthropological sense, indicating the "aesthetic embellishment of objects" through crafts like pottery, weaving, and metalwork rather than a Western concept of art that prioritizes aesthetic contemplation or forms like painting and sculpture. Similarly, the terms "Berber arts" or "North African arts" are used interchangeably with terms like "craft" or "artisanal production" to refer to these everyday art forms. See Abraham Rosman and Paula G. Rubel, "Art," in *The Dictionary of Anthropology*, ed. Thomas Barfield (Oxford and Malden, Mass.: Blackwell, 1997), 29–30.

2. The term *arts premiers* does not have a commonly used English equivalent. For this reason I use "first arts" in quotation marks or the French term. It can also be translated as "early arts." Further discussion of this term to follow.

3. Lisa Bernasek, "Representation and the Republic: North African Art and Material Culture in Paris" (Ph.D. diss., Harvard University, 2007).

4. Pierre Bourdieu and Randal Johnson, *The Field of Cultural Production: Essays on Art and Literature* (New York: Columbia University Press, 1993), 37.

5. The European collections of the Musée de l'homme have been transferred to the new Musée des civilisations de l'Europe et de la Méditerranée to open in Marseilles in 2012. The Musée de l'homme has retained its collections pertaining to archaeology and physical anthropology, and is now in the process of redefining itself to focus on prehistory, evolution, and man's relationship to the natural world. See Jean-Pierre Mohen, *Le nouveau Musée de l'homme* (Paris: Odile Jacob and Muséum national d'histoire naturelle, 2004). The MAAO closed at the end of 2002. Its building at Porte Dorée, built as part of the International Colonial Exposition of 1931, is now being used for a new museum of immigration, the Cité nationale de l'histoire de l'immigration.

6. Stephen Vernoit, ed., *Discovering Islamic Art: Scholars, Collectors and Collections, 1850–1950* (London: I.B. Tauris, 2000).

7. On collecting practices in North Africa and colonial arts policies, see Nadia Erzini, "Cultural Administration in French North Africa and the Growth of Islamic Art History," in *Discovering Islamic Art*, ed. Stephen Vernoit (London: I.B. Tauris, 2000), 71–84; Hamid Irbouh, *Art in the Service of Colonialism: French Art Education in Morocco, 1912–1956* (London: I.B. Tauris, 2005).

8. For background on colonial policies related to Berber ethnicity, see Patricia M. E. Lorcin, *Imperial Identities: Stereotyping, Prejudice and Race in Colonial Algeria* (New York: I.B. Tauris, 1999), passim, and Paul A. Silverstein, *Algeria in France: Transpolitics, Race, and Nation* (Bloomington: Indiana University Press, 2004), chapter 2.

9. Erzini, "Cultural Administration in French North Africa," 80–84.

10. On the early history of the Musée de l'homme, see Alice Conklin, "Civil Society, Science and Empire in Late Republican France: The Foundation of Paris's Museum of Man," *Osiris* 17 (2002); Benoit de l'Estoile, "'Des races non pas inférieures,

mais différentes: de l'exposition coloniale au Musée de l'homme," in *Les politiques de l'anthropologie: discours et pratiques en France (1860–1940)*, ed. Claude Blanckaert (Paris: L'Harmattan, 2001); and James Clifford, *The Predicament of Culture* (Cambridge, Mass.: Harvard University Press, 1988), chapter 4.

11. Musée d'ethnographie, *Instructions sommaires pour les collecteurs d'objets ethnographiques* (Paris: Musée d'ethnographie et mission scientifique Dakar-Djibouti, 1931), 8.

12. On salvage ethnography, see Jacob W. Gruber, "Ethnographic Salvage and the Shaping of Anthropology," *American Anthropologist* 72(6) (1970): 1289–1299; George W. Stocking, *The Ethnographer's Magic and Other Essays in the History of Anthropology* (Madison: University of Wisconsin Press, 1992); and Steven Conn, *Museums and American Intellectual Life, 1876–1926* (Chicago: University of Chicago Press, 1998), chapter 3.

13. On the history of the MAAO, see Patricia Morton, *Hybrid Modernities: Architecture and Representation at the 1931 Colonial Exposition, Paris* (Cambridge: Massachusetts Institute of Technology Press, 2000) and Musée national des arts d'Afrique et d'Océanie, *Le palais des colonies: histoire du Musée des arts d'Afrique et d'Océanie* (Paris: Réunion des musées nationaux, 2002).

14. Irbouh, *Art in the Service of Colonialism*, 59–62; Roger Benjamin, *Orientalist Aesthetics: Art, Colonialism, and French North Africa, 1880–1930* (Berkeley: University of California Press, 2003), chapter 8.

15. This is especially true of the jewelry collections of Paul Eudel and the Lelong textile collection. Eudel's collection was formed as part of a study of gold and silverworking in Algeria funded by the Algerian government in the early 1900s. See Paul Eudel, *L'orfèvrerie algérienne et tunisienne* (Alger: Adolphe Jourdan, 1902). The textiles (primarily carpets) collected by Dr. Lelong and his wife Thérèse Lemerle in Morocco between 1927 and 1937 were bought under the guidance of their friend Prosper Ricard, director of the Service des arts indigènes. See Mireille Jacotin, "Splendeur du Tapis Marocain: La collection du musée national des arts d'Afrique et d'Océanie," *L'estampille l'objet d'art*, no. 323 (1998): 41–49. Both collections figure prominently in the Musée du quai Branly's permanent exhibit.

16. Henri Terrasse and Jean Hainaut, *Les arts décoratifs au Maroc* (Casablanca: Afrique Orient, 2001 [1925]), 15. (All translations of quotations from French sources are my own.)

17. Augustin Berque, *Les arts indigènes algériens en 1924* (Alger: Pfister, 1924).

18. James Clifford, *Routes: Travel and Translation in the Late Twentieth Century* (Cambridge, Mass.: Harvard University Press, 1997); Akhil Gupta and James Ferguson, "Beyond "Culture": Space, Identity, and the Politics of Difference," in *Culture Power Place: Explorations in Critical Anthropology*, ed. Akhil Gupta and James Ferguson (Durham, N.C.: Duke University Press, 1997), 33–51.

19. There has been much literature on this shifting paradigm in relation to ethnographic and other types of museums. See, for example, Clifford, *Routes: Travel and Translation in the Late Twentieth Century*; Anna Laura Jones, "Exploding Canons: The Anthropology of Museums," *Annual Review of Anthropology* 22 (1993): 201–220; Ivan Karp and Steven Lavine, *Exhibiting Cultures: The Poetics and Politics of Museum Display* (Washington: Smithsonian Institution Press, 1991); Ivan Karp, Christine Mullen Kreamer, and Steven Lavine, *Museums and Communities: The Politics of Public Culture* (Washington: Smithsonian Institution Press, 1992); and Sharon Macdonald and Gordon Fyfe, eds., *Theorizing Museums: Representing Identity and Diversity in a*

Changing World (Oxford: Blackwell, 1996). One example of a museum where community involvement has been placed at the center of curatorial practice is the new National Museum of the American Indian in Washington, D.C., a museum that has addressed the paradigm shift through innovative exhibits that directly discuss the history of collecting and exhibition is the Musée d'Ethnographie de Neuchâtel in Switzerland.

20. On these museum projects, see Herman Lebovics, *Bringing the Empire Back Home: France in the Global Age* (Durham, N.C.: Duke University Press, 2004), chapter 5. For a general account of the creation of the Musée du quai Branly, see Sally Price, *Paris Primitive: Jacques Chirac's Museum on the Quai Branly* (Chicago: University of Chicago Press, 2007). The Cité nationale de l'histoire de l'immigration, opened in October 2007, does not have permanent museum collections but houses exhibits on the history of immigration in France, contemporary art, oral history archives, and a resource center for people researching their family history and origins. The Musée des civilisations de l'Europe et de la Mediterranée will open in Marseilles in 2012 in a newly constructed building overlooking the Mediterranean. The museum will house the collections of the Musée national des arts et traditions populaires, the European collections of the Musée de l'homme, and recently acquired collections from the southern Mediterranean region, including North Africa. The Musée du quai Branly will place some of their Maghribi collections on semi-permanent loan at the Marseilles museum, but the extent of these loans has yet to be determined. Another important state museum project that will have an impact on the exhibition of arts from North Africa is the renovation of the Louvre's Arts of Islam department, scheduled for completion in 2010. The Musée du quai Branly's Maghrib section will put some of its collections on semi-permanent loan at the Louvre as well.

21. Clifford, *The Predicament of Culture*, chapter 10.

22. The other two zones, of "inauthentic masterpieces" (such as mass culture and industrial design) and "inauthentic artifacts" (tourist arts), are less relevant because the museum context itself confers an assumption of authenticity on the objects it houses.

23. See also Sally Price, *Primitive Art in Civilized Places* (Chicago: University of Chicago Press, 1989).

24. Museum Director Stéphane Martin quoted in French Ministry of Culture and Communication, "Dossier: le futur Musée du quai Branly" (Paris: Minstère de la culture et de la communication, 2000), 2–3.

25. See Johannes Fabian, *Time and the Other: How Anthropology Makes Its Object* (New York: Columbia University Press, 1983) and Price, *Primitive Art in Civilized Places*, chapters 3 and 4.

26. Jacques Kerchache, *Art premier en Afrique* (Arras: Centre Noirot, 1981), and by the same author, "Les arts premiers de l'Est nigérien," *Connaissance des Arts*, no. 285 (1975): 67–73.

27. Nélia Dias, "Qu'est-ce que les 'arts premiers'?," *Les Grands Dossiers des Sciences Humaines* 3 (2006): 11.

28. The museum's official names have been Musée des civilisations et des arts premiers; Musée de l'homme, des arts et des civilisations; Musée des arts et des civilisations; and finally Musée du quai Branly after its location along the Seine. See Nélia Dias, "Esquisse ethnographique d'un projet: le Musée du quai Branly," *French Politics, Culture & Society* 19(2) (2001): 81–101 for an account of the evolution of the museum project and some of the debates involved.

29. For example, "Dossier: Musée des arts premiers: le chef-d'œuvre de Jean Nouvel," *Beaux Arts* 264 (2006): 58–81.

30. Stéphane Martin, "Preface," in *Musée du quai Branly Museum Guide Book* (Paris: Musée du quai Branly, 2006), 8. Tropes of travel, a "journey," and "discovery" are common in the official literature of the Musée du quai Branly.

31. "C'est un lieu marqué par les symboles de la forêt, du fleuve, et les obsessions de la mort et de l'oubli . . . C'est un endroit chargé, habité, celui où dialoguent les esprits ancestraux des hommes qui, découvrant la condition humaine, inventaient dieux et croyances." Jean Nouvel, "Présence-absence ou la dématérialisation sélective: Lettre d'intention de Jean Nouvel pour le concours international d'architecture (1999)," in *Un musée composite: une architecture conçue autour des collections*, ed. Musée du quai Branly (Paris: Musée du quai Branly, 2006), 1. This passage is from Jean Nouvel's original description of the building submitted for the architectural competition in 1999 and has been reprinted in many museum publications and on its website.

32. The festival of 'ashura is held on the tenth day of *Muharram*, the first month of the Muslim calendar. In some parts of North Africa celebrations of 'ashura include a masquerade, in which young men disguise themselves with masks and parade through the village or perform in a public square. See further discussion of 'ashura in E. Bernus, "Ashura," in *Encyclopédie Berbère*, volume VI, ed. Gabriel Camps (Paris: Edisud, 1990), 1231–1232.

33. Marie-France Vivier and Jean Lambert, "Parcours Maghreb: Formes, signes et sens (unpublished preliminary exhibit plans)," (Paris: Musée du quai Branly, 2001), 1. Jean Lambert eventually left the project and Marie-France Vivier became the main curator in charge of the North African collections, working in coordination with Hélène Joubert, head of the Africa section, and assisted by other curators working in the Africa section and on the Middle Eastern collections. Marie-France Vivier retired in October 2006 and was replaced by Hana Chidiac, who is now in charge of the collections from North Africa and the Near East. The creation of a "unité patrimoniale des collections Afrique du Nord et Proche Orient" at the Musée du quai Branly (rather than separating these two regions as was done earlier in the project) is unlikely to have an impact on the permanent exhibit's orientation.

34. Exhibit text "Art Citadin," North Africa section, Musée du quai Branly.

35. The term "nomadic art" is rather anachronistic as most of the peoples who created these arts are now primarily settled. See Jeremy Keenan, *The Lesser Gods of the Sahara: Social Change and Contested Terrain amongst the Tuareg of Algeria* (London and Portland, OR: Frank Cass, 2004).

36. See Gilles Boëtsch, Hélène Claudot-Hawad, and Jean-Noël Ferrié, "Des Touareg 'sauvages' aux Egyptiens 'urbains': les gradations de l'émotion exotique," in *Zoos humains: de la vénus hottentote aux reality shows*, ed. Nicolas Bancel et al. (Paris: Editions la Découverte, 2002), 142–150.

37. Interview with Marie-France Vivier at the Musée du quai Branly on June 29, 2006. Other information on the development of the Maghrib section comes from meetings and interviews carried out between December 2003 and June 2006. Mme. Vivier also kindly provided me with a number of internal reports on the development of the North Africa section and copies of all exhibit texts. I am grateful for her time and her openness to my research.

38. Ivan Karp, "Other Cultures in Museum Perspective," in *Exhibiting Cultures: The Poetics and Politics of Museum Display*, ed. Ivan Karp and Steven Lavine (Washington: Smithsonian Institution Press, 1991), 376.

39. Ibid., 375–376.

40. Exhibit text "Les expressions du sacré," North Africa section, Musée du quai Branly.

41. Ibid. The objects in this case are not primarily from Berber-speaking regions, but are used to evoke pre-Islamic practices and beliefs that are associated with Berber arts and culture elsewhere in the exhibit.

42. In previous exhibit plans this case was given the broader title "Life Cycles and Social Life," an indication that the objects exhibited here were meant to stand for a much larger conception of social life in North Africa.

43. Exhibit text "Autour des rituels," North Africa section, Musée du quai Branly.

44. Exhibit text "Mariage, mythes et jeux," North Africa section, Musée du quai Branly. This case also contains objects that illustrate the theme of games that I will not discuss here.

45. Musée du quai Branly Inventory Number 71.1942.28.3. This object is from the Musée de l'homme collection, and was donated by Joseph Herber, a doctor who worked in Morocco for many years. It is described in museum records as originating from the Beni M'tir in the Middle Atlas. The collector describes its use as a means of collective justice: when someone in the community committed a crime, a likeness would be made of him or her and displayed in a public place as punishment. See Marie Barthelemy Joseph Herber, "Poupées marocaines," *Archives berbères* 3(1) (1918): 18.

46. Dominique Champault, "Une oasis du Sahara nord-occidental, Tabelbala" (Ph.D. diss., Centre national de la recherche scientifique, Université de Paris, 1969), 140–141, 146–153.

47. Gabriel Camps, "Anzar," in *Encyclopédie berbère*, volume VI, ed. Gabriel Camps (Paris: Edisud, 1989), 795–797. See also Cynthia Becker, *Amazigh Arts in Morocco: Women Shaping Berber Identity* (Austin: University of Texas Press, 2006), 37–38.

48. "Ashura," in *Oxford Dictionary of Islam*, ed. John L. Esposito (Oxford: Oxford University Press, 2003). Oxford Reference Online. http://www.oxfordreference.com/views/ENTRY.html?subview=Main&entry=t125.e217 (accessed Dec. 20, 2008).

49. E. Bernus, "Ashura,"; and Champault, "Une oasis du Sahara nord-occidental, Tabelbala." On *Bilmawn*, see Abdallah Hammoudi, *The Victim and Its Masks: An Essay on Sacrifice and Masquerade in the Maghreb*, trans. Paula Wissing (Chicago: University of Chicago Press, 1993), passim.

50. This criticism is directed more at the framing of the museum as a repository for "first arts" than at the decisions of the North Africa section curators themselves, whose work has been confined by these parameters.

51. Musée du quai Branly, *La richesse des collections offerte à tous les regards: un musée passerelle, une cité culturelle* (Paris: Musée du quai Branly, 2006), 7.

Bibliography

Beaux Arts Magazine. "Dossier: Musée des arts premiers: le chef-d'œuvre de Jean Nouvel." *Beaux Arts* 264 (2006): 58–81.

Becker, Cynthia. *Amazigh Arts in Morocco: Women Shaping Berber Identity*. Austin: University of Texas Press, 2006.

Benjamin, Roger. *Orientalist Aesthetics: Art, Colonialism, and French North Africa, 1880–1930*. Berkeley: University of California Press, 2003.

Bernasek, Lisa. "Representation and the Republic: North African Art and Material Culture in Paris." Ph.D. diss., Harvard University, 2007.

Bernus, E. "Ashura." In *Encyclopédie Berbère*, volume VIII, ed. Gabriel Camps. Paris: Edisud, 1990, 1231–1232.

Berque, Augustin. *Les arts indigènes algériens en 1924*. Alger: Pfister, 1924.

Boëtsch, Gilles, Hélène Claudot-Hawad, and Jean-Noël Ferrié. "Des Touareg 'sauvages' aux Egyptiens 'urbains': les gradations de l'émotion exotique." In *Zoos Humains: de la Vénus hottentote aux reality shows*, ed. Nicolas Bancel, Pascal Blanchard, Gilles Boëtsch, Eric Deroo, and Sandrine Lemaire. Paris: Editions la Découverte, 2002, 142–150.

Bourdieu, Pierre, and Randal Johnson. *The Field of Cultural Production: Essays on Art and Literature*. New York: Columbia University Press, 1993.

Camps, Gabriel. "Anzar." In *Encyclopédie berbère*, volume VI, ed. Gabriel Camps. Paris: Edisud, 1989, 795–797.

Champault, Dominique. "Une oasis du Sahara nord-occidental, Tabelbala." Ph.D. diss., Université de Paris, 1969.

Clifford, James. *Routes: Travel and Translation in the Late Twentieth Century*. Cambridge, Mass.: Harvard University Press, 1997.

———. *The Predicament of Culture*. Cambridge, Mass.: Harvard University Press, 1988.

Conklin, Alice. "Civil Society, Science and Empire in Late Republican France: The Foundation of Paris's Museum of Man." *Osiris* 17 (2002): 255–290.

Conn, Steven. *Museums and American Intellectual Life, 1876–1926*. Chicago: University of Chicago Press, 1998.

Dias, Nélia. "Esquisse ethnographique d'un projet: le Musée du quai Branly." *French Politics, Culture & Society* 19 (2001): 81–101.

———. "Qu'est-ce que les 'arts premiers'?" *Les grands dossiers des sciences humaines* 3 (2006): 8–11.

Erzini, Nadia. "Cultural Administration in French North Africa and the Growth of Islamic Art History." In *Discovering Islamic Art: Scholars, Collectors and Collections, 1850–1950*, ed. Stephen Vernoit. London: I.B. Tauris, 2000, 71–84.

Esposito, John L., ed. *Oxford Dictionary of Islam*, s.v. "Ashura." Oxford: Oxford University Press, 2003. Oxford Reference Online. http://www.oxfordreference.com/views/ENTRY html?subview=Main&entry=t125.e217 (accessed Sept. 30, 2009).

Eudel, Paul. *L'orfèvrerie algérienne et tunisienne*. Alger: Adolphe Jourdan, 1902.

Fabian, Johannes. *Time and the Other: How Anthropology Makes Its Object*. New York: Columbia University Press, 1983.

French Ministry of Culture and Communication. "Dossier: Le futur musée du quai Branly." Paris: Minstère de la culture et de la communication, 2000.

Gruber, Jacob W. "Ethnographic Salvage and the Shaping of Anthropology." *American Anthropologist* 72 (1970): 1289–1299.

Gupta, Akhil, and James Ferguson. "Beyond 'Culture': Space, Identity, and the Politics of Difference." In *Culture Power Place: Explorations in Critical Anthropology*, ed. Akhil Gupta and James Ferguson. Durham, N.C.: Duke University Press, 1997, 33–51.

Hammoudi, Abdallah. *The Victim and Its Masks: An Essay on Sacrifice and Masquerade in the Maghreb*, trans. Paula Wissing. Chicago: University of Chicago Press, 1993.

Herber, Marie Barthelemy Joseph. "Poupées marocaines." *Les archives berbères* 3(1) (1918): 18.

Irbouh, Hamid. *Art in the Service of Colonialism: French Art Education in Morocco, 1912–1956.* London: I.B. Tauris, 2005.

Jacotin, Mireille. "Splendeur du Tapis Marocain: La collection du musée national des arts d'Afrique et d'Océanie." *L'estampille l'objet d'art* 323 (1998): 41–49.

Jones, Anna Laura. "Exploding Canons: The Anthropology of Museums." *Annual Review of Anthropology* 22 (1993): 201–220.

Karp, Ivan. "Other Cultures in Museum Perspective." In *Exhibiting Cultures: The Poetics and Politics of Museum Display,* ed. Ivan Karp and Steven Lavine. Washington, D.C.: Smithsonian Institution Press, 1991, 373–385.

Karp, Ivan, and Steven Lavine. *Exhibiting Cultures: The Poetics and Politics of Museum Display.* Washington, D.C.: Smithsonian Institution Press, 1991.

Karp, Ivan, Christine Mullen Kreamer, and Steven Lavine. *Museums and Communities: The Politics of Public Culture.* Washington, D.C.: Smithsonian Institution Press, 1992.

Keenan, Jeremy. *The Lesser Gods of the Sahara: Social Change and Contested Terrain amongst the Tuareg of Algeria.* London and Portland, OR: Frank Cass, 2004.

Kerchache, Jacques. *Art premier en Afrique.* Arras, France: Centre Noirot, 1981.

———. "Les arts premiers de l'Est nigérien." *Connaissance des Arts* 285 (1975): 67–73.

Lebovics, Herman. *Bringing the Empire Back Home: France in the Global Age.* Durham, N.C.: Duke University Press, 2004.

l'Estoile, Benoit de. "'Des races non pas inférieures, mais différentes': de l'Exposition coloniale au Musée de l'homme." In *Les politiques de l'anthropologie: discours et pratiques en France (1860–1940),* ed. Claude Blanckaert. Paris: L'Harmattan, 2001, 391–473.

Lorcin, Patricia M. E. *Imperial Identities: Stereotyping, Prejudice and Race in Colonial Algeria.* New York: I.B. Tauris, 1999.

Macdonald, Sharon, and Gordon Fyfe, eds. *Theorizing Museums: Representing Identity and Diversity in a Changing World.* Oxford: Blackwell, 1996.

Martin, Stéphane. Preface. In *Musée du quai Branly Museum Guide Book.* Paris: Musée du quai Branly, 2006, 8–9.

Mohen, Jean-Pierre. *Le nouveau Musée de l'homme.* Paris: Odile Jacob and Muséum national d'histoire naturelle, 2004.

Morton, Patricia. *Hybrid Modernities: Architecture and Representation at the 1931 Colonial Exposition, Paris.* Cambridge: Massachusetts Institute of Technology Press, 2000.

Musée d'ethnographie. *Instructions sommaires pour les collecteurs d'objets ethnographiques.* Paris: Musée d'ethnographie et Mission scientifique Dakar-Djibouti, 1931.

Musée du quai Branly. *La richesse des collections offerte à tous les regards: un musée passerelle, une cité culturelle.* Paris: Musée du quai Branly, 2006.

Musée national des arts d'Afrique et d'Océanie. *Le palais des colonies: histoire du Musée des arts d'Afrique et d'Océanie.* Paris: Réunion des musées nationaux, 2002.

Nouvel, Jean. "Présence-absence ou la dématérialisation sélective: Lettre d'intention de Jean Nouvel pour le concours international d'architecture (1999)." In *Un musée composite: une architecture conçue autour des collections,* ed. Musée du quai Branly. Paris: Musée du quai Branly, 2006, 1.

Price, Sally. *Paris Primitive: Jacques Chirac's Museum on the Quai Branly.* Chicago: University of Chicago Press, 2007.

———. *Primitive Art in Civilized Places.* Chicago: University of Chicago Press, 1989.

Rosman, Abraham, and Paula G. Rubel. "Art." In *The Dictionary of Anthropology*, ed. Thomas Barfield. Oxford: Blackwell, 1997, 29–30.

Silverstein, Paul A. *Algeria in France: Transpolitics, Race, and Nation.* Bloomington: Indiana University Press, 2004.

Stocking, George W. *The Ethnographer's Magic and Other Essays in the History of Anthropology.* Madison: University of Wisconsin Press, 1992.

Terrasse, Henri, and Jean Hainaut. *Les arts décoratifs au Maroc.* Casablanca: Afrique Orient, 2001 [1925].

Vernoit, Stephen, ed. *Discovering Islamic Art: Scholars, Collectors and Collections, 1850–1950.* London and New York: I.B. Tauris, 2000.

Vivier, Marie-France, and Jean Lambert. *Parcours Maghreb: formes, signes et sens* (unpublished preliminary exhibit plans). Paris: Musée du quai Branly, 2001.

9

Deconstructing the History of Berber Arts: Tribalism, Matriarchy, and a Primitive Neolithic Past

Cynthia Becker

In Marrakesh, exclusive art galleries flank the tree-lined boulevards of the Ville Nouvelle. These galleries exhibit local and European artists with international reputations and cater to a wealthy European, American, and Moroccan clientele. The small shops in Marrakesh's *madina* (old city) feature lesser-known artists who paint stereotypical scenes of Morocco, such as rolling dunes or veiled women. However, few collectors or tourists are exposed to the growing number of painters in Morocco who use their art as a tool to raise political awareness of the Imazighen in North Africa and beyond. These artists paint primarily for themselves, for Amazigh activists, and for a small number of foreigners supportive of the Amazigh cause. They exhibit in small galleries or at Amazigh cultural association meetings in towns such as Ouarzazate, Tinghrir, or Goulmima. Many are self-taught or have limited formal training.[1] The visual repertoire of these artists includes images of veiled Tuareg men atop camels and tattooed women adorned with silver and amber jewelry. While the subject matter of these paintings may be construed as a cliché that reinforces romanticized stereotypes, in fact it gives visual form to the artists' political ideas and allows them to express a nostalgic and idealized vision of the past.

Few contemporary Berber women practice tattooing or wear the heavy silver jewelry and large amber necklaces featured in these paintings; therefore, these artists consult anthropological and historical texts from the colonial era to learn about aspects of Berber arts and culture that no longer exist. The study of Berber artistic production began during the period of French colonization and resulted in the publication of numerous articles and books.[2] Ethnographic studies written during the colonial period by French social scientists and colonial officials typically included discussions of Berber artistic production buried in chapters on domestic architecture, clothing, labor, birth, marriage, and Berber arts.[3] Colonial scholarship generally divided Maghribi art into "urban" and "rural," and posited urban "Arab" artistic production as the antithesis of rural "Berber" art. Berber arts were divided according to tribal groupings: each tribe was thought to possess a unique artistic style, and a trained eye could recognize a particular tribe's woven carpets, hand-coiled ceramics, leatherwork, tattooing, and silver jewelry.[4] Furthermore, Berber arts were described as static, unchanging, and representing pre-Islamic beliefs in animism, magic, and the worship of the female fertility goddess, Tanit. For example, in his book *L'art des Berbères*, Georges Marçais writes:

> Archaic art, primitive art, rural Berbers practiced one and the other. Their surprising fidelity to traditions comes from a remote past and becomes apparent above all in the crafts that women practice.[5]

Scholars also characterized Berbers as superficially Muslim, fundamentally democratic, and ruled by women, as opposed to the fanatically religious, patriarchal, despotic, and uncivilized Arabs.

Colonial officials often took the approach of Eugène Guernier, a professor at the Political Science Institute at the University of Paris. Guernier wrote that Arabs, whose strength came from their centralized military organization, never emerged from feudalism, making it impossible for them to adapt to Western life and fully accept French rule. Berbers, on the other hand, who lived in mountain villages and followed rational and democratic ancestral customs derived from ancient Rome, were more open-minded and closer biologically and socially to Europeans. Guernier wrote that Berbers would be more likely than Arabs to embrace Western democratic ideologies and eventually be absorbed into French society.[6] At the same time, colonial scholars propagated the seemingly contradictory idea of the "noble" Berber savage that has "never been entirely tamed by any conqueror."[7] Evidence of this savagery consisted of such qualities as loyalty to the tribe, their language (Tamazight), and their customary law.

Although post-colonial scholarship has effectively critiqued much of this discourse and exposed the stereotypes used to justify colonial rule, revisionist scholarship has not effectively deconstructed Euro-American scholarship on Berber arts in the Maghrib.[8] Our understanding of the history of Berber arts remains cursory and superficial. Images of noble Berbers living an untouched existence in remote rural settings dominate the art historical literature. Scholars deny the influences of Islam, Arabs, trade, and commercialization, reinforcing the view that historical and cultural contact between Berbers and others resulted in an inauthentic or impure artistic form. Here I shall argue that the set of suppositions regarding the origins of Berber art generated during the colonial period continue to inform scholarship on Berber arts. I shall also examine the influence of colonial scholarship on contemporary painting by Amazigh political activists within the Maghrib, in order to show that artists intentionally draw on colonial myths to refute the idea that Maghribi nations have an essentially Arab-Islamic character.[9]

The Origins of Berber Art: The Search for Purity

Colonial scholarship on Berber art typically attempted to isolate and separate out the influence of Islam and Arab culture on Berbers in order to distinguish the "pure" pre-Islamic and pre-Arab aspects from those "impure" aspects derived from its adulteration by outside influences. Furthermore, in their search for the origins of Berber art, French colonial scholars compared Berber tattoo, ceramic, and textile motifs, all of which share stylistic similarities, to designs found in the ancient European world that suggest a European ancestry for the Berbers. For example, the French scholar Ernest Gobert wrote in 1956 that North African Berber tattoos resembled Neolithic pictograms in Spanish caves, such as the cave of La Pileta.[10] Scholars such as Mathéa Gaudry suggested that Berber motifs resembled those of ancient Egypt and Sparta.[11] Arnold Van Gennep, who wrote extensively about Kabyle ceramics in Algeria, went so far as to suggest that Berber arts owed their invention to a colony of people from Cyprus, or Cyprus-influenced Syria, who had traveled across North Africa around 2000 BCE and eventually arrived in Kabylia. He based his hypothesis on a comparison between early twentieth century Kabyle ceramics and those of Bronze Age Cyprus, suggesting that Berbers and Europeans shared an ancient history.[12] This scholarship implies that unlike Europeans, Berbers never managed to emerge from their Neolithic past.

The drive to identify pure, authentic forms of Berber art continued in post-colonial scholarship. Scholars of Berber art often take a salvage approach to scholarship, recording what they see as artistic forms on the verge of extinction. This sort of scholarship suggests that Berbers lived in relative isolation in North Africa for millennia. For example, the book *Imazighen: The Vanishing Traditions of Berber Women* features striking photographs taken by Margaret Courtney-Clarke in Morocco, Algeria, and Tunisia in the 1990s. Geraldine Brooks, author of the text, states that Berbers live now as they have for centuries, and a Berber weaver "draws on a repertoire of symbols that predates the Roman empire."[13] She goes on to state that intermarriage with Arabs, tourism, and radical Islamic movements threaten to "erode the individual character of Berber culture."[14] Such claims romanticize and de-historicize rural Berbers, reinforcing the idea that authentic Berber arts are those that remained untouched throughout the centuries.

A photographic book that attempts to document and valorize the so-called traditional Berber house before it disappears, but fails to provide historical and contextual documentation, is Mohand Abouda's 1985 book, *Axxam, maisons kabyles: espaces et fresques murales*.[15] This book features photographs of Kabyle home interiors adorned with wall paintings, giving a romantic and nostalgic image of Berber life. It fails to take into account the fact that thousands of Kabyles have migrated to France or Algiers, resulting in drastic changes in building practices. Jane Goodman writes that the traditional Berber house continues to be memorialized by scholars and Amazigh activists "even as it is torn down in Kabylia to make way for modern houses whose residents are absent for much of the year."[16] Visual influences on Berber art are due to trade, population movement, and cross-cultural exchange. Such change certainly occurred during the colonial period, but there is no reason to doubt that it also transpired in the pre-colonial past. Art historian Sidney Kasfir notes that "precolonial cultures were mutually dependent, interacted frequently, and shared many of their artistic traditions across ethnic boundaries."[17] Berbers, like other groups, exhibit cultural borrowing, and their art has been subject to historical change. Recognition of stylistic change over time does not make a society any less "authentic."

Berber Origins and Contemporary Artists/Activists

Contemporary Amazigh political activists also strive to identify the origins of Berber culture and to employ colonial scholarship to counter assertions that Morocco and Algeria are essentially Arab nations. In post-Independence Morocco, for example, nationalists feared that Berber particularism would threaten national unity. In Algeria, Arab nationalists made the claim that

Berbers in fact originated in the Middle East, predisposing them to "the East" rather than "the West" and resulting in the Berber assimilation into Arab society and the Berber acceptance of Islam.[18]

While French mythology surrounding the Berbers intended to align Berbers with Europe, it inadvertently provided members of the post-colonial Amazigh movement with a mythological system to promote their identity and revive their heritage. Amazigh activists use colonial-era scholarship to reveal the original Berber nature of the Maghrib. In an effort to purge evidence of Arabization from their culture, Amazigh activists sought to reformulate the Tamazight language so that it did not contain Arabic words. They also resuscitated the *tifinagh* script rarely used over centuries, and in the 1960s Amazigh activists began to write poetry, songs, and political slogans promoting it. Until the official adoption of *tifinagh* by the Royal Institute of the Amazigh Culture (IRCAM) in 2003, the use of *tifinagh* was considered a political act directed against the national government. For example, in 1994 seven members of the Moroccan Amazigh cultural association of Goulmima, Tilelli (meaning "freedom" in Tamazight), were arrested after publicly displaying banners with slogans written in *tifinagh* that promoted recognition of Morocco's Imazighen.[19] In 1997, the flag flown at the first transnational Amazigh World Congress in the Canary Islands included the *tifinagh* symbol for the letter yaz (English /z/), the central character in the word Amazigh (meaning "free man"); thus, it has come to symbolize freedom from oppression.

In addition, Amazigh painters commonly decorate their canvases with designs inspired by the *tifinagh* script that is now an icon of Berber culture. For example, the Amazigh artist Hamid Kachmar, who now lives in the United States, writes political messages on his canvases promoting the Amazigh cause. He also creates abstract designs reminiscent of *tifinagh* letters and decorative surface patterns similar to those found in Berber textiles.

One of the most prolific Moroccan calligraphers of *tifinagh* is Fouad Lahbib, an artist, writer, and researcher at the IRCAM in Rabat.[20] Lahbib, who exhibits under the Hebrew name Yeshou in order to reinforce the claim among Amazigh activists that the Imazighen have ancient Jewish origins, creates abstract calligraphy based on *tifinagh* script and what he refers to as "ancestral signs" such as tattoos and textile motifs. Using bold strokes, he uses red and black paint to create a massive *tifinagh*-inspired design at the center of his canvases, filling the surrounding space with words written in *tifinagh*.[21] His intention is to give artistic credibility to the *tifinagh* script, moving it out of the realm of folkloric decoration and into that of a "high art" on par with Arabic calligraphy. His brush strokes are loose and his fluid technique and bold colors convey a sense of freedom of movement. Lahbib assigns his works empowering titles such as *Libération* and *Courage* that suggest struggle against oppression.[22] Many contemporary Amazigh activists feel an affinity to the *tifinagh* script as distinct from the Arabic script they associate with this oppression.

Another claim of Berber scholars and activists is that the geometric designs that adorn Berber arts are derived from *tifinagh*, including the motifs adorning the facades of the adobe architecture of the Moroccan South.[23] Mohand Saidi, a politically active Berber artist, insists that the designs spell out words in *tifinagh*, suggesting that the adobe architecture of the oases of southern Morocco predates the arrival of Arabs in the Maghrib.[24] While it is tempting to assign a Berber origin to the adobe architecture that characterizes southern Morocco, it is important to remember that the oases of southern Morocco "reflect a checkerboard history of invasions, migrations, and intermixtures" among Berbers, Arabs, Jews, and *haratin*, making their origins impossible to determine.[25] In the Tafilalet oasis of southeastern Morocco, where I lived in the 1990s, Qsar Mezguida is inhabited by Ait Khabbash Berbers.[26] While geometric motifs resembling *tifinagh* letters adorn the *qsar*'s façade, this fortified village also has many features commonly attributed to Islamic architecture. According to local legend, Mezguida was built in the seventeenth century by Sultan Mawlay Isma'il. In fact, the *qsar* features a horseshoe arch portal and towers with crenellations that resemble Bab al-Khemis, the imperial city gate built by Mawlay Isma'il in Meknes. In the nineteenth century, Berbers were invited to live in Qsar Mezguida to provide security from invading Arab nomads. Jewish craftspeople also lived there, embroidering, silver-smithing, and tailoring for their Arab, Berber, and *haratin* neighbors, demonstrating the intense cultural exchange and migration that occurred in southern Morocco.

This connection between the earthen architecture of the *qsar* and urban imperial 'Alawi architecture is not surprising, since the Tafilalet oasis was a historically Arab stronghold and home of the reigning 'Alawi dynasty. However, horseshoe arches and crenellated towers also characterize adobe architecture traditionally regarded by scholars as Berber, such as the large fortified homes, called *tigermatin* in Tamazight, occupied by Berbers throughout the Dadès valley of southern Morocco. This example further demonstrates the complex nature of Berber art and architecture; the various stylistic influences on architecture inhabited by Berbers clearly reveal that Berbers responded to historical change and external influences. Disregarding these historical realities, Amazigh activists and artists cling to a belief that an original, authentic pre-Islamic and pre-Arab Berber aesthetic and culture continue into the present, replicating the French mythology used to legitimate the colonial system.

Berber Art, Rural Life, and Tribalism

Scholars of Maghribi art have tended to divide artistic production into urban (Arab) and rural (Berber) categories. Golvin's *Aspects de l'artisanat en Afrique du Nord* divides North African carpets into two groups: urban Hispano-Moorish (Arab) and rural Berber:

> In Morocco, Algeria and Tunisia, there are two distinct types of carpets: an urban carpet clearly influenced by Oriental or Hispano-Moorish art, a luxury object reserved for a bourgeoise; and a more rustic carpet used as a bed throughout the Middle Atlas and High Atlas by the nomadic populations.[27]

Jean Besancenot, who wrote about Moroccan costume, also followed this categorization. He traveled extensively in Morocco between 1934 and 1939, publishing *Costumes et types du Maroc* in 1942. This work contains sixty elaborately detailed colored plates based on his gouaches of men's and women's dress, as well as 229 black and white line drawings of headdresses, jewelry, shoes, and other bodily adornment. His illustrations placed his subjects on stark white backgrounds, removing them from any historical or social context. Besancenot organized his sketches into three basic categories: Berber dress, urban dress (meaning Arab), and Jewish dress. Berber dress was divided according to region and then sub-divided into tribal group, since, according to Besancenot, "each type of dress represents a tribal identity."[28] Scholars have recognized Besancenot's book as a collection of "dazzlingly beautiful yet thoroughly accurate images of one of the more vulnerable aspects of Moroccan traditional culture."[29] While Besancenot's work is invaluable for studying historic styles of dress, his use of "tribe" as a conceptual unit in distinguishing among styles is problematic. This "one tribe, one style" method of categorization is based on the idea that tribes are self-contained, autonomous units with uniform rules for artistic production linked to primordial identities, without taking into account outside influences.[30]

Nowhere is the use of tribal categories more evident than in the study of Berber textiles. During the Protectorate period, Prosper Ricard wrote a multi-volume study of Moroccan carpets entitled *Corpus des tapis marocains* with the goal of revitalizing and standardizing Moroccan textile production. Ricard and his staff of military officers painstakingly interviewed Berber carpet weavers in order to identify the technical and decorative aspects of woven textiles according to the tribal group. Each volume of the *Corpus* concentrated on a different region of Morocco and offered patterns and descriptions outlining the designs, composition, and colors of woven textiles, including illustrative photographs and meticulously drawn grid patterns for each tribal style.

Weavers who worked within the guidelines established in the *Corpus* and whose carpets featured the decorative motifs and compositions assigned to a particular tribal group qualified for an official stamp that allowed the carpet to be exported abroad. Historian Hamid Irbouh argues that the motivation for Ricard's project was the erroneous idea that arts in Morocco had been in crisis since the late nineteenth century due to competition from European manufactured goods.[31] The state stamp was instituted in order to "guarantee the authenticity of origin, the good quality, and the indigenous character of Moroccan carpets."[32] Ricard's project contributed to the narrative that aesthetic mixture suggested inauthenticity.

Ricard's *Corpus* continues to influence carpet production within Morocco, although its effects have not been studied.[33] Between 1988 and 1992, the Ministry of Handicrafts published a multi-volume study of Moroccan carpets based on Ricard's original *Corpus*. Entitled *Le nouveau corpus de tapis marocains*, this government-sponsored publication features color photographs of carpets, diagrams indicating colors and motifs, as well as technical descriptions of knotting and weaving techniques, fringe styles, and weaving materials. Each volume includes a map showing the geographic borders of each tribe with whom the carpet is identified. The publication is meant to be an artistic and technical guide for both weavers and agents in charge of the control of stamps. However, as noted by Roger Benjamin, most Moroccan carpets are currently sold outside of government-sponsored shops and often feature "irregular design and uneven materials," indicating that many contemporary weavers work outside of government standards.[34] Art historian Niloo Imami Paydar notes that the abstract nature of Berber motifs "enables them to embody a wide range of meanings that are flexible in their implications," and that Berber weavers frequently experiment with new motifs, incorporating them into their own repertoire of designs. The portable nature of textiles means that rugs can be easily transported from region to region, resulting in the dispersion of patterns across a wide geographic area.[35] My own research supports these assertions. I found that the names of textile motifs not only varied from generation to generation but also from weaver to weaver in the same region. Women often named motifs after objects, plants, animals, or reptiles present in their contemporary environment.[36]

The technique of classifying Berber art forms by tribe is evident in coffee table art books devoted to Berber art. For example, the book *Bijoux berbères au Maroc* (1989), intended to complement Besancenot's tome, is widely considered the jewelry collectors' Bible.[37] The book classifies jewelry by region, function, tribal group, and date of production. It contains fourteen pages of explanatory text, 474 color images of individual pieces of jewelry, and a one-page bibliography. It speaks to an audience of collectors concerned with provenance and connoisseurship and suggests that each Berber tribe has an artistic style that is unchanging and bounded. Carpet and jewelry stores in Moroccan souks prominently display this book, targeting buyers who see similarities between the market goods and the images in the texts, thereby enhancing the value of the object and its perceived authenticity. Books of this genre rarely contain photos of Berber women wearing this jewelry, stripping it of its cultural and historical context and distancing the object from its role in the complex visual semiotic system in which jewelry is only one artistic element of women's dress.

One example of how cultural borrowing influenced jewelry styles can be seen among the Ait Khabbash. A sub-group of the Eastern High Atlas Ait Atta, the Ait Khabbash arrived in the Tafilalet from the Jebel Saghro in the early nineteenth century and forced into submission the Arabs who lived scattered in villages throughout the oasis.[38] Approximately 6,000 Jews lived in the Tafilalet in the late nineteenth century, occupying the separate quarters (*mallahs*) of several qsur (sing. *qsar*), with the largest concentration in the town of Rissani.[39] Arabs, Berbers, and Jews in the Tafilalet were connected through an elaborate system of exchange and patronage. Jews and Berbers shared similarities in dress. Ait Atta brides throughout southeastern Morocco wore a distinct horn-like headdress (see figure 9.1, second woman from the left) that resembled those formerly worn by Jewish women in the region.[40] Jewish silversmiths molded the heavy Berber silver bracelets and fibulae commonly worn by Berber women in the area. One wonders whether the Berber client or the Jewish artisan designed Berber women's jewelry. More importantly, this example demonstrates the influence of Jewish styles of dress on Berber wedding dress and the cross-fertilization between Jewish jewelers and Berber clients. Berber jewelry has long had both an aesthetic and commercial component, as Jewish silversmiths made specific styles of jewelry for their Berber clientele. However, Berber arts continue to be classified in an ahistorical fashion, as if they were never influenced by outside contact.

A further example of outside influences on Berber dress is evident in the indigo-dyed veils embroidered with vegetal and geometric motifs evoking female fertility worn by Ait Khabbash women who live in the Tafilalet oasis of southeastern Morocco. These women no longer wear the indigo wraparound garments (*ahruy*) or woven wool shawls (*taghnast*) common to Berber women in early twentieth century Morocco.[41] Increased contact with the heavily veiled Arab women of the Tafilalet oasis in the 1960s shaped their decision to move to long-sleeved dresses under their wraparound garments, then to drape large veils over their woven shawls, and eventually to abandon the shawls altogether. In the Tafilalet oasis, the connection people made between Arabic speakers and the

FIGURE 9.1. Marriage dance of the Ait Yazza (a sub-group of the Ait Atta) of Mellab. This Berber bride (standing second from the left) dances with her sister-in-law and two young girls. Photo by Mireille Morin-Barde in *Coiffures féminines du Maroc: au sud du Haut Atlas.* Aix-en-Provence: Édisud, 1990.

Prophet Mohammed gave Arab women's dress a religiously conservative valence. Ait Khabbash women, however, "Berberized" the veils by adding colorful embroidered patterns reminiscent of their ancestors' facial and wrist tattoos; they also attached glimmering silver-colored sequins.[42] The increased availability of market goods in the colonial period, and manufactured fabric and colorful wool thread in particular, promoted a distinctly Ait Khabbash style of dress. The Ait Khabbash, like many other Berber groups, borrow aspects of Arab culture while maintaining a strong sense of their own heritage and Muslim identity. Their aesthetic culture reflects this complicated reality. Scholarly descriptions of Berber art that fossilize Berbers into tribal categories and continue to connect twentieth century Berber arts to prehistoric Europe or ancient Rome fail to consider the subtle social encounters and negotiations that influence artistic production.

Symbolism and Matriarchy

The colonial-era tendency to interpret Berber motifs as visual manifestations of pre-Islamic beliefs accords with what historian and archaeologist Gabriel Camps calls "Berber permanence."[43] Camps argues for an unconscious, millennia-old "Berberness" that shapes artistic production.[44] As evidence, Camps compares patterns engraved on shell fragments and ostrich eggs found in excavations dating from 8000 BCE with contemporary Berber textile, pottery, and facial tattoo designs. Using material excavated from a third-century BCE archaeological site in Tiddis, Algeria, he illustrates how the artistic rendering of three-dimensional objects evolved into the geometric schematization common to twentieth-century Berber arts. The figurative pattern of the ducks on the left, he argues, gradually transitioned into three triangles with hook-like protuberances emerging from their tops on the right (see figure 9.2).[45]

According to Camps, Berber designs were schematized over time. He collected the names given to Berber motifs in order to recover their original meaning. Tattoo motifs also captured the imagination; scholars meticulously sketched the tattoos found on the female forehead, nose, chin, cheeks, chest, and arms, making inventories of Berber motifs and creating elaborate charts (see figure 9.3).

Berber motifs were interpreted as protective symbols against the evil eye and other metaphysical forces.[46] Triangular or diamond motifs were compared to ancient representations of the Phoenican-Cathaginian fertility goddess Tanit. Hence, the motifs made of repeating triangles or diamonds with lateral protruding lines resembling arms, as seen in sketch number 2 in figure 9.3, were interpreted as vestiges of the Berbers' pre-Islamic

FIGURE 9.2. From Gabriel Camps, *Les Berbères: mémoire et identité*. Paris: Errances, 1995, 211.

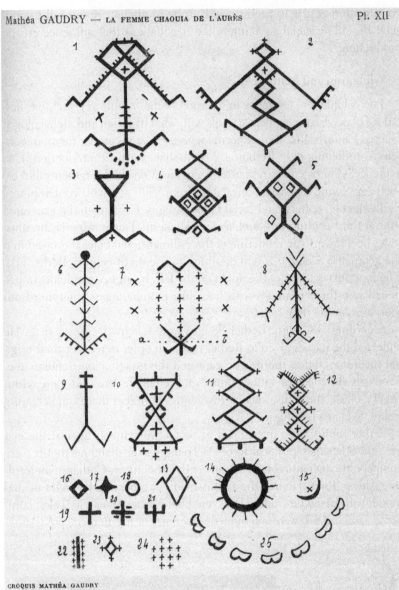

CROQUIS MATHÉA GAUDRY

TATOUAGES. — INDICATIONS DES PARTIES DU CORPS SUR LESQUELLES ILS ONT ÉTÉ RELEVÉS :

1 à 5 front ; 6 à 12, menton (le n° 7 commence sous la lèvre inférieure, la ligne *a b* marque l'endroit où il passe sous le menton) ; 13-14, joues ; 15, entre le pouce et l'index ; 16 à 24, visage, doigts, seins ; 25, cou.

FIGURE 9.3. From Mathéa Gaudry, *La femme chaouia de l'Aurès: étude de sociologie berbère*. Paris: Librairie Orientalist Paul Geuthner, 1929, plate XII.

worship of Tanit. By extension, scholars also interpreted a single vertical line filled with lateral protruding lines (sketches 6 and 8) as the representation of a palm frond, and subsequently, an expression of Tanit, sometimes depicted on ancient stelae (upright stone slabs) holding what appears to be a palm branch.[47]

Berber artistic designs were read to suggest other forms of pre-Islamic worship. According to Julio Cola Alberich, a circle motif, such as the number 14, represented the sun and was evidence of an ancient Berber sun-worshipping cult.[48] The presence of the cross motif in Berber art (numbers 17, 19, 20, 23, and 24) was held up as proof that Berbers practiced Christianity before Islam.[49] The intention was to distance Berbers from Arabs and Islam by suggesting that Berbers were superficially Muslim and lived in a world colored by ancient forms of spirituality.

Much of contemporary art historical scholarship mines textile motifs for evidence of ancient Berber religious beliefs. Paul Vandenbroeck, for example, compared the oval or lozenge design commonly found on Berber textiles to paintings from the Neolithic sites of La Pileta in Spain and Çatalhöyük in Turkey, the latter often interpreted as a demonstration of matriarchy. Vandenbroeck interpreted the lozenge design common to Berber art as a uterus, and the oval shape surrounded by zigzags as a vagina experiencing the contractions of childbirth.[50] Vandenbroeck apparently drew upon French scholarship that interpreted many of the schematic designs within Neolithic caves as stylized vulva symbols and applied these interpretations to Berber art, suggesting that Berber art contains vestiges of an ancient matriarchal religion.[51]

Amazigh Artists and Matriarchy

Amazigh activists have connected their cause to the struggles of the Tuareg in the Sahel. They held up an ideal image of the Tuareg as less influenced by Arab cultural traits and Islam than North African Berbers, reinforcing the view that centuries of Arabization and the influence of Islam have resulted in the corruption of Berber culture and the oppression of women.[52] Activists point to Tuareg women's sexual freedom and right to divorce, and the fact that the Tuareg practice matrilineal descent. Notably, Tuareg men rather than women veil their faces. However, Danish anthropologists Johannes and Ida Nicolaisen argue that popular accounts erroneously romanticize the Tuareg, giving the impression that "Tuareg society is dominated by unveiled and free women, while the veiled men play a less significant role."[53] Nicolaisen and Nicolaisen argue that matrilineal organization coexists with patrilineal descent. In addition, they state that matrilineality should not be equated with matriarchy, and, among the Tuareg,

male dominance is actually expressed by male face veiling since this practice among the Tuareg increases social status.[54] Tuareg women own their
own domestic livestock, tents, and household utensils and exert considerable influence over household matters, but men hold leadership roles on
all other social levels and make decisions for the group.[55]

Contemporary Amazigh activists are less concerned with these anthropological complexities and typically embrace the characterization of Tuareg as matriarchal. This characterization can be seen in the 2004 still life
painting by Mohamed Mallal, an Amazigh activist, poet, musician, and
school teacher, featuring a fringed leather bag similar to those created today by Tuareg women (figure 9.4). In the background he painted a draped
piece of indigo fabric; below it, he recreated a carpet with solid colored
bands. He also included faint letters written in the *tifinagh* script on the
top right corner of his canvas. Although the *tifinagh* letters do not spell out
particular words, they are intended to solidify the connection between the
objects and their creators. In both the popular imagination and in colonial-
era literature, only Tuareg women know how to write using the *tifinagh*
script.[56] In fact, while women often teach the *tifinagh* script to children,
the reality is that both literate men and women are proficient in *tifinagh*
script.[57]

FIGURE 9.4. Mohamed Mallal, Untitled, 2004, acrylic on canvas, 80×92 cm.
Courtesy of the artist. Photo by Cynthia Becker.

Mallal's painting suggests a kinship with the Tuareg; his subject choice of a leather bag created by female leather workers expresses his perceived notion that Tuareg women exert considerable power and status within their society. In my discussions with Mallal, he felt that outsiders view Berbers as a primitive people who live an archaic lifestyle in their isolated and remote mountain villages.[58] In addition to his painting on canvas, Mallal performs with a musical group that uses modern instruments such as electric guitar, saxophone, and drums to sing about the Amazigh cause. His choice of artistic media and his production of music videos reinforce his desire to demonstrate that Berber culture is compatible with the modern world. Paradoxically, he often paints stereotypical and romanticized images of Berber and Tuareg culture, including veiled men on camels and the symbol of Tanit (as seen in the center of figure 9.4).

By romanticizing Tuareg culture and suggesting that their arts contain vestiges of an ancient religion that lauded women, Mallal's art reiterates activists' views that women are guardians and carriers of Amazigh identity. As sociologist Fatima Sadiqi has noted, as a "language of cultural identity, home, the family, village affiliation, intimacy, traditions, orality, and nostalgia to a remote past, Berber [language] perpetuates attributes that are considered female in the Moroccan culture."[59] Since Berber women are more likely than men to be unschooled, monolingual Tamazight speakers, they are responsible for teaching the spoken language to their children.

Berber women carry considerable prestige within their households, but they are also restricted by societal constraints that imagine women as keepers of purity and tradition. Berber women who remain virgins until marriage and give birth to many children achieve high status. Berber women act out the respect and status accorded to motherhood by incorporating fertility symbols into their woven carpets, clothing, tattoos, hairstyles, and ceremonial wedding dress. Arts, therefore, demonstrate the crucial role women play in propagating and preserving Berber identity. In addition, tattoo and textile motifs are often parallel, and the act of "humanizing" textiles with motifs similar to those on their own bodies equates women's physical reproductive powers as mothers with their artistic reproductive powers as conservers of Berber societies.

More specifically, in southeastern Morocco, women who work with wool are highly respected; it is said that a woman who makes forty carpets during her lifetime is guaranteed safe passage into heaven after she dies. Wool used to weave carpets has considerable *baraka* ("divine blessing") since it is natural, God-given, and crucial to everyday life. The loom and the act of weaving are also believed to have *baraka*. When the warp threads are attached to the vertical loom, women believe the carpet is metaphorically born and acquires a soul, echoing women's role in human reproduction.[60] According to anthropologist Brinkley Messick, some Berber weavers physically straddle the warp threads and beams of the loom before they are raised, symbolizing the metaphorical birth of the textile.[61] In southeastern Morocco, women told me that a textile then moves through youth, maturity, and old age as it is woven. Women have the power of life over a weaving, and when the weaver finishes it, she cuts it from the loom and splashes it with water, as if washing the deceased before burial. This anthropomorphization of the textile underlines women's reproductive and creative powers and, by equating textiles with the giving of human life, reinforces women's centrality to the propagation of Berber society.[62]

Certain colors used in Berber art can also be interpreted as referring to female fertility. Although variations exist among Berber regions, hues of red, green, yellow, and black are commonly used by women in southeastern Morocco, strengthening the correlation between these colors and objects found in the natural environment, such as dates ripening on a palm tree. Berber brides are commonly dressed in red, green, yellow, and black textiles, which they compare to the colors of the rainbow, a metaphor of female fertility.[63] The word for rainbow in Tamazight is *tislit n unzar*, "bride of the rain." The word *anzar* is a masculine noun for rain. Berber women once held "bride of the rain" ceremonies where they attached a reed of bamboo to a large wooden soup ladle to create a cruciform shape that they then dressed as a bride, carrying it through the village while asking for donations of food, tea, sugar, and dates while singing songs that asked God to send rain. They eventually proceeded to a dry riverbed, where they turned the figure upside down and put it head first into the riverbed.

Despite the fact that Arabs in North Africa also performed such ceremonies, Edward Westermarck suggested that it had a pre-Islamic origin.[64] Other scholars mentioned that the ceremony referred to a practice in which the "bride of the rain" represented a rain goddess, or the personification of the earth as a bride to be impregnated by the rain.[65] In the *Encyclopédie berbère*, Camps recounts a story told in the Kabyle region of northeastern Algeria that may explain the ceremony's inception. Anzar, the king of the rain, wished to marry a beautiful girl whom he saw bathing nude in a river. She refused him, infuriating Anzar, who retaliated by drying up all the rivers, streams, and wells. In order to save her people from disaster, she yielded to Anzar's blackmail and water flowed again.[66] Laoust interpreted the "bride of the rain" ceremony as celebrating the symbolic marriage of the puppet dressed as a bride to Anzar.[67] The scholar Nadia Abu-Zahra confronted these interpretations and suggested that the desire to identify the ceremony's pre-Islamic pagan origins fails to consider its

FIGURE 9.5. Mohamed Ezziani, *Fertility*, 2000, acrylic on canvas, 65 × 50 cm. Courtesy of the artist. Photo by Cynthia Becker.

social and spiritual implications and ignores its importance as a fertility and purification rite.[68] My own interpretation is that the creation of a bride for Anzar from an object associated with fluids and nourishment (a ladle) and a plant typically linked to a wet climate (bamboo) suggest a connection between rainfall, the fruitfulness of the land, and female reproductive power, thus extolling women's generative powers.

The bride of the rain ceremony serves as a subject for Amazigh activist-artists. Mohamed Ezziani, a self-taught artist living in Tinghir in southeastern Morocco pays tribute to women's artistic traditions in his acrylic painted canvas entitled *Fertility* (figure 9.5). The painting's title and its motifs evoke women's life-giving powers. On the left-hand side of the canvas, Ezziani painted a blue sky and used vertical zigzag lines to evoke rainfall. On the right, he painted vertically oriented geometric shapes, reminiscent of those seen in the chart in figure 9.3, that evoke grain growing under a sunny sky. The central design consists of an image within an image; its outer form resembles a woman's silver fibula, and a large ceramic container fits inside the fibula. Containers represent fertility, as they hold water, grain, and olive oil. He also paints four fibulas on both sides of a vertical axis that make reference to the female body. Women's bodies can also be interpreted as metaphorical containers. This painting, like the work of many Amazigh artists, lauds women as tradition-bearers and features designs drawn from women's tattoos, textiles, and ceramics. It illustrates how Amazigh painters celebrate women's roles in shaping Berber identity.

Conclusion

The historiography of Berber artistic production has been used here to demonstrate how past discussions are echoed in contemporary visual and written discourses of Berber identity. Amazigh painter-activists who connect their work to an imagined pre-Islamic past often borrow from colonial interpretations of Berber art to counter Arabo-Islamic national narratives. These artists, whose audience includes Amazigh activists and supporters of the Amazigh cause, tend to privilege pre-Islamic and pre-Arab aspects of Amazigh culture over other elements. They view Arab culture as an oppressive system imposed upon them by force that destroyed many aspects of Berber culture, including their indigenous religion. They paint subjects that reinforce assumptions that Berber society is tribal, matriarchal, and unchanged from pre-Islamic times to support the claim that Berbers are the indigenous inhabitants of North Africa whose rights must be granted. Recent publications on the history of Berber art often propagate colonial-era stereotypes and also claim that authentic Berber art is made up of aesthetic forms that have remained unchanged for millennia.

These tendentious arguments are due in part to the nature of academic scholarship in North America and Europe, in which Berber arts conform to neither Islamic nor African art history. As art historians Sheila Blair and Jonathan Bloom write, the academic discipline of Islamic art history is "normally restricted to the 'core' Islamic lands between Egypt and central Asia from the seventh to the eighteenth century, with occasional forays into Spain, Sicily, and India or later periods."[69] Art historians of Africa, on the other hand, tend to marginalize Berber Maghribi arts, as evidenced in their absence in general surveys of the field.[70] The recently published text-book *A History of Art in Africa* is an exception, as it contains a section on Berber and Tuareg art in a chapter entitled "The Maghreb and the Ancient Mediterranean World."[71] Judith Perani and Fred Smith explained the absence of North Africa from their textbook entitled *The Visual Arts of Africa* because, according to them, these arts were "related more to the Middle East than to other parts of Africa."[72]

The study of the history of Berber art in the Maghrib has fallen through the disciplinary cracks, and as a result, our understanding of Berber art is often repetitive and superficial. Paradigms developed during the colonial era have persisted long after their usefulness is past. As we have seen, Amazigh painter-activists have appropriated these outmoded themes and reproduced stereotyped and mythologized images of Berber artistic forms. As Berber art evolves in response to processes of political and social change, artist-activists have adopted new media, such as painting on canvas. Although they tirelessly strive to preserve their Amazigh heritage through the promotion of a nostalgic and idealized vision of the past, contemporary Amazigh artists are engaged in the creation of a new aesthetic form that exemplifies dynamism, inventiveness, and resilience.

Notes

1. Here I use the term Amazigh (pl. Imazighen), meaning a "free person," to refer to political activists, who prefer this to the word Berber.

2. Two of the most prolific writers on Berber arts are Lucien Golvin, who wrote *Les tissages nord-africains d'après les collections du Musée Stéphane Gsell* (Alger: Imprimerie Officielle, 1958) and *Aspects de l'artisanat en Afrique du Nord* (Paris: Presses Universitaires de France, 1957), about the textile and the craft industry in Algeria, and Prosper Ricard, who wrote extensively about Berber and Arab textiles in Morocco. See, for example, Prosper Ricard, *Corpus des tapis marocains*, 4 vols. (Paris: Librairie Orientaliste Paul Geuthner, 1923–1927). Jean Herber and E. G. Gobert wrote numerous articles on tattooing: Jean Herber, "Tatouages marocains," *Archives berbères* (1920), 58–66; Jean Herber, "Tatouages marocains; Tatouages et religion," *Revue d'histoire des religions* 83 (1921): 68–83; Jean Herber, "Origine et signification des tatouages marocains," *L'Anthropologie* 37 (1927): 517–525; Jean Herber, "Les tatouages de la face chez la Marocaine," *Hespéris* 33 (1946): 323–351; E. G. Gobert, "Notes sur les tatouages indigènes de la région de Gafsa," *Revue tunisienne* 18 (1911): 32–41; and E. G. Gobert, "Remarques sur les tatouages nord-africains," *Revue africaine* 100 (1956): 501–517. Other books on Berber art include Georges Marçais, *L'art des Berbères* (Alger: Imprimerie Officielle, 1956); Louis Poinssot and Jacques Revault, *Tapis tunisiens*, 4 vols. (Paris: Horizons de France, 1937–1957).

3. Colonial-era ethnographies on Berber culture include Edmond Doutté, *Magie et religion dans l'Afrique du Nord* (Alger: A. Jourdan, 1908); Émile Laoust, *Mots et*

choses berbères: notes de linguistique et d'ethnographie: dialectes du Maroc (Paris: A. Challamel, 1920); and Edward Westermarck, *Ritual and Belief in Morocco*, 2 vols. (New York: University Books, [1926] 1968).

4. I use the term "arts" rather than "crafts" to refer to the silver jewelry, woven textiles, painted house interiors, and ceramics created by Berbers, as "crafts" implies a hierarchal distinction between it and the so-called high arts (painting and sculpture).

5. Marçais, *L'art des Berbères*, 3–4.

6. Eugène Guernier, *La Berbérie, l'Islam et la France: le destin de l'Afrique du Nord* (Paris: Éditions de l'union française, 1950), 353–354.

7. Jeanne D'Ucel, *Berber Art: An Introduction* (Norman: University of Oklahoma Press, 1932), 49.

8. For a critical discussion of colonial scholarship, see Edmund Burke III, "The Image of the Moroccan State in French Ethnological Literature: A New Look at the Origin of Lyautey's Berber Policy," in *Arabs and Berbers*, ed. Ernest Gellner and Charles Micaud (London: Duckworth, 1972): 175–200; Patricia Lorcin, *Imperial Identities: Stereotyping Prejudice and Race in Colonial Algeria* (London: I.B. Tauris, 1995); James McDougall, "Myth and Counter-Myth: 'The Berber' as National Signifier in Algerian Historiographies," *Radical History Review* 8 (Spring 2003): 66–88; and Paul A. Silverstein, *Algeria in France: Transpolitics, Race, and Nation* (Bloomington: Indiana University Press, 2004).

9. This paper concentrates on Moroccan artists. For information about Amazigh painters across North Africa and the Sahel, see Cynthia Becker, "Matriarchal Nomads and Freedom Fighters: Transnational Amazigh Consciousness and Moroccan, Algerian, and Nigerian Artists," *Critical Interventions* 5 (2009): 70–101.

10. Gobert, "Remarques sur les tatouages nord-africains," 501–517.

11. Mathéa Gaudry, *La femme chaouia de l'Aurès: étude de sociologie berbère* (Paris: Librairie Orientaliste Paul Geuthner, 1929), 45.

12. Arnold Van Gennep, *Études d'ethnographie algérienne* (Paris: Ernest Leroux, 1911), 66.

13. Margaret Courtney-Clarke and Geraldine Brooks, *Imazighen: The Vanishing Traditions of Berber Women* (New York: Clarkson Potter Publishers, 1996), xiv.

14. Courtney-Clarke and Brooks, *Imazighen*, xv.

15. Mohand Abouda, *Axxam, maisons kabyles: espaces et fresques murale* (Goussainville, France: M. Abouda, 1985).

16. Jane E. Goodman, *Berber Culture on the World Stage: From Village to Video* (Bloomington: Indiana University Press, 2005), 93.

17. Sidney Kasfir, "One tribe, one style? Paradigms in the historiography of African art," *History in Africa* 11 (1984): 177.

18. For a discussion of the logic that governed the claim that Algeria was a predominantly Arab and Islamic nation, see James McDougall, "Myth and Counter-Myth," 66–88, and his contribution to the present volume.

19. Three of the seven men, all of them teachers, were sentenced to prison. Widespread publicity and public outrage led to a reduction of their sentences by the Moroccan king, and the three were released two months after their arrest. See Bruce Maddy-Weitzman, "Contested Identities: Berbers, 'Berberism,' and the State in North Africa," in *Middle Eastern Minorities and Diasporas*, ed. M. Ma'oz and Gabriel Sheffer (Portland, Ore.: Sussex Academic Press, 2002), 153–178.

20. The Royal Institute of the Amazigh Culture (IRCAM) was created in 2001 by King Muhammad VI of Morocco. The creation of this institute is both supported and criticized by Imazighen within Morocco (see Silverstein, this volume), but it did result in the first official recognition of Morocco's Amazigh population and played an important role in enhancing public visibility of Amazigh issues within Morocco.

21. Fouad Lahbib, interview with author, Rabat, Morocco, June 20, 2006.

22. When I met with Lahbib, he could only show me photos of his works; he had sold all of his canvases.

23. For a discussion of how *tifinagh* survived in North Africa in carpet patterns, pottery decorations, and silver jewelry designs, see Annette Korolnik-Andersch and Marcel Korolnik, *The Color of Henna: Painted Textiles from Southern Morocco* (Stuttgart: Arnoldschen, 2002), 26.

24. Mohand Saidi, interview with author, Errachidia, Morocco, June 25, 2004.

25. See William Curtis, "Type and Variation: Berber Collective Dwellings of the Northwestern Sahara," *Muqarnas* 1 (1983): 182, and Silverstein, this volume.

26. A *qsar* is a fortified village with narrow streets and two- and three-story flat-roofed dwellings. The buttressed village walls have a singular monumental entrance and numerous watchtowers. See Curtis, "Type and Variation," 181–209.

27. Golvin, *Aspects de l'artisanat*, 74.

28. Jean Besancenot, *Costumes of Morocco* (New York: Kegan Paul International, 1990), 9.

29. James Bynon, "Preface," in Jean Besancenot, *Costumes of Morocco* (London: Kegan Paul International, 1990), 7.

30. Sidney Kasfir, "One tribe, one style? Paradigms in the historiography of African art," *History in Africa* 11 (1984): 172.

31. Hamid Irbouh, *Art in the Service of Colonialism: French Art Education in Morocco, 1912–1956* (London: I.B. Tauris, 2005).

32. These are reproduced in Ricard, *Corpus des tapis marocains*, volume I, 1923.

33. For more information about weaving in general and the influence of commercialization on weaving in Morocco, see Brinkley Messick, "Subordinate Discourse: Women, Weaving, and Gender Relations in North Africa," *American Ethnologist* 14 (1987): 210–225.

34. Roger Benjamin, *Orientalist Aesthetics: Art, Colonialism, and French North Africa, 1880–1930* (Berkeley: University of California Press, 2003), 210.

35. Niloo Imami Paydar, "Weavings for Rural Life," in *The Fabric of Moroccan Life*, ed. N. Paydar, and I. Grammet (Indianapolis: Indianapolis Museum of Art, 2002), 142–147.

36. Cynthia Becker, "Amazigh Textiles and Dress in Morocco: Metaphors of Motherhood," *African Arts* 39(3) (2006): 46.

37. David Rouach, *Bijoux berbères au Maroc* (Paris: ACR Édition, 1989).

38. See Ross E. Dunn, *Resistance in the Desert* (Madison: University of Wisconsin Press, 1977), 74; and David Hart, *Dadda 'Atta and his Forty Grandsons: The Socio-Political Organization of the Ait 'Atta of Southern Morocco* (Boulder, Colo.: Westview Press, 1981), 15.

39. Dunn, *Resistance in the Desert*, 87.

40. Berber women in southeastern Morocco today rarely wear the silver jewelry of the past. The decline in the use of silver began with the emigration of the Jewish population of the Tafilalet in the 1950s and 1960s. In the town of Rissani, some elderly Muslim jewelry vendors told me that they apprenticed with Jewish silversmiths

in order to learn their jewelry-making techniques and to continue the tradition of silver-smithing. However, by the 1960s, most Berbers in the Southeast had abandoned their nomadic lifestyles and settled into villages and towns, resulting in increased contact with Arabs and exposure to urban Moroccan jewelry styles. Because of Jewish emigration and the influence of Arab jewelry preferences, Berber demand for silver jewelry in southeastern Morocco ended in the 1980s. As gold became more popular, Arab silversmiths abandoned their workshops in order to open boutiques for gold jewelry. See Cynthia Becker, *Amazigh Arts in Morocco: Women Shaping Berber Identity* (Austin: University of Texas Press, 2006), 116.

41. Ibid., 40.

42. Ibid., 69.

43. Gabriel Camps, *Berbères: aux marges de l'histoire* (Paris: Éditions des Hespérides, 1980), 213.

44. Camps, *Berbères. Aux marges de l'histoire*, 213; and Camps, *Les berbères: Mémoire et identité* (Paris: Errances, 1995), 199.

45. Camps, *Mémoire et identité*, 209–210.

46. On Berber motifs and their connection to the evil eye, see James Bynon, "Berber Women's Pottery: Is the Decoration Motivated?," in *Colloquies on Art & Archaeology in Asia No. 12*, ed. J. Picton (London: University of London, 1984), 147; and Westermarck, *Ritual and Belief*, volume I, 467.

47. E. G. Gobert, "Notes sur les tatouages des indigènes tunisiens," *L'Anthropologie* 34 (1924): 57–90; and Georges Marcy, "Origine et signification des tatouages des tribus berbères," *Revue de l'histoire des religions* 102 (1931): 13–66.

48. Julio Cola Alberich, *Amuletos y tatuajes marroquíes* (Madrid: Instituto de Estudios Africanos, 1949, 116–117.

49. d'Ucel, *Berber Art*, 198.

50. Paul Vandenbroek, *Azetta: l'art des femmes berbères* (Paris: Flammarion, 2000), 81.

51. See Cynthia Eller, *The Myth of Matriarchal Prehistory* (Boston: Beacon Press, 2000) for a critique of cave painting scholarship and other issues concerning female matriarchy in the ancient world.

52. The Tuareg and Berbers share a common ancestry and speak related languages, commonly referred to under the overarching term Tamazight. Morocco has the largest Amazigh population (40–60%) followed by Algeria (25%). The Tuareg occupy a vast Saharan region and live in Niger, Mali, Algeria, Burkina Faso, and Libya. Estimates of their numbers range between 600,000 and 1,600,000. See Michael Brett and Elizabeth Fentress, *The Berbers* (Oxford: Blackwell, 1996), 3. The idea of a transnational Amazigh identity is relatively new among Imazighen in Morocco and is largely due to the internet. In 1992 the electronic mailing list *Amazigh-Net* was established, allowing Imazighen with internet access to communicate, share information, and establish a sense of community across national borders. On *Amazigh-Net* and the transnational Amazigh imaginary, see David Crawford and Katherine E. Hoffman, "Essentially Amazigh: Urban Berbers and the Global Village," in *The Arab-Islamic World: Interdisciplinary Studies*, ed. Kevin Lacey and Ralph Coury (New York: Peter Lang, 2000), 117–133. Several dozen websites have emerged recently that are concerned with the question of Amazigh identity and strategies to implement Tamazight into each nation's educational curriculum and mass media.

53. Johannes Nicolaisen and Ida Nicolaisen, *The Pastoral Tuareg: Ecology, Culture, and Society*, 2 vols. (New York: Thames and Hudson, 1997), volume II: 677.

54. Ibid.

55. Ibid., 2: 712–717.

56. See, for example, Henri Duveyrier, *Les Touareg du Nord* (Paris: Challamel, 1864).

57. Nicolaisen and Nicolaisen, *The Pastoral Tuareg*, volume II: 717–718.

58. Mohamed Mallal, interview with author, Ouarzazate, Morocco, June 10, 2004.

59. Fatima Sadiqi, *Women, Gender and Language in Morocco* (Leiden: Brill, 2003), 225.

60. Sadiqi, *Women, Gender and Language*, 20–29.

61. Messick, "Subordinate Discourse," 210–225.

62. Becker, *Amazigh Arts in Morocco*, 34.

63. Ibid.

64. Westermarck, *Ritual and Belief*, 2, 269.

65. S.v. "Anzar," in *Encyclopédie berbère*, ed. Gabriel Camps (Aix-en-Provence: Édisud, 1989), volume VI: 795–797; and Laoust, *Mots et choses berbères*, 227–228.

66. "Anzar," *Encyclopédie berbère*, volume VI: 795–797.

67. Laoust, *Mots et choses berbères*, 238.

68. Nadia Abu-Zahra, "The Rain Rituals as Rites of Spiritual Passage," *International Journal of Middle East Studies* 20(4) (1988): 510–511.

69. Sheila S. Blair and Jonathan M. Bloom, "The Mirage of Islamic Arts: Reflections on the Study of an Unwieldly Field," *The Art Bulletin* 85(1) (2003): 157.

70. See, for example, Peter Garlake, *Early Art and Architecture in Africa* (Oxford: Oxford History of Art, 2002); Werner Gillon, *A Short History of African Art* (New York: Viking, 1984); Judith Perani and Fred Smith, *The Visual Arts of Africa* (Upper Saddle River, N.J.: Prentice Hall, 1998); and Frank Willett, *African Art* (London: Thames & Hudson, 2002).

71. Monica Blackmun Visonà, Robin Poyner, Herbert M. Cole, Michael D. Harris, Rowland Abiodun, and Suzanne Preston Blier, *A History of Art in Africa* (Upper Saddle River, N.J.: Prentice Hall, 2007).

72. Perani and Smith, *The Visual Arts of Africa*, ix.

Bibliography

Abouda, Mohand. *Axxam, maisons kabyles: espaces et fresques murales.* Goussainville, France: M. Abouda, 1985.

Abu-Zahra, Nadia. "The Rain Rituals as Rites of Spiritual Passage." *International Journal of Middle East Studies* 20(4) (1988): 507–529.

Alkoum, Abderrahim. *Le Nouveau corpus des tapis marocains.* 6 vols. Casablanca: Ministère de l'Artisanat et des Affaires Sociales, Direction de l'Artisanat, 1988–1992.

Becker, Cynthia. *Amazigh Arts in Morocco: Women Shaping Berber Identity.* Austin: University of Texas Press, 2006.

———. "Amazigh Textiles and Dress in Morocco: Metaphors of Motherhood." *African Arts* 39(3) (2006): 42–55, 96.

———. "Matriarchal Nomads and Freedom Fighters: Transnational Amazigh Consciousness and Moroccan, Algerian, and Nigerian Artists." *Critical Interventions* 5 (2009): 70–101.

Benjamin, Roger. *Orientalist Aesthetics: Art, Colonialism, and French North Africa, 1880–1930.* Berkeley: University of California Press, 2003.

Besancenot, Jean. *Costumes of Morocco*. New York: Kegan Paul International, 1990.

Blair, Sheila, and Jonathan M. Bloom. "The Mirage of Islamic Arts: Reflections on the Study of an Unwieldly Field." *The Art Bulletin* 85(1) (2003): 152–184.

Brett, Michael, and Elizabeth Fentress. *The Berbers*. Oxford: Blackwell, 1996.

Burke, Edmund, III. "The Image of the Moroccan State in French Ethnological Literature: A New Look at the Origin of Lyautey's Berber Policy." In *Arabs and Berbers*, ed. Ernest Gellner and Charles Micaud. London: Duckworth and Co., 1972, 175–200.

Bynon, James. "Berber Women's Pottery: Is the Decoration Motivated?" In *Colloquies on Art & Archaeology in Asia No. 12*, ed. J. Picton. London: University of London, 1984, 136–161.

———. "Preface." *Costumes of Morocco*, ed. Jean Besancenot. London: Kegan Paul International, 1990.

Camps, Gabriel. *Berbères: aux marges de l'histoire*. Paris: Éditions des Hespérides, 1980.

———. *Encyclopédie berbère*. Ed. Gabriel Camps. Aix-en-Provence: Édisud, 1989.

———. "La céramique des sculptures berbères de Tiddis." *Libyca Anthropologica* 4 (1956): 155–203.

———. *Les Berbères: mémoire et identité*. Paris: Errances, 1995.

Cola Alberich, Julio. *Amuletos y tatuajes marroquíes*. Madrid: Instituto de Estudios Africanos, 1949.

Courtney-Clarke, Margaret, and Geraldine Brooks. *Imazighen: The Vanishing Traditions of Berber Women*. New York: Clarkson Potter Publishers, 1996.

Crawford, David, and Katherine E. Hoffman. "Essentially Amazigh: Urban Berbers and the Global Village." In *The Arab-Islamic World: Interdisciplinary Studies*, ed. Kevin Lacey and Ralph Coury. New York: Peter Lang, 2000, 117–133.

Curtis, William J. R. "Type and Variation: Berber Collective Dwellings of the Northwestern Sahara." *Muqarnas* 1 (1983): 181–209.

D'Ucel, Jeanne. *Berber Art: An Introduction*. Norman: University of Oklahoma Press, 1932.

Dunn, Ross E. *Resistance in the Desert*. Madison: University of Wisconsin Press, 1977.

Duveyrier, Henri. *Les Touareg du Nord*. Paris: Challamel, 1864.

Eller, Cynthia. *The Myth of Matriarchal Prehistory*. Boston: Beacon Press, 2000.

Garlake, Peter. *Early Art and Architecture of Africa*. Oxford: Oxford University Press, 2002.

Gaudry, Mathéa. *La femme chaouia de l'Aurès: étude de sociologie berbère*. Paris: Librairie Orientaliste Paul Geuthner, 1929.

Gellner, Ernest. "Introduction." In *Arabs and Berbers*, ed. Ernest Gellner and Charles Micaud. London: Duckworth, 1972, 11–24.

Gobert, E. G. "Les pierres talismaniques (folklore tunisien)." *Journal de la Société des Africanistes* 16 (1946): 39–48.

———. "Notes sur les tatouages des indigènes Tunisiens." *L'Anthropologie* 34 (1924): 57–90.

———. "Notes sur les tatouages indigènes de la région de Gafsa." *Revue tunisienne* 18 (1911): 32–41.

———. "Remarques sur les tatouages nord-africains." *Revue africaine* 100 (1956): 501–517.

Golvin, Lucien. *Aspects de l'artisanat en Afrique du Nord.* Paris: Presses Universitaires de France, 1957.

———. *Les tissages nord-africains d'après les collections du Musée Stéphane Gsell.* Alger: Imprimerie Officielle, 1958.

Goodman, Jane E. *Berber Culture on the World Stage: from Village to Video.* Bloomington: Indiana University Press, 2005.

Guernier, Eugène. *La Berbérie, l'Islam et la France: le destin de l'Afrique du Nord.* Paris: Éditions de l'Union française, 1950.

Hart, David. *Dadda 'Atta and his Forty Grandsons: The Socio-Political Organization of the Ait 'Atta of Southern Morocco.* Boulder, Colo.: Westview Press, 1981.

Herber, Jean. "Les tatouages de la face chez la marocaine." *Hespéris* 33 (1946): 323–351.

———. "Les tatouages du dos au Maroc." *Revue africaine* 91 (1947): 118–122.

———. "Les tatouages du pied au Maroc." *L'Anthropolgie* 33 (1923): 87–102.

———. "Notes sur les tatouages au Maroc." *Hespéris* 36 (1949): 11–46.

———. "Origine et signification des tatouages marocains." *L'Anthropologie* 37 (1927): 517–525.

———. "Tatouages marocains." *Archives berbères* (1920): 58–66.

———. "Tatouages marocains. Tatouages et religion." *Revue d'histoire des religions* 83 (1921): 68–83.

———. "Tatoueuses marocaines." *Hespéris* 35 (1948): 289–297.

Irbouh, Hamid. *Art in the Service of Colonialism: French Art Education in Morocco, 1912–1956.* London: I.B. Tauris, 2005.

Kasfir, Sidney. "One Tribe, One Style? Paradigms in the Historiography of African art." *History in Africa* 11 (1984): 163–193.

Keenan, Jeremy. "Power and Wealth are Cousins: Descent, Class and Marital Strategies among the Kel Ahaggar (Tuareg. Sahara). Part I." *Africa: Journal of the International African Institute* 47(3) (1977): 242–252.

Korolnik-Andersch, Annette, and Marcel Korolnik. *The Color of Henna: Painted Textiles from Southern Morocco.* Stuttgart: Arnoldschen, 2002.

Laoust, Émile. *Mots et choses berbères: notes de linguistique et d'ethnographie: dialectes du Maroc.* Paris: A. Challamel. 1920.

Lorcin, Patricia. *Imperial Identities: Stereotyping, Prejudice, and Race in Colonial Algeria.* London: I.B. Tauris, 1995.

Maddy-Weitzman, Bruce. "Contested Identities: Berbers, 'Berberism,' and the State in North Africa." In *Middle Eastern Minorities and Diasporas,* ed. M. Ma'oz and Gabriel Sheffer. Portland, Ore.: Sussex Academic Press, 2002, 153–178.

Marçais, Georges. *L'art des Berbères.* Alger: Impr. Officielle, 1956.

Marcy, Georges. "Origine et signification des tatouages des tribus berbères." *Revue de l'histoire des religions* 102 (1931): 13–66.

McDougall, James. "Myth and Counter-Myth: 'The Berber' As National Signifier in Algerian Historiographies." *Radical History Review* 8 (Spring 2003): 66–88.

Messick, Brinkley. "Subordinate Discourse: Women, Weaving, and Gender Relations in North Africa." *American Ethnologist* 14 (1987): 210–225.

Morin-Barde, Mireille. *Coiffures féminines du Maroc: au sud du Haut Atlas.* Aix-en-Provence: Édisud, 1990.

Nicolaisen, Johannes, and Ida Nicolaisen. *The Pastoral Tuareg: Ecology, Culture, and Society,* 2 vols. New York: Thames and Hudson, 1997.

Paydar, Niloo Imami. "Weavings for Rural Life." In *The Fabric of Moroccan Life*, ed. N. Paydar and I. Grammet, 142–147. Indianapolis: Indianapolis Museum of Art, 2002.

Perani, Judith, and Fred T. Smith. *The Visual Arts of Africa: Gender, Power, and Life Cycle Rituals*. Upper Saddle River, N.J.: Prentice-Hall, 1998.

Poinssot, Louis, and Jacques Revault. *Tapis tunisiens*, volume I. *Tapis du Kairouan*. Paris: Horizons de France, 1937.

———. *Tapis tunisiens*, II. *Tapis bédouins à haute laine*. Paris: Horizons de France, 1950.

———. *Tapis tunisiens*, III. *Tissus décorés de Gafsa et imitations*. Paris: Horizons de France, 1953.

———. *Tapis tunisiens*, IV. *Tissus ras décorés de Kairouan, du Sahel et du Sud Tunisien*. Paris: Horizons de France, 1957.

Prussin, Labelle. "Judaic Threads in the West African Tapestry: No More Forever?" *The Art Bulletin* 88(2) (2006): 328–353.

Rabaté, Jacques, and Marie-Rose Rabaté. *Bijoux du Maroc: du Haut Atlas à la vallée du Draa*. Aix-en-Provence: Édisud, 1996.

Reswick, Irmtraud. "Traditional Textiles of Tunisia." *African Arts* 14(3) (1981): 56–65.

Ricard, Prosper. *Corpus des tapis marocains*. 4 vols. Paris: Paul Geuthner, 1923–1934.

Ricard, Prosper, and Marcel Vicaire. *Corpus des tapis marocains*. vol. 5. Paris: Service des Metiers et Arts Marocains, 1950.

Rouach, David. *Bijoux berbères au Maroc*. Paris: ACR Édition, 1989.

Sadiqi, Fatima. *Women, Gender and Language in Morocco*. Leiden: E. J. Brill, 2003.

Silverstein, Paul A. *Algeria in France: Transpolitics, Race, and Nation*. Bloomington: Indiana University Press, 2004.

Vandenbroeck, Paul. *Azetta: l'art des femmes berbères*. Paris: Flammarion, 2000.

Van Gennep, Arnold. *Études d'ethnographie algérienne*. Paris: Ernest Leroux, 1911.

Visonà, Monica Blackmun, Robin Poyner, Herbert M. Cole, Michael D. Harris, Rowland Abiodun, and Suzanne Preston Blier, A *History of Art in Africa*. Upper Saddle River, N.J.: Prentice Hall, 2007.

Westermarck, Edward. *Ritual and Belief in Morocco*. 2 vols. New York: University Books, [1926] 1968.

Willett, Frank. *African Art*. London: Thames and Hudson, 2002.

CONTRIBUTORS

Cynthia Becker is Associate Professor of African Art History, Boston University. Her publications include *Amazigh Arts in Morocco: Women Shaping Berber Identity* and *Desert Jewels: North African Jewelry and Photography from the Xavier Guerrand-Hermès Collection* as well as numerous articles.

Lisa Bernasek is a research fellow at the Subject Centre for Languages, Linguistics and Area Studies, U.K. and author of *Artistry of the Everyday: Beauty and Craftsmanship in Berber Life*. In 2004 she co-curated the exhibit *Imazighen! Beauty and Artisanship in Berber Life*, held at the Peabody Museum of Archaeology and Ethnology.

David Crawford is Associate Professor of Sociology and Anthropology at Fairfield University and author of *Moroccan Households in the World Economy: Labor and Inequality in a Berber Village*.

Mohamed El Mansour is Professor of History at Mohammed V University, Rabat, Morocco. He is author of *Morocco in the Reign of Mawlay Sulayman* and many articles on Moroccan social and religious history.

Mokhtar Ghambou is Assistant Professor of English at Yale University. He teaches and writes on postcolonial theory and comparative literature, as well as Orientalism, minority discourse, Mediterranean studies, and migration. His forthcoming book is *Nomadism and Its Frontiers*.

Jane E. Goodman, an anthropologist, is Associate Professor of Communication and Culture at Indiana University. She is author of *Berber Culture on the World Stage: From Village to Video* (Indiana University Press, 2005) and editor (with Paul Silverstein) of *Bourdieu in Algeria: Colonial Politics, Ethnographic Practices, Theoretical Developments*.

Katherine E. Hoffman is Associate Professor of Anthropology at Northwestern University. She is author of *We Share Walls: Language, Land, and Gender in Berber Morocco* and Associate Editor of the *Journal of Linguistic Anthropology*.

James McDougall is University Lecturer in Twentieth Century History and a Fellow of Trinity College, University of Oxford. He is a member of the editorial advisory board of the *Journal of African History*, a former member of the editorial committee of *Middle East Report*, and author of *History and the Culture of Nationalism in Algeria*.

Susan Gilson Miller is Associate Professor of History at the University of California, Davis. Her books include *The Architecture and Memory of the Minority Quarter in the Muslim Mediterranean City*, edited with architect Mauro Bertagnin.

Paul A. Silverstein is Associate Professor of Anthropology at Reed College. He is author of *Algeria in France: Transpolitics, Race, and Nation* (Indiana University Press, 2004) and editor (with Ussama Makdisi) of *Memory and Violence in the Middle East and North Africa* (Indiana University Press, 2006).

INDEX

Printed and bound by CPI Group (UK) Ltd, Croydon, CR0 4YY

13/04/2025

14656544-0003